SHE PREACHED THE WORD

She Preached the Word

WOMEN'S ORDINATION IN MODERN AMERICA

Benjamin R. Knoll
and Cammie Jo Bolin

OXFORD
UNIVERSITY PRESS

OXFORD
UNIVERSITY PRESS

Oxford University Press is a department of the University of Oxford. It furthers
the University's objective of excellence in research, scholarship, and education
by publishing worldwide. Oxford is a registered trade mark of Oxford University
Press in the UK and certain other countries.

Published in the United States of America by Oxford University Press
198 Madison Avenue, New York, NY 10016, United States of America.

Library of Congress Cataloging-in-Publication Data
Names: Knoll, Benjamin R., 1983– author. | Bolin, Cammie Jo, 1994– author.
Title: She preached the word : women's ordination in modern America /
Benjamin R. Knoll, Cammie Jo Bolin.
Description: New York, NY : Oxford University Press, 2018. |
Includes bibliographical references and index.
Identifiers: LCCN 2017057416 (print) | LCCN 2018016053 (ebook) |
ISBN 9780190882372 (updf) | ISBN 9780190882389 (epub) | ISBN 9780190882396 (online resource) |
ISBN 9780190882365 (hardcover : alk. paper)
Subjects: LCSH: Ordination of women—United States. | Women in church work—United States. |
Women clergy—United States. | United States—Church history.
Classification: LCC BV676 (ebook) | LCC BV676 .K58 2018 (print) | DDC 262/.14082—dc23
LC record available at https://lccn.loc.gov/2017057416

9 8 7 6 5 4 3 2 1

Printed by Sheridan Books, Inc., United States of America

For my daughters.

B.R.K.

To all the women who continue to lead in congregations, whether they are ordained or not.

C.J.B.

Mary Magdalene, you know, walked with him just as the twelve disciples did. You know, he loved her and taught her just as he did his twelve disciples. She preached the word, just as [the] twelve disciples did. (Interview 45)

Contents

Acknowledgments

THERE ARE SEVERAL individuals to whom we owe an immense debt of gratitude for their contributions and assistance on this project. Paul Djupe, Mark Chaves, Ryan Cragun, Andre Audette, Andrew Lewis, Mirya Holman, and Georgie Weatherby gave us extensive feedback on early iterations of our project at various academic conferences. The Political Science Department of the University of Kentucky invited us to present early findings at a workshop luncheon and gave us very helpful and constructive comments. Dave Redlawsk provided invaluable advice on designing and implementing the public opinion surveys that constitute the backbone of this book. Matthew Pierce, Chris Haskett, and Shayna Sheinfeld provided insight on the gender dynamics of non-Christian congregations in the United States. For guidance and suggestions related to gender theory and gender research in the social sciences, we thank Tiffany Barnes, Tracy Osborn, Sara Egge, and Ellen Prusinski. Charles Hokayem and Bruce Johnson provided frequent assistance with our empirical analyses while Leah Marie Silverman provided us constructive feedback on the introductory chapter. We especially extend our thanks to Rev. Amy Dafler Meaux of Trinity Episcopal Church in Danville, Kentucky, who gave us several hours of her time on numerous occasions to chat about her experiences and themes related to the book, including the interpretation of some of our empirical findings.

Beau Weston, Joshua (not Jason!) Ambrosius, Corwin E. Smidt, Laura Olson, Katie Knoll, and Jennifer Mansfield read early drafts of the manuscript and provided us with extensive recommendations for improvement. We thank Laura Olson especially for her guidance and suggestions on some of the key theoretical framings of the book—Chapter 6 exists due to her input. We appreciate Theo Calderara at

Oxford University Press for his efforts in working with us throughout the extensive review and publishing process as well as his input and comments on the manuscript. Thanks to Amanda Fernandez and Sangeetha Vishwanathan for their sharp editing eyes and input on our prose. We are particularly indebted to our friend and editor Jana Riess, who was with this project from beginning to end. Jana gave us feedback when the project was merely a three-page outline, guided us through the publishing process, and then read drafts of each chapter while providing comments on everything from the book's arguments and evidence down to the appropriate use of *which* versus *that*. This book is much stronger thanks to the time and effort that each of these individuals provided along the way.

We thank Centre College for the robust institutional support to carry out this project. We received financial support from the College's John Marshall Harlan Research Fund, Faculty Development Committee, Center for Teaching and Learning, and the Social Sciences Division. The primary writing of this book took place during a Stodghill research leave during the Spring 2016 semester. More important, the vast majority of the data featured in this book, both quantitative and qualitative, were collected by Centre College students through undergraduate research modules that were built into several different courses and summer experiences. In all, over two hundred undergraduate students at Centre College, along with students from Boyle County High School in Danville, Kentucky, spent thousands of hours making tens of thousands of telephone calls (usually in good humor) throughout 2015 and 2016 to collect the survey data featured in this book. We also appreciate Christopher Paskewich and Ryan New for letting us "borrow" their students to collaborate with us on this endeavor. In addition, Nicole Pottinger contributed an extensive literature review of the causes and consequences of gender egalitarianism (now part of Chapter 3) as part of an independent study course. We thank the administrators and faculty of Centre College for their support of undergraduate research projects such as these.

A few Centre College graduates deserve special acknowledgement: Matthew Baker, Dexter Horne, Margaret "Maggie" Kaus, Katie Solomon, Kelli South, and Joseph "Gray" Whitsett. As part of a senior research seminar in the Fall 2015 semester they each worked dozens of hours to collect and transcribe the seventy-three oral interviews featured in this book. Their course papers were a major source of background research for the section of Chapter 2 on the contemporary dynamics of gender leadership in the various American religious traditions. Further, our weekly seminar discussions inspired a number of ideas that eventually made their way into this work in one form or another. This book would not have been possible without the contributions of these six outstanding students.

On a personal level, Cammie Jo Bolin would like to thank the women of 30 Brock and her roommates who listened to her excitement and frustration throughout the writing process. They serve as a constant reminder of why women can and should lead. She would also like to thank her parents Evelyn and Duane and her brother Wesley for being egalitarians in a complementarian congregation. Benjamin Knoll would like to thank Rene Rocha, Caroline Tolbert, Dave Redlawsk, and Tracy Osborn, who several years ago taught him how to do academic research and frame it in such a way that at least a few people find interesting. He also thanks his wife Katie for her infinite patience and understanding as he devoted nearly four years of his life to pursue this project from beginning to end. Finally, he appreciates his mother Lora for being his original example of a woman who can overcome obstacles, show leadership, and influence the lives of others for the better.

SHE PREACHED THE WORD

We had an older man that came up to me,
and he says, "Do you know we're gonna
have a woman priest?" I says, "Yeah, I do."
And I says, "So?" (Interview 36)

1

INTRODUCTION

The Need for a New Perspective

IN APRIL 2016 a video link appeared on the Facebook wall for *Sojourners*, an Evangelical Christian magazine with a decidedly leftist, social justice orientation. The one-minute video was titled "7 Reasons Men Should Not Be Pastors" and featured a series of women making tongue-in-cheek statements about why men should not be ordained to the ministry, based on a list first authored by the late David Scholer who taught at Fuller Theological Seminary in Pasadena, California.

The first woman in the video looks directly into the camera and says with only a hint of irony, "Men can still be involved in church. They just don't need to be ordained. The children's ministry is *always* in need of male leadership." The next woman continues the theme: "Some men are handsome. They could be too distracting for us on Sunday . . ." The next adds, "They're too emotional to be priests or pastors! Go to a March Madness game and *tell* me I'm wrong." One by one a variety of women present their arguments:

- "Male pastors who have children might be distracted by the responsibility of being a parent."
- "Jesus was betrayed by a man! How can men be trusted to lead?"
- "About once a month male pastors get *really* cranky."

- "Men are still vitally important to the life of the church. I mean, they could sweep sidewalks, or repair the church roof. They could even lead worship on Father's Day!"

At the conclusion of the video, some of the women featured earlier in the video reappear and make their point: "So yeah, we hear stuff like this all the time. / *All* the time. / But it's 2016. / So don't be that guy. / Support women in the church." Within two weeks the video post had been "liked" by more than 17,000 Facebook users, generated more than 1,600 comments, been shared by more than 34,000 people, and been viewed more than three million times.[1]

Only a few months earlier, Canadian Archbishop Paul-Andre Durocher had proposed the ordaining of women as deacons (but not priests) at a high-profile three-week Vatican summit on the Roman Catholic Church's teachings on the family (Boorstein 2015a). Over the previous two years Pope Francis had generated headlines for his progressive approach to issues such as poverty, refugees, immigrants, and the environment as well as his commitment to bureaucratic reform in the Vatican hierarchy. Those who hoped that this agenda of reform would extend to women's ordination in the Catholic Church were disappointed when the archbishop's proposal was not adopted by the summit.

Pope Francis had previously expressed little optimism that this proposal would make headway when he spoke to reporters on the issue: "The Church has spoken and says no . . . that door is closed" (Allen 2015). To the surprise of many, however, he opened the door just a little in May 2016 by telling representatives of a global network of nuns that he would support the creation of a special commission to study the possibility of ordaining women as deacons (Povoledo and Goodstein 2016). He fulfilled this promise on August 2, 2016, when he appointed six women and seven men to a panel to study the role of women in early Christianity so as to inform discussions on the possibility of women becoming deacons in the Catholic Church. One panel member, Hofstra University scholar Phyllis Zagano, had written earlier that "there were women ordained as deacons in the early church. That is a historical fact" (McKenna 2016).

This special commission has sparked much conversation and renewed speculation about the future role of women in the Catholic Church (Poggioli 2016), and supporters of women's ordination to the priesthood have found hope in the creation of the commission (Miller 2016b). The Women's Ordination Conference, for example, released a statement in 2016 describing the commission as an "important step for the Vatican in recognizing its own history of honoring women's leadership" (Lavanga 2016). In November 2016, however, the Pope was asked about women and the priesthood following a trip to Sweden where he met Antje Jackelén, the first female archbishop of the Church of Sweden. Pope Francis responded that "St. Pope John Paul II had the last clear word on this and it stands." John Paul II had previously declared that "the [Catholic] Church has no authority whatsoever to confer priestly ordination on women and that this judgment is to be definitively held by all the Church's faithful" (Bacon 2016). When the reporter asked: "Forever, forever?" Pope Francis replied: "Never, never. If we read carefully the declaration by St. John Paul II, it is going in that direction."

Of course we cannot know whether the Catholic Church will stand firm on its males-only clerical policies "forever, forever" as the reporter asked, but in the meantime, the organization Roman Catholic Womenpriests continues to ordain women in defiance of the Vatican and they officiate at masses in some parts of the country (Brady 2015). Other Catholic organizations have sought a more moderate path, including the DeaconChat initiative cosponsored by the Association of U.S. Catholic Priests, FutureChurch, and Voice of the Faithful. DeaconChat seeks to begin a variety of conversations at the local level regarding the possibility and role of women in the Catholic diaconate (McKenna 2017).

Elsewhere, delegates to the 60th General Conference of the Seventh-day Adventist Church fiercely debated in 2015 a resolution to allow regional church bodies to extend ordination to women pastors. Supporters pointed to historical precedent, arguing that one of Adventism's key founders, Ellen Gould White, was a woman. They also pointed out that some regional conferences in the United States had already moved forward to ordain women. Ultimately, the Conference voted "no" on the resolution, 1,381 to 977 (Banks 2015a). In response, some male Adventist pastors requested to change their own status to "commissioned" but not "ordained" pastors in a show of solidarity with their female colleagues who desire ordination (Banks 2015b).

In 2009 Rabbi Avi Weiss, a Modern Orthodox Jew, founded Yeshivat Maharat in New York City, a rabbinical school specifically for women (Heilman 2015). Lila Kagedan became the first officially ordained female rabbi to graduate and serve in an Orthodox congregation (Moghe and Pomrenze 2016). In response, the Rabbinical Council of America, which represents Modern Orthodox Judaism in the United States (Orthodox Jews comprise about 3% of all Jews in the United States), passed a resolution in October 2015 that stated, "RCA members with positions in Orthodox institutions may not ordain women into the Orthodox rabbinate, regardless of the title used; or hire or ratify the hiring of a woman into a rabbinic position at an Orthodox institution; or allow a title implying rabbinic ordination to be used by a teacher" (Winston 2015). Nevertheless, the Modern Orthodox Jewish School Yeshivat Maharat continues to operate and ordain female rabbis in defiance of the RCA's resolution.

In June 2014 leaders of The Church of Jesus Christ of Latter-day Saints (LDS, also referred to as "the Mormon church") excommunicated activist Kate Kelly for vigorously advocating for female ordination through the organization Ordain Women (Boorstein and Robinson 2014). As part of Kelly's advocacy, she participated prominently with hundreds of other women who gathered at the church's semiannual General Conference to request tickets to the all-male priesthood session (their requests were denied). She was excommunicated by three male Mormon priesthood holders in her local congregation who explained that she had participated in "conduct contrary to the laws and order of the Church." They explained to Kelly that while she was entitled to her opinions on women and the priesthood, "the problem is that you have persisted in an aggressive effort to persuade Church members to your point of view and that your course of action has threatened to erode the faith of others" (Harrison 2014). A year later, a leaked internal training document for the LDS governing hierarchy identified Ordain Women as "leading people away from the Gospel," its pernicious influence on par with pornography, sexual promiscuity, "lack of righteousness," secularism, and "false prophets" (Melander 2015).

At the same time, the LDS Church began inviting women to offer prayers in these semiannual General Conferences in 2013 (Berkes 2013) and adopted the faith's annual women's meeting as an official session of General Conference in 2014 (Walch 2014). Leaders also announced in 2015 that more congregational decision-making, including the planning of worship services, would be delegated to a leadership council that included representatives from the various women's ministry groups in local congregations (Stack 2015). That same year, women representatives were invited to join several of the LDS Church's major governing committees (Walch 2015). On the ground, the Mormon Women Project (www.mormonwomen.com) is a grass-roots effort to offer oral interviews, resources, and religious education supplements to raise the profile of women's voices in Mormon devotionals, sermons, and classrooms.

Gender conversations are also happening in other faith traditions. There are currently more than three million Muslims in the United States, but local imams (congregational leaders) worldwide are almost entirely men. Worshipers traditionally self-segregate in the mosque according to gender: men position themselves toward the front, while women assemble at the back or in a separate room entirely. In April 2017 the Qal'bu Maryam Women's Mosque opened in Berkeley, California. Its founder, Rabi'a Keeble, aimed to create an Islamic worship space that was intentionally egalitarian when it came to gender roles. At Qal'bu Maryam, women lead prayers during worship services and everyone is invited to mingle; there is no segregation by gender. According to Keeble, "Women need to be empowered to do what they're called to do. If your calling is to be an imam, come try it out. Come study, and no one is going to tell you that because you're female you can't do it" (Blumberg 2017).

Meanwhile, women have been serving as pastors and priests in a variety of other religious denominations in the United States for several decades, if not more than a century. According to researchers, the first formal ordination of a woman occurred in 1853 when Antoinette Brown was ordained as a Congregational minister (Schneider and Schneider 1997, chap. 3; Zikmund, Lummis, and Chang 1998, 9). She later resigned from the ministry over "internal strife" but joined the Unitarian Church, where she continued to preach (Nesbitt 1997, 23). Olympia Brown was the first woman ordained as a Universalist minister, and today more than half of Unitarian-Universalist clergy are women, including the Reverend Susan Frederick-Gray, who was elected in June 2017 to be the first female president of the Unitarian Universalist Association (Banks 2017).

Multiple Christian denominations began to ordain women for the first time in the second half of the nineteenth century. In 1866, for example, Helenor Alter Davisson was "recommended to the Annual Conference as a suitable person to preach the gospel or, at least a small work," thereby becoming the first woman to be ordained within the Methodist tradition in the United States (Shoemaker 2003). The American Baptist Churches USA began ordaining women in the 1870s (American Baptist Churches USA 1989). In 1886 Anna Bartlett became the first woman to be ordained to the ministry in the Free Will Baptist denomination (Schneider and Schneider 1997, 77). In 1914 the Assemblies of God formally recognized women's ordination, but this stance did not equate to full equality for women within the denomination, as women were barred from voting within the organization until 1920 (Nesbitt 1997, 23).

Coincident with the rise of the secular feminist movement in the United States, many denominations began ordaining women in the mid-twentieth century (see Lehman 1993, chap. 1). The African Methodist Episcopal Church, for example, began ordaining women in 1948, more than half a century after the denomination's 1887 decision to reverse the ordination of Sarah Ann Hughes, who had been made a deacon two years previously. In 1956 Maud Keister Jensen became the first pastor in the United Methodist Church, and Margaret Ellen Towner was the first woman to be ordained in the American Presbyterian Church, which is now part of the PC(USA). A group of women known as the Philadelphia 11 were "irregularly" ordained as priests in the Episcopal Church in 1974, before ordination was officially extended to all women in that denomination in 1976. Thirty years later, Katharine Jefferts Schori became the first woman to serve as the denomination's presiding bishop from 2006 to 2015 (Kuruvilla 2014). This followed closely on the heels of

Sharon Watkins's election as the first female general minister and president of the Disciples of Christ in 2005; Watkins was also the first woman to lead a Mainline Protestant denomination in the United States. In 2017 Teresa Hord Owens was elected as her successor, becoming the denomination's first woman of color to serve in that capacity (Kennel-Shank 2017).

Despite the strides that women have made in the leadership positions of these denominations, however, a recent survey revealed that women still make up less than a third of their congregation's pastors and priests (Hersh and Malina 2017; Quealy 2017). We haven't arrived at a point of leadership gender parity even in congregations and denominations that ordain women. Why is this the case? Does a congregation's policy on gender and leadership drive the opinions of its members, or is it the other way around? What effects might the gender imbalance in America's pulpits have on the lives and attitudes of American worshipers? These are some of the key questions that we seek to answer in this book.

WOMEN AND LEADERSHIP IN AMERICAN SOCIETY

Conversations about the role of women and leadership in American society have not been limited to religious organizations, but have also taken place in politics, business, and the workplace, especially over the last thirty-odd years. The 1992 elections, for example, marked a new milestone in women's political leadership when four women were elected to the Senate. The election of Carol Moseley Braun from Illinois, Barbara Boxer from California, Dianne Feinstein from California, and Patty Murray from Washington signified the greatest number of women elected to the Senate in the same year. Joining senators Barbara Mikulski (Maryland) and Nancy Kassebaum (Kansas), they raised the number of women in the Senate to a record high of six, which later rose to seven after Kay Bailey Hutchison of Texas won a special election. The year 1992 further stood out as a year of women's political advancement, as Boxer and Feinstein made California the first state to have two female senators serving simultaneously. These gains in leadership were not confined to the Senate; the number of women in the House of Representatives rose from thirty to forty-eight the same year. Because of the widespread success of female candidates, 1992 was popularly dubbed the "Year of the Woman" which has since served as a reference point in scholarship about women's representation, empowerment, and political involvement.

The success of the Year of the Woman was understood to be a response, in part, to the Senate's handling of Anita Hill's sexual assault allegations and Clarence Thomas's subsequent appointment to the Supreme Court in 1991. One reporter following the election described women candidates as being "thrust forward by

Anita Hill–inspired outrage and helped along by anti-incumbency sentiment" and "in contention as never before" (*Time* 1992). At least one of the newly elected senators, Patty Murray, indeed decided to run after watching the Senate's response to Anita Hill's allegations. Senator Murray recently recalled her perception of the hearing: "It was so stark, watching these men grill this woman in these big chairs and looking down at her." After seeing how the judiciary committee responded to Anita Hill, Senator Murray had made up her mind. "I just said, I am going to run for [U.S.] Senate . . . because they need somebody there who is going to say what I would say if I was there" (Newton-Small 2016).

Congresswomen in the House of Representatives were similarly motivated by the Senate's treatment of Anita Hill. In fact, a group of congresswomen were largely responsible for the Senate's permitting Anita Hill to testify. After hearing that the Senate Judiciary Committee was refusing to let Anita Hill testify in Clarence Thomas's nomination hearings, female representatives in the House took turns giving "one-minute" speeches on the subject. Meanwhile, several congresswomen left the floor of the House, notified the press, and hurried over to the Senate, where, as Congresswoman Louise Slaughter described, they "told Senator Biden that Anita Hill had to speak. And she did." Then-Representative Barbara Boxer described the effect of their charge when stating, "because we made that walk over to the Senate, there were hearings, and America saw the way Anita Hill was treated, saw that there wasn't one woman on the committee, that only two percent of the members of the Senate were women. It set off a chain of events . . . things have changed mightily" (Chase 2014).

Many expected that 2016 would be another Year of the Woman, as Democratic presidential nominee Hillary Clinton consistently led in the polls throughout the election cycle against Republican nominee Donald Trump. Similar to the Anita Hill incident that was a precursor to the 1992 Year of the Woman, the release of an *Access Hollywood* tape in October made public Trump's lewd comments and descriptions of actions toward women that many claimed constituted sexual assault (Fahrenthold 2016). Although Trump dismissed his comments as "locker room talk" (Severns 2016), the conversation on the tapes was part of a pattern of sexist rhetoric from the Republican candidate throughout the campaign season (Cohen 2017), which made issues of sexism and gender frequent topics of discussion throughout the election cycle. Many expected that Trump's sexual assault controversy, like that of Clarence Thomas a generation earlier, would motivate women to turn out in droves to vote against him. Ellen Malcolm, the founder of Emily's List, a group devoted to electing pro-choice women, described the hopes of many when she said that even though "the circumstances are different," the election would be "just as historic as it was in 1992" (Carney 2016).

After pollsters and pundits confidently predicted a watershed Year of the Woman in 2016, Donald Trump's Electoral College victory stunned the nation and world alike. While the election was not without notable accomplishments for women's advancement—for example, the number of women of color in the Senate quadrupled (Cauterucci 2016) and Hillary Clinton became the first woman in U.S. history to win the popular vote for president—the highest glass ceiling remained intact. Moreover, despite the prevalence of sexism and misogynistic campaign rhetoric throughout the election cycle, gender was not a substantial predictor of voter choice on Election Day. Although exit polls showed that 54% of all women voters supported Clinton (compared to 41% who supported Trump), among white women, 52% voted for Trump and 43% voted for Clinton. Voting patterns in the 2016 election were shaped more by partisanship, religiosity, education, and race/ethnicity, as in previous elections, than by female solidarity.

In many ways, the results of the 2016 election fit a larger pattern in society. Specifically, second-wave feminism in the 1960s spurred a general trend toward gender equality in both the private and public spheres, which continued through the 1970s and 1980s. However, the trend stalled in the 1990s and 2000s (England 2010). For example, data from the Census Bureau shows that women earned, on average, about 60% of men's wages from 1960 to around 1980; the number climbed to about 70% in 1990, when it began to slow. It took another twenty-five years for women's earning to be 80% of men's (Corbett and Hill 2012). This effect is also apparent in terms of women's participation in the workforce. Data from the U.S. Department of Labor shows that in 1960 women comprised only 33% of the labor force in comparison to nearly 47% in 2015. Once again, these increases in employment were sharpest in the 1960s through the early 1980s before stalling in the 1990s and early 2000s. In 1990, for example, 45.2% of the labor force was occupied by female workers, compared to 46.8% in 2015—showing virtually no change over a quarter century. According to one recent estimate, the percentage of women in the work force is projected to hold steady at about 46% through 2060 (Fry and Stepler 2017).

This stalling effect can be seen in corporate leadership positions as well. In 1980 there were no women in the top executive positions in Fortune 100 organizations, but by 2001, 11% were women. Despite this increase, the percentage of women leading corporations both on boards and in management positions has stagnated. For the last decade the percentage of women on all corporate boards in the United States has hovered around 12%, while women hold only 9% of top management positions (Warner 2014).

As previously discussed, the 1992 Year of the Woman dramatically increased the number of women in Congress. It ushered in a decade of women gaining increased political prominence, culminating in California Representative Nancy Pelosi's being elected House minority whip in 2002. While the 1990s saw a dramatic increase in the number of women representatives, growth slowed in the 2000s and early 2010s. In fact, the 2016 election was notable in that there were *no* overall gains in female representation: the gain of one woman in the Senate was offset by the loss of one in the House of Representatives. According to a report by the Institute for Women's Policy Research, if gains in political gender representation in Congress continue at the current rate, women will not achieve equal representation until 2117 (Hess et al. 2015).

WOMEN AND LEADERSHIP IN AMERICAN RELIGIOUS ORGANIZATIONS

While women have arguably gained greater position, voice, and influence in the professional and political worlds throughout the twentieth and early twenty-first centuries, gender imbalances remain strong in the leadership of many religious denominations and congregations throughout the United States. The stalling effect observed in politics and the workplace can also be seen in American congregations. Figure 1.1, for example, shows the proportion of female clergy in the United States based on U.S. Census and Current Population Survey workforce data. These surveys are based on self-reported data, meaning that anyone who claims "clergy" as an occupation is counted. (This theoretically includes clergy currently assigned to congregations as well as those who are not as well as other supporting or associated clergy in congregations.) According to Figure 1.1, women made up less than 1% of

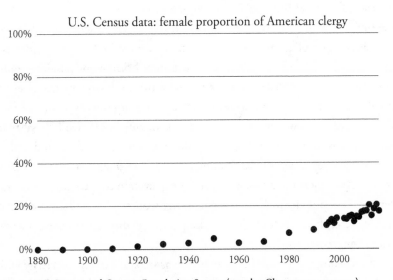

FIGURE 1.1 U.S. Census and Current Population Survey (see also Chaves 1997, page 15)

clergy in America until the 1920 Census and less than 5% through the 1970 Census. Between 1970 and 1995, the proportion of women clergy increased from 3.5% to 11%. According to Census data, the proportion of clergy who are female has averaged around 15% since the mid-1990s.

Other congregational surveys show a similar pattern. The 2015 National Congregations Survey showed that while about three out of every five of American congregations allow women to serve as the head clergyperson, women serve as the "senior or solo pastoral leader" in only 11% of congregations (Chaves, Mark and Eagle 2015). Smidt (2016) shows that women made up only 12% of Protestant clergy in 2009. A 2016 study by Eitan Hersh and Gabrielle Malina estimates that women make up about 15% of Christian and Jewish congregational clergy (Hersh and Malina 2017; Quealy 2017).

This is especially noteworthy given that women outnumber men in American pews: among those who attend religious services at least once a week, 57% are women and 43% who are men, according to the 2014 Pew Religious Landscape Survey. Indeed, scholars have noted that "although religious institutions long excluded women from clerical leadership . . . women have consistently been more devout and more religiously active than men" (Burns, Schlozman, and Verba 2001, 17). Researcher Tobin Grant compiled statistics of religious adherents and found that a majority of religiously active women in the United States belong to denominations with male-only leadership policies (Grant 2015). Other research has shown that women are also less likely than men to serve as lay leaders or ministers in their congregations (Burns, Schlozman, and Verba 2001, 90). Given that over half of American congregations allow women to serve as the chief religious leader, why are so few leadership positions currently occupied by women?

One obvious reason for this gender gap in American congregational leadership is sincerely held theological beliefs about the relationship between gender and religious ordination. Based on scripture, tradition, or both, many religious traditions and institutions either discourage or outright prohibit women from serving as ordained clergy in their congregations. Theological arguments as to the merit of female ordination, however, are not the focus of our book. We believe that this particular motivation is best left to theologians, church leaders, and individual congregants as they weigh the competing rationales of their sacred texts, traditions, beliefs, etc. Also, there remains a wide gender gap even in congregations that do have gender-inclusive policies in place and encourage women to serve in those capacities. Something else, then, must be driving the persistent disparity in the leadership of America's congregations.

One nontheological possibility may be the association of female clergy with liberal political views and Democratic political leanings in the United States. Chaves

(1997) describes how a religious organization's stance on female clergy signals to others the church's position on the political ideological spectrum. According to Chaves, the decision to open the pulpit or priesthood to women signals to other denominations and organizations that they are committed to "modernist" theological priorities instead of "traditionalist" orientations. This is useful, he argues, because congregations and denominations need information about each other in order to form coalitions to work for shared goals and priorities.

The research of Deckman et al. (2003) and Olson et al. (2005) falls in line with Chaves's (1997) findings. While Chaves found that a church's acceptance of clergywomen is perceived as acceptance of a liberal/progressive agenda, Deckman et al. found that clergywomen tend to be more liberal than clergymen. Their examination of a random sample of six Mainline Protestant denominations found that about 80% of female clergy identify with the Democratic Party in comparison to a little under half of male clergy (623). Moreover, when presented with political issues, the clergywomen gave more liberal responses than the male clergy on every question. Not only did clergywomen tend to be more left leaning, they were also more politically active than clergymen, adopting positions on topics such as abortion and gay rights "that directly contradict those of the religious right" (625). Olson et al.'s (2005) extension of the sample beyond Mainline Protestant denominations to include Jewish traditions further confirmed these patterns.

Can partisan politics, then, help explain the gender gap in church leadership? Do Republicans and conservatives tend to oppose female clergy due to the perception (and/or reality) that clergywomen are political liberals? If so, could this account for lower rates of female clergy in American congregations given that political conservatives also tend to be more religiously active (Cooperman and Smith 2015) and likely more invested in the decision-making processes of their congregational leadership? Given that female clergy are more likely to hold liberal political and theological views (Smidt 2016), are Democrats more likely to support female clergy than Republicans in the United States?

Yet another possible explanation for the religious gender gap in congregational leadership pertains to the validity of stated support for equality. In other fields, such as politics and business, stated support for women in leadership roles is much higher than in actual practice. In principle, almost everyone says that they are happy to vote for a woman for president or other elected offices (Malone 2016), and yet women are still vastly underrepresented in the halls of Congress and the White House as well as in the state legislatures and governors' mansions of the various U.S. states. Research has also shown that sexism still influences voting choices, including in the 2016 election (Wayne, Valentino, and Oceno 2016). In business, people routinely say that women can excel if given the opportunity to lead (Pew Research Center

2015) and should receive equal pay for equal work (Patten 2015), yet women are underrepresented on corporate boards and management positions, and they make less than 80 cents for every dollar a man is paid—and even less than that if they are women of color (Patten 2016).

While more than half of all religious congregations in the United States allow women to serve as the principal religious leader, men still retain leadership in roughly nine out of ten congregations in the United States (Chaves and Eagle 2015). Could this be because more people say they support ordaining women in the abstract than actually support female clergy in practice?

The disproportionate paucity of female religious leaders in American congregations, even in congregations with female-inclusive leadership policies, may also be attributed to the prevalence of gender stereotypes and the relative shortage of female role models in positions of religious authority in the lives of young girls. There is no shortage of research and evidence showing that young people internalize the signals they pick in their childhood environment. This was recently illustrated by an analysis published in the journal *Science,* which showed that six-year-old boys are more likely to believe that men are "really, really smart" than six-year-old girls are to believe the same about women. The authors attribute this effect to the pervasive influence of gender stereotypes that in turn diminish the likelihood that young girls seek out activities that they understand to be only for children who are also "really, really smart" (Bian, Leslie, and Cimpian 2017).

When young girls and boys grow up in an environment where women in positions of religious authority are uncommon, rare, or even absent, they may internalize an expectation that positions of religious leadership are for men only, thereby discouraging women and girls from seeking out opportunities to exercise leadership in religious settings later in life. This may affect enrollment rates in seminaries and other religious training programs, which may result in the continued disproportionate number of male religious leaders in American congregations. We know, for example, that women make up approximately one-third of enrollees in Masters of Divinity programs in Mainline Protestant seminaries and only about one-fifth of enrollees of these programs in Evangelical Protestant seminaries (Miller 2013).

In sum, the last fifty years have seen uneven advancement in gender equality in American religious congregations. Multiple American denominations and congregations of various religious traditions have adopted inclusive leadership policies. The same can be said of employers, businesses, and government regarding women's opportunities in those areas. At the same time, the strides of the 1960s through the early 1990s in many of these fields, including religion, seem to have slowed or even halted in some cases. Why is this, specifically when it comes to gender and leadership in American congregations? While traditional theological orthodoxy is undoubtedly a significant part of the answer, there are other compelling explanations that may also help to explain this. These include the possibility that American worshipers are more supportive of female clergy in principle than in practice, that female clergy tend to not appeal to political conservatives (who make up the majority of American churchgoers these days), or even that young women do not pursue the ministry simply because it never occurred to them that it was a possibility. Here we hope to shed new light on these questions and many others.

THE NEED FOR A NEW PERSPECTIVE

Our goal is to speak to some of these wider questions about women, leadership, and society. We also investigate specific scholarly questions of female clergy and their interactions with their congregations. Researchers took an interest in studying female clergy in the 1980s and 1990s after a number of Mainline Protestant denominations began to extend the priesthood to women in the 1950s, 1960s, and 1970s. They wanted to answer questions such as, "Are women pastors different from male pastors in their ministry styles?" and "How do career patterns compare between male and female clergy? Are they equally as likely to be hired, and are they paid the same when they are?" (See, e.g., Carroll, Hargrove, and Lummis 1983; Chaves 1997; Lehman 1980, 1981, 1985, 1986, 1987, 1993; Lummis and Nesbitt 2000; Nesbitt 1997; Zikmund, Lummis, and Chang 1998.)

Scholarly interest in this topic dropped off somewhat in the late 1990s, though, as female ordination became more common in many Christian denominations throughout the United States. As can be seen in this chapter's introduction, the issue has regained traction in recent years, as the conversation has begun to focus on women's ordination in denominations and congregations that maintain their male-only clerical policies in a society that is increasingly coming to see gender discrimination as unacceptable, both in the secular/public and religious/private spheres. As most of the pioneering scholarly work on female ordination is now nearly twenty years old, we believe the time is ripe for a new perspective on this issue, especially considering that the currents of American religion have continued to change in a number of important ways in this period, most notably with the rise of the "Nones" (those with no formal religious affiliation) and the continued self-sorting of the American public along religious as well as political lines.

One of our primary goals, in addition to updating some of the scholarly research on women in religious leadership, is to contribute to the ongoing public conversation on this topic. We have noticed that supporters and opponents of female ordination are quick to make assertions about how people think about women at the pulpit and the predicted effects of a female priest on parishioners. These assertions are often overly broad generalizations that are extrapolated from a few anecdotal examples or personal experiences. While these personal observations are valuable, we seek to add systematic, comprehensive, and generalizable empirical evidence to these discussions, as hard data on the topic of women's ordination is often hard to come by.

We ask two key scholarly questions in this book: 1) What explains support for (or opposition to) women serving as the principal leader in American religious congregations? and 2) What effect do female clergy and congregational policies regarding female clergy have on the personal empowerment, religious attitudes, and behaviors of parishioners in those congregations? The answers to these questions will help us contextualize wider debates about women and leadership in American society: why are women underrepresented in American religious congregations, even in the congregations that allow them to serve in head leadership capacities? How might the trends we uncover regarding gender affect other broader trends of religion on society?

In our research we use a "mixed-methods" social science approach (Jick 1979) that draws upon a variety of academic disciplines, including sociology, political science, gender studies, and religious studies. We especially emphasize that the analysis presented in this book draws on completely novel quantitative and qualitative data that we collected throughout 2015 and 2016 via the Gender and Religious Representation Survey. Through a series of nationally representative public opinion surveys, we collected data on gender in religious representation from hundreds of American congregants from all major religious traditions, including those that currently ordain women and those that do not. Most previous research has been restricted to analysis of denominations within Mainline Protestantism, and understandably so, given that in the twentieth century this tradition pioneered extending clerical positions to women. More recent research has investigated these questions focused on other single denominations in isolation (Cragun et al. 2016; Martínez, Rodríguez-Entrena, and Rodríguez-Entrena 2012; Nesbitt 1997). As Lehman (1987) pointed out, however, it is essential that we broaden our sample given that gender interacts with religious leadership in *all* traditions, whether they ordain women or not.

In order to get a more personal and nuanced understanding of how gender and leadership interact in religious settings, we also spent several months in 2015 conducting face-to-face interviews with people in the pulpits as well as in the pews. Through this series of conversations with both clergy and congregants from a range of religious traditions, we allowed individuals to tell their stories, which provided us with an array of perspectives to enhance our understanding of this topic. Together with the public opinion survey data, these interviews allow us to take a broad as well as a deep look at our questions. To our knowledge, the research we present in this book is the first nationally representative and comprehensive analysis of support for female ordination and its effects among American churchgoers that includes perspectives from *all* major American religious traditions.

In contrast to most previous work on this topic, we also examine this question from an individual level of analysis, meaning that we take individual people as the key "unit" and examine how various demographic, religious, political, and contextual factors affect their attitudes and behaviors in congregations. Others have focused on the question of clergywomen from a denominational perspective (e.g. Chaves 1997) and we refer to such research throughout as we examine similar questions from the complementary perspective of people in the pews. This will add more breadth and depth to our existing knowledge on the issue. In sum, our key question is not why some denominations or congregations choose to ordain women while others do not. Instead, we ask, "What do parishioners think of the topic of female ordination?" "How supportive are they of women being allowed to serve in the pulpit in their congregations?" "Are they empowered or disempowered by the presence of female clergy?" "Does women's ordination influence parishioners' levels of self-esteem, education, church attendance, spirituality, or feelings of identity or trust in their congregational leadership?" These questions are important not only because they contribute to ongoing conversations on the role of women in religious institutions, but also because they shed light on some of the wider questions about the role and advancement of women in American society.

Another novel contribution of our approach is that we broaden our understanding of the topic by looking beyond the role of the principal leader in a congregation. Most previous research has focused on women who serve in the capacity of the head pastor or priest. We certainly include this aspect of congregational leadership in our analysis, but we also examine congregational policies about women's ability to serve as pastors or priests in the first place. Does it matter if the congregation allows women to serve as the principal leader, even if the individual currently occupying that role is a man? We also examine the lay leadership in a congregation: what proportion of the small-group and ministry leaders are women? Does this affect the religious attitudes and behavior of those in the congregation?

Finally, most previous research on this topic has been performed by sociologists who specialize in the sociology of religion. Here we draw heavily upon their pioneering work and add to it many insights and theoretical contributions from the discipline of political science. Both of us are primarily political science scholars and have been able to think about this question from a different theoretical framework. For example, political scientists often consider questions such as leadership, representation, and identity in political communities and nations. Much research has shown that representation has an important effect on political behavior and attitudes: minority groups clearly benefit when they are represented by someone who shares their group identity. Racial and ethnic minorities, for instance, are more likely to vote and feel invested in the political system when their member of Congress shares their background. In many ways we will explain in this book, we see a parallel between gender leadership in the political sphere and gender leadership in the religious sphere.

We are thus able to make a novel theoretical contribution to the study of female clergy that combines the strengths and approaches of different academic disciplines. We show that the same forces that drive the relationship between gender and leadership in politics can also produce a similar effect in religious communities. We also show that the reverse is sometimes true: gender and leadership in religious organizations can have important effects on religious behaviors of political groups. As we will see later on, liberals and Democrats can be negatively affected in their religious attitudes and behavior when their congregations do *not* allow women to serve as pastors or priests; however, contrary to what we might expect, conservatives and Republicans are largely unaffected by the gender of their congregational religious leader. Similarly, women tend to have lower levels of self-esteem than men when their most influential clergy member in childhood was a man, but have levels of self-esteem *equal* to men when their most influential religious leader was a woman. In short, gender representation matters in the private sphere just as it does in the public sphere.

We stress again that we will not spend much time in this book assessing the theological arguments related to women's ordination. Others more able than we are already actively engaged in that particular question (e.g. Belleville et al. 2005; Cunningham, Hamilton, and Rogers 2000; Macy 2007; Payne 2009; Shepherd, Anderson, and Shepherd 2015; Torjesen 1993; Willard 2010). Rather, our goal is to provide empirical evidence that will help inform these discussions and also speak to normative, philosophical, or theological perspectives. We do argue, however, that the evidence we present in this book merits strong consideration by those in a position to make such decisions as they seek to best achieve the goals of their organizations. While we found evidence that could be used to support either position, ordaining women produces many "upsides" with little to no "downside" in terms of its effects on significant religious behaviors and attitudes. In fact, our data show that male-only clerical policies in American congregations can even sometimes have disempowering and harmful effects on some groups in the pews.

PLAN FOR THE BOOK

This chapter has provided an overview and motivations for our research project. One of the key takeaways is that women's access to leadership positions has been expanding over the last century in American religious congregations just as it has in the secular and professional world. Similar to those worlds, though, the advancements toward greater equality in gender representation that followed the second-wave feminism of the 1960s has stalled in recent decades. There remains a clear gender gap in that women continue to be strongly underrepresented in congregational leadership positions, including in those congregations that allow women to serve as the principal religious leader. This gender gap is even more puzzling when considering the widespread stated support for gender equality. We want to understand better why this is case as well as the effects that it has on those in the congregations.

Chapter 2 explores both the historical and contemporary "lay of the land" of women's ordination in American religious congregations. We show how the extension of ordination to women has developed throughout American history and also look at recent statistics on how many congregations currently permit women to serve in the pulpit and how many currently have a clergywoman in that office. We also take a brief look at stated preferences for gender and leadership in these congregations: how many people say they would prefer a man or woman as their personal religious leader?

Chapter 3 focuses on the question of "why" in terms of support for women's ordination. We will take a deep dive into our face-to-face interviews to uncover the common themes and patterns of explanations that people give to justify either their support for or opposition to women's ordination. We uncover a few key themes that are common to individuals in a variety of religious traditions, including scriptural authority, personal experiences, and gender stereotypes about the gifts and talents that men and women possess.

Chapter 4 then turns to the "who" of support for women's ordination: who supports and who opposes female clergy in their congregations? We will examine our nationwide public opinion survey to uncover the factors associated with support and opposition, paying special attention to personal demographics, religious behavior and attitudes, congregational context, and political orientations. Our results show that support for female ordination is much more a function of congregational context and religious and political orientations than it is of demographics, most notably gender.

Chapter 5 returns to the evidence presented in the preceding chapter and asks whether it is reasonable to expect that the data is revealing a fully accurate picture of the prevalence of support for female ordination in the United States. After all, gender and leadership, especially in religious communities, is often a sensitive and controversial issue. When asked in a telephone survey whether they were in favor of women being allowed to serve as clergy in their own congregations, some respondents might feel social pressure to say "yes," when in reality are more hesitant. After all, who wants to appear sexist? We take advantage of a survey tool called a list experiment to see if there is any evidence that support for female ordination is either over- or underreported in our public opinion surveys. We find that this is indeed the case: support for female clergy is likely overreported among our survey respondents, meaning that there are fewer supporters of female ordination among those who attend religious services than our public opinion surveys would lead us to believe.

Chapter 6 then begins to explore our second question: what effect do female clergy have on those in the pews? More specifically, we examine whether female clergy can serve as positive role models during childhood and adolescence in ways that enhance levels of personal and societal empowerment as adults. Are girls and young women affected by influential female religious leaders in their lives such that as adults they have higher levels of self-esteem or self-efficacy? Do they have higher levels of education and employment than otherwise would be the case?

Chapter 7 focuses more specifically on how gender leadership affects people's interactions with their religious congregations. Do women in the pulpit have any effect on the religious attitudes or behaviors of those in their congregations? One of the many arguments that supporters of female ordination use is that female clergy can empower the women (especially younger women) in their congregations such that they are motivated toward higher levels of religious engagement and activity. On the other hand, opponents of female ordination sometimes argue that women clergy may drive away more theologically tradi-tional folks, which might lead to stagnation in congregational growth and loss of identity. While anecdotes of this nature abound, our goal is to discover whether there is any systematic evidence one way or another on this important question. In interviews, we find that while people are eager to say that the gender of their particular pastor or priest does *not* matter, they are quick to offer observations on ways they believe it *does* matter.

Chapter 8 turns back to the public opinion survey data to approach the same question from a quantitative perspective. In general, our evidence shows that the presence of female clergy, policies regarding female clergy, and lay female leader-ship in congregations do matter in terms of people's level of religiosity, spirituality, and trust in and identification with their congregations. These effects, though, are more modest than often asserted. Most interestingly, we find that the effects are pre-sent not only among women but among certain political and theological subgroups as well.

Our final chapter assesses the evidence that we have presented in light of current conversations regarding female ordination in American congregations as well as wider societal forces at play. We will also consider our evidence in light of previous research on female ordination. We conclude by offering some thoughts to religious congregational leaders and decision-makers on this issue that affects more than half of the members of their congregations.

A NOTE ON TERMINOLOGY

"Sex" versus "gender." Scholars of gender studies as well as many interested readers are aware of the important conceptual differences between "sex" and "gender"; sex is a biological characteristic, while gender is a social construct (Unger 1979). Accordingly, some have intentionally avoided the term "female clergy" or "female priest" in favor of "women clergy" or "woman priest" for this reason (e.g. Sentilles 2009). We recognize this important distinction, yet choose to use the terms interchangeably in this book almost purely to provide variety in the labels we use, which can often be repetitive. In doing so, we in no way mean to imply that the distinctions between sex and gender are irrelevant or unimportant to topics such as this.

Religious terms. The population of interest to our research is adult Americans who attend religious services. We refer to this group interchangeably as "churchgoers," "attenders," "those who attend religious services," "worshipers," etc. Again, this is primarily a stylistic choice. We are aware that "church" has a specifically Christian connotation and that it is inaccurate to describe those of other faiths who attend synagogues, mosques, temples, as "churchgoers." Nonetheless, only about 7% of our sample of adult Americans who at least occasionally attend religious services identify with some non-Christian tradition (Judaism, Islam, Buddhism, etc.), very close to the 5.9% found by the 2014 Pew Religious Landscape Survey that identify as Jews, Muslims, Buddhists, and so on. Given that reality, we try to alternate among "churchgoers," "worshipers," "parishioners," "congregants," "church attenders," and "religious service attenders" while acknowledging that not all terms are completely applicable in all instances.

We also recognize that there is a wide variety of terms used to refer to clergy and congregational leaders in various religious contexts in the United States. Depending on the context, the appropriate title might be priest, pastor, rabbi, imam, preacher, rector, dastoor, bishop, manbo, elder, abbot, swami, minister, reverend, or something else. We also recognize that words like "ordination" or "priesthood" are more appropriate in some contexts than in others. Given the diversity in terminology, we have opted to use "pastors and priests" or "clergy" as our primary terminology given that Christian congregations still make up a majority of adherents among American worshipers today. While we use these terms somewhat interchangeably throughout, we again acknowledge that not all terms are equally appropriate in each circumstance.

NOTE

1. As of the time of writing, the video is available at: https://www.facebook.com/Sojourners Magazine/videos/10153602912467794/

2

WOMEN'S ORDINATION IN AMERICA

A Contemporary Overview

WOMEN HAVE BEEN acting as religious leaders and preachers since before the American Revolution. In 1637 Anne Hutchinson led a group of religious followers after being banished from the Massachusetts Bay Colony to settle the area that is now Rhode Island. Nearly four hundred years later, women's religious leadership is widely, though not universally, accepted in the United States. The most recent major expansion in the number of American denominations ordaining women occurred in the 1970s, with the Lutheran Church in America, the American Lutheran Church, Reform Judaism, the Mennonite Church in North America, and the Episcopal Church all ordaining women during that decade. Conservative Judaism followed in 1983. (For a more comprehensive treatment of the history of female ordination in the United States, see Schneider and Schneider 1997.)

These changes in the 1970s brought an increase in both female enrollment in seminaries and in the number of women clergy in these denominations. On the national level, the Census Bureau showed that in 1970 only 3% of clergy were women, which grew to 10% by 1990 (Chaves 1997). Lehman (1993, 15) reports that this rapid expansion of ordination to women throughout Mainline Protestantism in the 1970s generated a good deal of pushback and retrenchment. Some proponents continued to press for women's ordination, while others found the backlash too much and so abandoned the cause entirely.

Why did some denominations choose to admit women to their leadership offices throughout the twentieth century, while others did not? What characteristics are shared by traditions and congregations that followed the path of ordination? Do male and female clergy differ in their career paths or ministry styles? How common are clergywomen in American congregations today? Who attends congregations led by women? This chapter will address each of these questions and more. We will proceed by giving an overview of policies and practices on gender and leadership in contemporary American religious congregations and then summarize the findings of previous research on the topic of women's ordination. We then introduce and describe a novel public opinion survey dataset that will allow us to look broadly and dive deep into recent trends and patterns of women's ordination in the United States as well as public opinion on female ordination and its effects on those in the pews.

WOMEN AT THE PULPIT: POLICIES AND PRACTICES IN AMERICAN CONGREGATIONS

Table 2.1 shows which major denominations in the United States have, as of the time of this writing, policies in place that generally allow the ordination of women to ministry positions and which have male-only leadership policies. Here and throughout this book we categorize American religions following the approach of Putnam and Campbell (2012) and the Pew Research Organization. Religious traditions canvassed include Evangelical Protestants (Baptists, Pentecostals, etc.), Mainline Protestants (Presbyterians, Episcopalians, Methodists, etc.), Historically Black Protestants, Catholics, and Nones.

Evangelical Protestantism. According to the 2014 Pew Religious Landscape Survey, Evangelicals currently comprise about 25% of the total U.S. population and consist of Baptists (including the Southern Baptist Convention), Pentecostals, and Restorationists of various kinds. As the name suggests, Evangelical Protestantism is characterized by an emphasis on evangelizing, or sharing the word of God with others. In contrast to Mainline Protestantism or Catholicism, Evangelical Protestantism places less of an emphasis on ritual and sacraments aside from baptism and communion, and instead focuses on conversion, which is often described as "being saved" or "born-again" (Fowler et al. 2013).

As in all religious traditions, there is variation among Evangelicals when it comes to gender and cultural norms. There are currently three general camps: Fundamentalists, Complementarians, and Egalitarians. Fundamentalists emphasize the inherent differences between men and women and prescribe strict gender roles accordingly. From the perspective of Fundamentalists, the man is the

TABLE 2.1

Policies on female ordination in American denominations and religious traditions[a]

Generally <u>permit</u> female clergy	Generally <u>prohibit</u> female clergy
African Methodist Episcopal	Churches of Christ
American Baptist Church	Islam
Assemblies of God	Jehovah's Witnesses
Buddhist	Jewish: Orthodox
Christian Science	Latter-day Saints (Mormon)
Community of Christ	Missouri/Wisconsin Synod
Disciples of Christ	Lutheran Church
Episcopal Church	Orthodox Church
Evangelical Lutheran Church in	Presbyterian (non-PCUSA)
America	Roman Catholic Church
Jewish: Reform and Conservative	Seventh-day Adventist Church
Movements	Southern Baptist Convention
Mennonite Church USA	
Pentecostal Church of God	
Presbyterian Church (USA)	
Progressive Baptist	
Salvation Army	
Society of Friends (Quakers)	
Unitarian Universalist	
United Church of Christ	
United Methodist Church	

[a] *Source:* Grant 2015; Kuruvilla 2014; Masci 2014.

leader both in the public and private spheres, while the woman is to be submissive. Complementarians also view men and women as having different roles, but place a greater emphasis than Fundamentalists on the equality between sexes. For Complementarians, these different roles are not forced but rather encouraged as part of their "Christian duty" (Hankins 2009). In contrast, Egalitarians see marriages as equal partnerships and allow room for women to assert a more dominant role in everyday life and church leadership (Hankins 2009). They tend to focus more on the context of the Biblical passages that call for women to be submissive to their husbands, and also to emphasize Ephesians 5:21, which calls for men and women to "be subject to one another out of reverence for Christ" (New Revised Standard Version [NRSV]).

The Fundamentalist and Complementarian views of gender and leadership are most common within Evangelical denominations. In 1964, Addie Davis became the first woman to be ordained in the Southern Baptist Church (SBC) (Allen 2014). In 1984 the SBC reversed their stance with a resolution against the ordination of women, declaring, "that we not decide concerns of Christians doctrine and practice by modern cultural, sociological, and ecclesiastical trends or by emotional factors; that we remind ourselves of the dearly bought Baptist principle of the final authority of Scripture in matters of faith and conduct; and that we encourage the service of women in all aspects of church life and work other than pastoral functions and leadership roles entailing ordination," a stance which was reaffirmed in 2000 (Southern Baptist Convention 1984). While the Southern Baptist Convention does not endorse the ordination of women, individual congregations are left to decide for themselves whether to ordain women. The vast majority tend to follow the male-only endorsement of the wider SBC (Zikmund, Lummis, and Chang 1998, 10). According to the executive committee of the SBC, only about 30 of the convention's 40,000 congregations are currently headed by women, or 0.075% (Chapman 2016). That said, a few Evangelical denominations ordain women, including the Pentecostal Assemblies of God and the Cooperative Baptists.

Mainline Protestantism. About 15% of the American public identifies with a Mainline Protestant tradition. This family of Protestantism is generally characterized by ritual and tradition (such as creeds, communion, and baptism), semi-hierarchical structures, interpretation of the Bible as the inspired word of God (as opposed to the literal word of God), and progressive stances on social issues. The five largest Mainline Protestant denominations in the United States are the United Methodist Church, the Evangelical Lutheran Church in America, the American Baptist Churches USA, the Episcopal Church, and the Presbyterian Church (USA). Each of these denominations has granted full ordination rights to women since at least the 1970s. Women's ordination is therefore no longer a controversial topic within these denominations; contemporary discussions tend to focus instead on issues of LGBT (Lesbian Gay Bisexual Transgender) ordination and same-sex marriage.

Roman Catholicism. The Roman Catholic Church is Christianity's largest branch, accounting for over one billion members worldwide (BBC News Services 2013) and over 65 million in the United States (about 20% of the total U.S. population) by most estimates. While Evangelicals tend to be politically conservative and Mainliners tend to be more progressive, political ideology and partisanship among Catholics vary widely, largely mirroring trends within American society as a whole. Catholicism operates within a strict institutional hierarchy. Seated in Rome, the church is based on a hierarchical structure that includes a pope, bishops, and priests. Due to this hierarchical structure, official doctrinal change can be a slow process that often leads to disconnects between opinions among the laity and those of church leaders.

In terms of women's ordination, official Catholic doctrine states that because Jesus elected only men among his twelve apostles and because the college of bishops represents the apostles on Earth today through the process of apostolic succession, the ordination of women is not possible. As seen in the introductory chapter, however, some within the church favor the introduction of women into the deaconate and/or the priesthood.

Historically Black Protestantism. Roughly 7% of the American public identifies with denominations within the Historically Black Protestant religious tradition. These include churches within the Baptist family (e.g., National Baptist Convention, Progressive Baptist Convention, and Missionary Baptist), Pentecostal family, and Methodist family (e.g., African Methodist Episcopal). This tradition emerged in the nineteenth century as an alternative to the segregation and exploitation rooted in slavery that characterized the American religious landscape. In the northern states, independent Baptist church leaders began to separate from white Baptist churches, creating a loose association of black ministries (Mellowes 2010). Black Methodist and Pentecostal congregations soon followed suit to establish a strong system of networks and conventions. Historically Black Protestant churches have served as visible engines of social change to fight oppression and counter racial injustices.

Women have traditionally played an active role within these denominations, many of which currently ordain women, including churches within the National Baptist Convention and the African Methodist Episcopal denomination. Due to the diversity of denominations that are grouped under the category of "Historically Black Protestant," it is no wonder that there is a wide range of opinions on the topic of female ordination. There are several black women's ministries that were developed in the early twentieth century and continue to lobby for the interests of black women and their representation among the clergy (e.g., the National Association of Colored Women, the Young Women's Christian Association, and the Women's Missionary Union).

Other Christian denominations. About 3% of Americans belong to one of a variety of smaller Christian traditions and denominations. These include the Church of Jesus Christ of Latter-day Saints (Mormonism), Jehovah's Witnesses, Seventh-day Adventists (also referred to as the Adventist Church), Christian Scientists, Orthodox Christians (Greek, Russian, etc.), and many others. These denominations differ from each other in that they represent a wide variety in beliefs and traditions, but they are similar in that they are often (although not always) non-Trinitarian and often depart radically from traditional Christian doctrines. With the notable exception of Christian Science, these minority traditions generally have a strong commitment to male-only clergy.

For example, within the Adventist Church women are unable to serve in official clerical roles and are often relegated to other leadership roles such as teaching, community organizing, or counseling. In 2015 the General Conference of the Adventist Church voted not to ordain women after five years of debate and activism. Despite this ruling, some North American Adventist congregations have begun to ordain women to serve as leaders although they are not officially recognized on a denomination-wide level (Banks 2015; Boorstein 2015).

The Ordain Women organization has been a visible proponent of women's ordination in the LDS Church, which has a male-only leadership policy. In the LDS Church, there is no professional clergy and young boys are ordinarily ordained as "deacons" at the age of twelve, "priests" at the age of sixteen, and "elders" around age eighteen, after which they may serve in nearly all the leadership positions in their congregations. Similar to other denominations with a male-only priesthood, women have supporting leadership roles in auxiliary organizations such as the Relief Society, the church's worldwide women's group. Activist Kate Kelly was excommunicated by the LDS Church in 2014 after she led a rally of hundreds of Mormon women in Salt Lake City, Utah, which drew media attention to what she described as inequalities within policies related to church leadership (Boorstein and Robinson 2014).

Women are not admitted to the priesthood in various branches of the Orthodox Church in the United States, for reasons similar to those given by the Catholic Church (Matthewes-Green 2007; Matusiak 2017). Nevertheless, discussions about the role of women in church structure and governance are ongoing. Following the lead of the Orthodox Church in Africa, there appears to be openness to inviting women to serve as deacons in the Greek Orthodox Church in America (Clark 2017).

Judaism. About 2% of Americans identify with some branch of Judaism, a monotheistic religion that holds the Torah as its primary text and the covenantal relationship between God and Israel as a foundational component of belief. American Judaism is generally divided into three categories: Orthodox, Conservative, and Reform. About 10% of American Jews identify with the Orthodox tradition, 18% with Conservative Judaism, and 35% with the Reform movement, while another 30% identify with no denomination in particular (Lugo et al. 2013). The Reform and Conservative traditions permit women to serve as rabbis, while only men can be rabbis within the Orthodox tradition. In Orthodox and some Conservative synagogues, men and women are physically separated, while Reform Judaism rejects this practice because of a firm belief in equality between men and women (Elliott 2005). Conservative Judaism occupies a middle ground between the Orthodox and Reform traditions. Since 1983 women have been allowed to be rabbis within the Conservative tradition, but there remain some differences between men and women in religious contexts (e.g., men and women are still separated during services in some congregations). In other contexts, women traditionally occupy a central role in the weekly Shabbat ritual observed at home, and Orthodox women are empowered to ritually administer the *mikveh* purification ceremony to other women.

Other non-Christian religions. About 4% of the American public identifies with a non-Christian/non-Jewish religious tradition. Of these, Islam represents about 1%, Buddhism and Hinduism both at about 0.7%, and "New Age" faiths at about 1.5%, according to the 2014 Pew Religious Landscape Survey. Most of these New Age faiths, including Unitarian Universalists and Pagan/Wiccan communities, routinely allow women to act in a leadership capacity as often as men.

Islam, like Judaism and Christianity, falls under the tradition of Abrahamic religions. It follows the word of Allah as given to the Prophet Muhammad and is based on five main pillars: Shahada (the declaration of faith), prayer, alms giving, fasting, and the Hajj (the pilgrimage to Mecca). None of the three main sects within Islam (Sunni, Shia, and Sufi) permit women to act as imams, lead prayer, or deliver the khutbah (sermon). Some scholars of Islam, such as Amina Wadud, though, have argued that Islam can be supportive of female leaders. In 2005 Wadud led Friday prayer and delivered the khutbah in New York City (Elliott 2005).

Buddhism is a religious tradition that focuses on inner cleansing and meditation. American Buddhism differs from Buddhism in other contexts through its increased focus on everyday mindfulness rather than the "unattainable quest for enlightenment" (Seager 2012, 188). In Western settings Buddhism has adopted several ideals of liberal democracy and as a consequence has deemphasized the need for strict monastic hierarchies. This results in a unique context that encourages leadership to be accessible to all, so women as well as men are allowed to lead in worship.

The Purusarthas (i.e., the objects/goals of human pursuit) are foundational to Hinduism and include Dharma (ethics and duty), Artha (prosperity and work), Kama (emotions), and Moksha (liberation). Through meditation and rituals of prayer and worship, as well as rites of passage, one works toward attaining a balance of these four goals. Although women do not serve as priests in the Hindu tradition, they are expected to lead in their families, maintain the family shrine, and teach Hindu traditions and values to their children. In an American context, while Hindu women are more likely to work outside the home, they have begun also to share in official religious capacities and are more likely to serve on temple boards of directors than women in India are.

CHARACTERISTICS OF TRADITIONS AND CONGREGATIONS THAT SUPPORT WOMEN'S ORDINATION

With this overview in mind, we can now examine in more detail the motivating factors behind the expansion of women's ordination over the last two centuries. As discussed, the 1970s was the last period of major expansion of women's ordination in American congregations. These changes in institutional policies coincided with rapid societal changes toward greater inclusion for women in wider secular society and politics. Some have investigated the factors that caused some denominations to ordain women while others stayed with their male-only leadership policies. Both Carroll et al. (1983) and Chaves and Cavendish (1997) identify societal trends such as modernization and feminism as key factors that motivated a number of denominations to begin to ordain women in the 1970s.

Perhaps the most extensive look at this question was conducted by Chaves (1997), who examined both external and internal factors associated with women's ordination in American religious institutions. Drawing on both historical and comparative evidence, Chaves gathered an extensive amount of data to perform a "systematic quantitative study of the one hundred largest Christian denominations in the United States." He concludes that there are a few primary factors that predict which denominations choose to ordain women and which do not. For example, denominations with a more literal view of scripture are more likely to oppose women's ordination, as are denominations with a strong degree of sacramentalism (i.e., holding a belief in transubstantiation, that bread and wine do not merely symbolize Jesus's body and blood but rather mystically *become* his body and blood during communion).

He also finds that institutions that are decentralized in their leadership structure are more likely to move to ordain women sooner because decentralization allows greater autonomy for local congregations to experiment with women's ordination. Finally, Chaves (1997) finds that the presence of an autonomous women's ministry group is associated with earlier adoption of female ordination. When women become accustomed to exercising power within an organization they can use their platform to advocate for additional privileges and rights. Lummis and Nesbitt (2000) further add that it usually takes the support of a majority of women in an institution to overcome barriers to join together as a group to advocate. They conclude that institutions with male-only leadership will likely not change if a majority of women in those communities are not on board with the prospect of clergywomen.

Perhaps the most intriguing conclusion reached by Chaves (1997) is that the choice of a denomination to ordain women or not has a strong symbolic significance.

"Rules about women's ordination have become one of the primary markers of a denomination's cultural location," he writes (40). It is one of the many ways that institutions communicate their values and priorities to each other as they negotiate religious alliances and coalitions in a pluralistic society. In other words, women's ordination acts as a signaling device that institutions use to advertise whether they are more modernist or traditionalist in their theology and culture. Those that maintain male-only leadership are able to communicate that they are taking a stand against modernity. In contrast, both Chaves (1997) and Lehman (1993) see the choice for a denomination to ordain women as an internalization of some of the fundamental assumptions of secular humanism and Enlightenment liberalism.

CAREER TRAJECTORIES AND LEADERSHIP STYLES OF CLERGYWOMEN

As we explained in the introductory chapter, most research on women's ordination in the United States has been performed by sociologists who specialize in the field of religion. They were primarily interested in clergy themselves, and examined, for example, how men and women clergy compare in their career patterns and ministry styles. Their pioneering research established a baseline and context to which our research now contributes.

Although women are now permitted to be ordained in many religious denominations, scholarship on their career trajectories reveals inequalities in both opportunity and experience between clergywomen and clergymen. Overall, clergywomen have more difficulty finding work (Chang 1997; Lehman 2002; Nesbitt 1997), make less money (Carroll, Hargrove, and Lummis 1983; Grant 2016; Lehman 2002; Zikmund, Lummis, and Chang 1998), receive fewer benefits (Lehman 2002), and are more likely to remain in lower-level clerical jobs longer than men (Carroll, Hargrove, and Lummis 1983; Lehman 2002; Lummis and Nesbitt 2000; Sullins 2000). Moreover, female clergy are more likely than male clergy "to begin [as or] remain rural pastors or assistants in the larger congregations" (Lummis and Nesbitt 2000, 446).

The difference in pay is worth some elaboration. Zikmund et al. (1998, 73) found that clergywomen made 9% less than clergymen in the 1980s and 1990s, even after controlling for such factors as age, experience, education, number of hours worked, level of job, denomination, and size of church (Zikmund et al. 1998, 73). More recently, Grant (2016) found that clergywomen make, on average, seventy-six cents for every dollar that male clergy make, which is slightly lower than the pay gap in 2015 for women working full time (seventy-nine cents for every dollar that men working full time earn, see Institute for Women's Policy Research 2016).

A 1998 study of more than five thousand surveys from clergy in Protestant denominations shows that clergywomen perceive that they are seen by others as effective and are satisfied with their jobs at rates comparable to clergymen (Zikmund, Lummis, and Chang 1998). While these rates of job satisfaction are positive, they do not excuse the reality just described: persistent pay gaps and placement discrimination. Zikmund et al. (1998) see the persistence of these inequalities as a result of a widespread assumption in the 1990s that the "gender barrier" was gone and so institutions made fewer systematic attempts to equalize hiring.

Other scholars have examined the extent to which male and female clergy are systematically different in their ministry styles. So far this body of research has produced only mixed results. Zikmund et al. (1998), for instance, conducted surveys with 250 male and female pastors from fifteen Christian denominations and found consistent differences in perceptions of male and female pastors' leadership styles. Respondents perceived women as "caring [more] than men about the individual lives of members of the congregation, [and being] more pastorally sensitive, more nurturing and more likely to draw on personal experiences in preaching, teaching and counseling" (55). Moreover, they said that women's leadership styles were more cooperative than "hierarchical or authoritarian" (56).

A study of full-time Protestant pastors found that despite working the same hours per week, clergywomen "generally allocate a higher percentage of time toward pastoral care and administering the work of the church, and less time toward preaching and preparing for worship" (McMillan 2002). Charlton (1997) found a greater level of interest from clergywomen than clergymen in "special ministries—chaplaincies, pastoral counseling, [and] directing service agencies" (611). Politically, male and female clergy differ in terms of both ideology and behavior. Female clergy are more likely to be liberal, Democrats, and active in politics than are male clergy (Deckman et al. 2003). They are more attentive to women's issues, have more progressive theological views, and are more likely to prioritize social justice initiatives (Djupe and Gilbert 2003; Olson, Crawford, and Deckman 2005; Smidt 2016). Clergywomen appear to experience higher levels of stress and "role strain" than their male counterparts due in large part to opposition from laity, but clergywomen also report feeling supported by clergymen and church executives (Lehman 2002). Similarly, Carroll et al. (1983) found that clergywomen were more likely than clergymen to report difficulty in "being themselves," relaxing, and finding close friends—likely associated with the fact that there are so few female clergy in comparison to male clergy. Their study also reported that clergywomen had a more difficult time than clergymen in managing a work-life balance, but this difference was slight. Despite these differences, both male and female clergy tend to be satisfied and committed to both their jobs and their communities (Carroll, Hargrove, and Lummis 1983; Zikmund, Lummis, and Chang 1998).

Other research, though, has found less evidence of any major substantive differences in leadership styles between clergymen and clergywomen. One of the most extensive studies of this topic was performed by Lehman (1993), which indicates only very qualified, context-based support for differences in leadership behavior between the sexes. Lehman found that women were more likely than men to value empowering laity, less likely to be legalistic when dealing with ethical issues, and less likely to "[prefer] making decisions using formal or rational criteria." However, each of these differences was very slight (29). "With regard to authority, status, preaching, interpersonal style, or dealing with social issues," however, Lehman found no evidence for differences between clergymen and clergywomen (29). Instead, these differences were dependent on contexts such as whether the pastor was in a senior or solo position as well as the date of seminary completion (30). (See also Purvis 1995; Simon and Nadell 1995).

THE GENDER AND RELIGIOUS REPRESENTATION SURVEY

As we explained in the previous chapter, most empirical research on women's ordination was performed in the last half of the twentieth century. Here and throughout this book we rely heavily on more extensive and recent data that comes from the Gender and Religious Representation Survey, a combined series of four nationally representative telephone and internet public opinion polls conducted throughout 2015 and the fall of 2016. This is a novel source of data on women and leadership in America's congregations that we collected for this book. The survey includes adult Americans from all major American religious traditions who report attending religious services at least "seldom." These include respondents from all major Christian denominations in the United States as well as non-Christian denominations (Judaism, Islam, Buddhism, Hinduism, etc.). It also canvasses those who identify as "None," that is, those who declare no formal religious affiliation but attend religious services at least once in a while.[1] (These include self-identified atheists and agnostics as well as those who identify as "nothing in particular." For some, religion is an important part of their lives, and for others it is not.) So long as they say that they attend religious services at least once in a while, regardless of their religious affiliation or identity, they are included in our surveys. According to the 2014 Pew Religious Landscape survey, this captures 86.1% of the total adult American population. Thus, these results should not be interpreted to mean that this is the effect for *all* adult Americans, but rather the approximately eight out every nine who say that they attend services at least occasionally.

Wave 1 of the survey was conducted in spring of 2015 and Waves 2 and 3 were collected in fall of 2015. Waves 1 and 2 were telephone-based surveys and Wave 3 was an internet-based survey collected to help balance out demographic biases in the telephone survey; Wave 3 also contained additional questions that are analyzed later in the book. Combined, these three waves of the survey produced 1,334 usable responses, which are the primary source for the quantitative analysis used throughout this book. Wave 4 was collected in the fall of 2016 and is a combination of 815 usable telephone and internet surveys. This wave of the survey contained unique questions that allowed us to glean additional insights. All four waves contained basic measures of respondents' demographic and religious characteristics and the gender of their current congregational leader as well as the gender policy of their current congregation. In each case throughout this book, our survey data is weighted to account for response biases in gender, race/ethnicity, and age. (More comprehensive and specific details on this survey's methodology can be found in the Data Appendix. We refer interested readers there for a comprehensive explanation of the survey, sample sizes, question wording, etc.)

In our surveys we measured congregational gender leadership in three ways: 1) whether a woman is currently serving as the congregation's "principal religious leader" (Waves 1–4); 2) whether women are *permitted* to serve in that capacity, regardless of the gender of the current leader (Waves 1–4); and 3) the proportion of the small group, ministry, vestry, council, and other lay leaders in the respondent's congregation that is composed of women (Waves 1–3). We opted to use the phrase "principal religious leader" deliberately in our survey so that it would fit just about any congregation regardless of its specific policies or leadership titles ("pastor," "priest," "rabbi," "imam," etc.).[2]

FEMALE CLERGY: MORE COMMON IN PRINCIPLE THAN IN PRACTICE

Figures 2.1 and 2.2 show the results of our survey on these three measures of gender leadership. On first pass, our survey results show that slightly over half (54.8%) of Americans who attend religious services report at least occasionally attending a service in a congregation that permits a woman to be the principal religious leader. Despite this, less than one in ten (9.1%) currently attend services in a congregation with a clergywoman in the pulpit. It is important to note that this figure does not include congregations in which women serve as an assistant pastor or youth leader, or in some other supportive capacity. Here and throughout we focus primarily on women serving as the head or chief pastor or priest in a congregation. The figures we recorded are similar to figures reported earlier by Chaves and Eagle (2015) in the

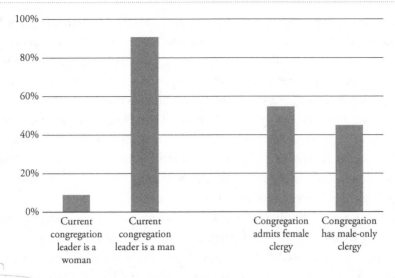

FIGURE 2.1 Gender and Religious Representation Survey

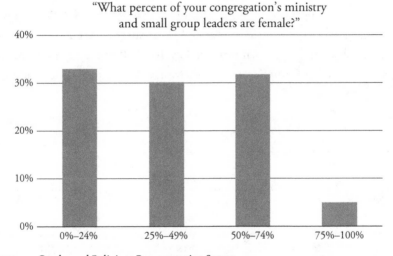

FIGURE 2.2 Gender and Religious Representation Survey

2012 National Congregation Survey. That study showed that 58% of congregations allow women to serve as the head clergyperson but only 11% of congregations currently have a woman serving in that capacity. We can also observe that, on average, only about a third of our sample (36.8%) attend a congregation in which women make up at least half of the lay leadership.

We can break down these figures further by the respondents' religious traditions. As before, we use the categories of Evangelical Protestant, Mainline Protestant,

Catholic, etc. Unfortunately, our survey did not capture a sufficient number of Jews, Mormons, or non-Christians (due to their small proportion of the wider population) to be able to speak individually to those religious traditions with any degree of confidence. In other words, these smaller groups are included in our overall analyses throughout this book but there are not enough of them to be able to say definitively, for instance, what percentage of Jewish/Buddhist/Hindu congregations in the United States have female leaders (more details are available in the Data Appendix). Nonetheless, we are able to drill down further within the larger religious traditions that account for about 85% of both the American population and our survey respondents. The results are presented in Figure 2.3.

Here we see that Mainline and Black Protestants report both the highest rates of congregational policies allowing for female clergy (75.7% and 66.1%, respectively) in their congregations as well as the highest proportion of congregations with women actually serving as their head pastor or priest (15.3% and 13.5%, respectively). In all, 10.1% of Protestant survey respondents report that they attend a congregation with a female leader, which is similar to the 12% of Protestant clergy who are female, as reported by Smidt (2016, 40). Smidt also notes that 19% of Mainline clergy and 2% of Evangelical clergy were female when his last survey was conducted in 2009. We also can observe that women make up less than half of the lay leadership body (the parish council in Catholic parishes, the vestry in Episcopal congregations, the

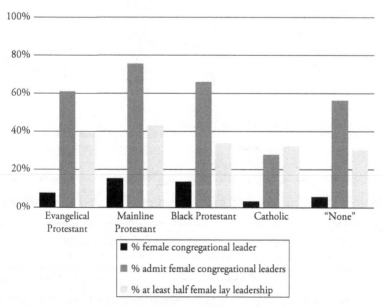

FIGURE 2.3 Gender and Religious Representation Survey

ward council in LDS congregations, or the equivalent collection or board of ministry and group leaders in any given congregation) in all major American religious traditions.

It is interesting to note as well that a little over a quarter of American Catholics claimed that their congregations allow women to serve as the "principal religious leader" and that about 3% report having a woman serving in that capacity. It is well known, however, that the Roman Catholic Church has a male-only priesthood. How might we explain this? First, we should remember that, as Chaves (1997) has shown, in American congregations there is a good deal of "decoupling" between policies and practice. Many traditions and congregations that do not ordain women in principle actually do in practice allow women to serve as the head congregational leader to some degree or another, while there are many congregations that theoretically permit women to serve but rarely do so in practice. Second, Wallace (1992) explains that there are indeed some Catholic parishes in the United States in which women have been assigned to function as the primary leader in a "priestless parish" because a male priest is unavailable for some reason. These women fulfill the pastoral and organizational (but not sacramental) duties traditionally performed by priests, including visiting parishioners in the hospital and in their homes, providing spiritual counseling, organizing classes, and supervising the parish budget. According to the Centre for Applied Research in the Apostolate, approximately 2.2% of Catholic parishes in 2016 had someone other than a full-time priest assigned to perform the chief pastoral duties because full-time priests were unavailable. About a third of these are estimated to have either a religious sister or a lay woman assigned as the principal congregational leader, which makes for about 0.7% of all Catholic parishes in the United States.[3] These realities help explain our survey finding that 3% of Catholic respondents say that the leader of the congregation they attend most often is female.

What of the 28% of Catholics who report that their congregations would permit women to serve as their principal leaders, even if women are not actually serving in that capacity? This is very likely higher than is actually the case, but perhaps is also to some extent due to this same "decoupling" phenomenon: some Catholic parishes may have women serving in some sort of informal or unofficial principal leadership capacity. It is also possible that there is some "social desirability" effect at play: there are likely some Catholics who are aware that the male-only priesthood in the Catholic Church may appear parochial in a more egalitarian society and thus might feel pressure to report to interviewers that their congregations permit women to serve as priests to try to avoid embarrassment. It is also possible that some Catholics (and non-Catholics for that matter) simply have an inaccurate understanding of gender policies in the congregations they attend. Finally, it is possible

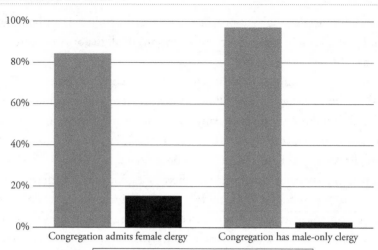

FIGURE 2.4 Gender and Religious Representation Survey

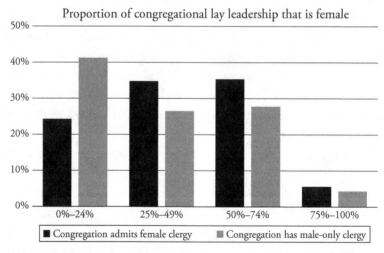

FIGURE 2.5 Gender and Religious Representation Survey

that some of these Catholics may identify as Catholic but attend a non-Catholic congregation that permits women to serve in this capacity. Regardless of the cause, it is notable that over a quarter of American Catholics report to surveyors that their congregations permit women to serve as the principal religious leader when it is well known that this is not the case.

We can also examine in Figures 2.4 and 2.5 how female pastors and the proportion of female congregational leaders are distributed among congregations that do and do not have policies that allow women to serve as the principal leader. This allows us to look even further beyond the wider religious tradition to individual congregations and individuals in those congregations, since, as we have discussed, leadership in policy and principle does not always match leadership in practice.

Here we see a few more trends worth noting. Earlier we showed that in the congregations attended by those in our survey, women served as the chief leader in about 9% of them. As we would expect, this proportion is concentrated almost entirely in the congregations that *allow* women to serve in that capacity, in which they lead in about 16% of those congregations. Interestingly, about 3% of our survey respondents who attend congregations that *do not* allow female clergy claim to have women serving as their congregation's principal leader, further evidence of the decoupling effect discussed earlier.

We also see that the proportion of women serving in the lay leadership of the respondents' congregations depends to some extent on the policies in place for women to be the head congregational leader. Generally speaking, women make up a larger proportion of the lay leadership in congregations in which the position of head pastor or priest is also open to women. Figure 2.5 also shows that there is stark difference at the low end of the spectrum: in about 40% of congregations with male-only clergy, women make up less than a quarter of the lay leadership, compared to about 25% of congregations that permit female clergy.

In sum, a few general trends are evident from our survey results. Between two-thirds and three-quarters of Protestants report attending congregations that permit women to serve as the pastor or priest, as well as more than a quarter of Catholics. Despite the generally widespread inclusivity of congregational gender policies in the United States, actual implementation of these policies is much more limited. Just under 10% of American churchgoers attend congregations headed by women, and these are primarily Mainline and Black Protestants whose rate of female clergy is only a little higher at about 15%.

Gender representation in lay congregational leadership is not much better: women hold at least half of the leadership positions only about a third of the time, regardless of the religious tradition. That said, women make up at least 25% of the congregational lay leadership about three-quarters of the time among Protestants and a little over half the time among Catholics and Nones. When we look at specific congregations instead of wider religious traditions, though, we see that this is dependent somewhat on the policies in place for gender leadership in those congregations: there are more female lay leaders and ministers in congregations in which women can serve as the head leader and fewer in those in which that position is restricted only to men.

WHO ATTENDS CONGREGATIONS WITH FEMALE CLERGY?

Aside from a person's religious affiliation, are there any other religious, demographic, or political factors associated with attending a congregation with a female pastor or priest? Table 2.2 presents the proportion of each group who attend a congregation led by a woman or who attend a congregation in which the position of principal congregational leader is open to a woman.

Table 2.2 shows that women are slightly more likely to attend congregations led by women (10.6% versus 7.2%), yet at the same time are slightly less likely than men

TABLE 2.2

Demographic patterns in attendance of congregations with female clergy or gender-inclusive leadership policies[a]

	Attend a congregation led by a woman (%)	Attend a congregation with gender-inclusive leadership policy (%)
TOTAL	9.1	54.8
Attend once a week or more	10.8	50.7
Attend less than once a week	7.4	59.1
Theological traditionalist	9.2	52.0
Theological moderate/ progressive	9.1	56.2
Women	10.6	52.0
Men	7.2	58.1
Age 50+	9.9	57.0
Age under 50	8.4	47.9
White	7.0	53.9
Black	14.2	65.6
Latino	11.7	50.7
College education	9.3	59.0
Less than college education	8.8	51.2
Democrats and leaners	13.5	60.1
Republicans and leaners	4.8	50.0
Political liberals	12.6	60.7
Political conservatives	5.8	50.0

[a] *Source:* Gender and Religious Representation Survey.

to attend congregations that allow women to serve as the principal religious leader (52% versus 58.1%). Race and ethnicity also make an important difference: African Americans are more likely than either whites or Latinos to attend a congregation led by a woman or one that has gender inclusive leadership policies. It is notable that about two-thirds of African Americans attend congregations that allow women to serve as the pastors or priests, compared to a little over half of whites and Latinos. About one in seven churchgoing African Americans currently has a woman pastor, compared to about one in eight Latinos and one in fifteen whites. Those with college degrees are a little more likely to attend a congregation that allows a woman to serve as clergy but are no more likely to actually attend a congregation with a female pastor.

There are also some important religious differences apparent here. Compared to infrequent church attenders, frequent attenders are more likely to have a female pastor but less likely to attend a congregation that permits female clergy (10.8% versus 7.4% and 50.7% versus 59.1%, respectively). Interestingly, theological traditionalists are only a little less likely to attend congregations with women clergy than are theological moderates or progressives (52.0% versus 56.2%), although they are no more or less likely actually to have a woman congregational leader in their current congregations.

Finally, some striking political patterns are apparent here. Democrats and liberals are about 10% more likely to attend congregations that allow women to serve as clergy than Republicans and conservatives (60.1% and 60.7% versus 50.0% and 50.0%, respectively). They are also more likely to attend congregations that have women clergy (13.5% and 12.6% versus 4.8% and 5.8%, respectively). We will explore the reasons for this in the following chapters.

SUPPORT FOR FEMALE CLERGY

In our Gender and Religious Representation Survey we asked respondents to tell us their preferences on gender policy in their religious congregations. Specifically, we asked: "Would you strongly prefer, somewhat prefer, somewhat NOT prefer, or strongly not prefer that the congregation you attend most often permit women to serve as the principal religious leader?" If asked for clarification, the surveyor explained to the respondent that "principal religious leader" refers to the chief pastor or priest in most congregations.

Figure 2.6 shows that support for female clergy among Americans who attend religious services is strong, with more than seven out of ten respondents (72.3%) reporting that they either somewhat or strongly prefer that women be permitted to serve as the principal leader of their congregations. We can also observe in Figure

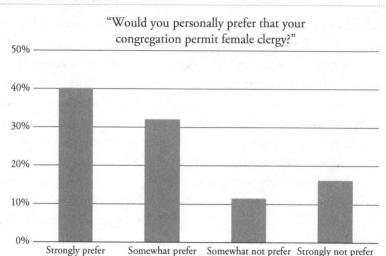

FIGURE 2.6 Gender and Religious Representation Survey

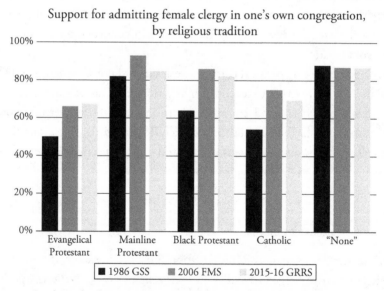

FIGURE 2.7 Gender and Religious Representation Survey and Figure 8.3 in Putnam and Campbell (2012); "GSS" is the "General Social Survey," "FMS" is the "Faith Matters Survey," and "GRRS" is the Gender and Religious Representation Survey; Note: "Catholics" for 2006 Faith Matters survey is specifically "Anglo Catholics."

2.7 that this support is widespread across religious traditions: support for female clergy is at 67.5% among Evangelicals, 84.9% among Mainline Protestants, 82.3% among Black Protestants, 69.5% among Catholics, and 86.8% among Nones. These levels of support for female ordination are comparable to those found in the 2006 Faith Matters Survey, which asked respondents: "Agree/disagree: Women should be

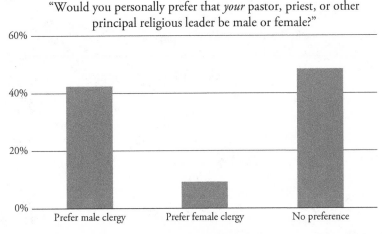

"Would you personally prefer that *your* pastor, priest, or other
principal religious leader be male or female?"

FIGURE 2.8 Gender and Religious Representation Survey

allowed to be priests or clergy in my house of worship" (Putnam and Campbell 2012, 635). Figure 2.7 also shows support in each religious tradition in the 1986 General Social Survey. From this we see that it has increased by about 10% to 15% among Evangelicals, Black Protestants, and Catholics since the 1980s, but stayed about the same among Mainline Protestants and Nones, who already registered high levels of support. Our findings are more or less in line with those reported by Putnam and Campbell (2012) in the 2006 Faith Matters Survey, although support for female ordination is somewhat lower in our results.[4]

While levels of support for female ordination are somewhat higher among Mainline Protestants, Black Protestants, and Nones than among Evangelical Protestants and Catholics, these results show that clear majorities of all major American religious traditions support the idea of female clergy in their congregations. We can confirm that Putnam and Campbell's (2012) characterization of Americans as "religious feminists" remains accurate. Moreover, these results fall in line with the broader national trend of high levels of support for measures of women's equality that we discussed in Chapter 1. It seems that at least in the abstract, support for gender equality in the religious sphere is similar to support for equality in the private and public spheres.

PREFERENCES FOR A WOMAN AS RESPONDENTS' PERSONAL CLERGYPERSON

As a final analysis of attitudes toward female clergy in the United States, we can examine questions asked in Wave 4 of our Gender and Religious Representation

TABLE 2.3

Personal preference for gender of one's own congregational leader[a]

	Prefer male clergy (%)	Prefer female clergy (%)	Doesn't matter (%)
TOTAL	42.4	9.2	48.4
Male	49.4	6.9	43.7
Female	36.2	11.4	52.4
Evangelical	49.5	7.6	42.9
Mainline	29.0	7.9	63.1
Black Protestant	45.9	9.0	45.2
Catholic	45.9	9.5	44.6
Congregation allows female clergy	32.2	9.8	48.1
Congregation has male-only clergy	52.9	10.0	37.0
Prefers congregation to allow female clergy as a policy	30.0	13.5	56.5
Prefers congregation to have male-only clergy as a policy	90.9	0.7	8.4

[a] *Source:* Gender and Religious Representation Survey.

Survey in fall 2016. We asked our respondents: "Regardless of the policies of your particular congregation, would you personally prefer that *your* pastor, priest, or other principal religious leader be male or female?" In all, Table 2.3 shows that 42.4% respondents said that they would prefer a male congregational leader, while a female leader was preferred by only 9.2% of respondents. The remaining 48.4% volunteered that they did not have a preference one way or another or "didn't know." As we might expect, there is a moderate degree of difference when it comes to the individual's gender. About half of men indicate that they would like a clergyman in their personal congregation, compared to only about 7% who say they would rather have a clergywoman. Interestingly, only about 11% of women say that they would personally favor a clergywoman, while more than a third (36.2%) claim a preference for a man to be their personal congregational leader.

It is interesting to note in Table 2.3 that this does not change much depending on one's indicated religious identification. Roughly half of Evangelicals, Black Protestants, and Catholics alike all report desiring a man to be their pastor or priest, and less than 10% report opting for a woman congregational leader, with the rest indicating no preference one way or another. Mainline Protestants, on the other hand, are less likely to indicate a desire for a male leader and more likely instead to say that it does not matter. Interestingly, about the same proportion of Mainline Protestants say they would prefer a woman pastor or priest. We also see that personal preferences for a clergywoman are roughly the same at about 10%, regardless of whether the individual's congregation has a gender inclusive policy, although the frequency of "doesn't matter" responses increases for those in congregations that allow female clergy.

Perhaps most telling in Table 2.3 is that among those who would like it better if their congregation allowed women to serve as the principal religious leader, only about one in seven would prefer that their *own* congregational leader were a woman, while about one in three still wants a man to serve in that capacity (although a little over half say that it would not matter either way). Not surprisingly, we see that preference for a clergyman in one's personal congregation is nearly universal among those who desire that their congregation allow only men to serve as clergy, although nearly one in ten say that it would not matter either way.

We can further examine this by estimating the likelihood of indicating a preference for either a male or female clergyperson over a "doesn't matter" opinion while statistically controlling for various other factors that might make a difference. Possible factors included one's gender (as we can see in Table 2.3 that women are slightly more likely to prefer women clergy and vice versa), current congregational policies permitting female clergy, whether the individual's current clergyperson is a male or female, level of religious service attendance, religious belief orthodoxy, political partisanship and ideology, and standard demographics (age, race/ethnicity, income, education). We also included control variables for non-Christian religious affiliation, as leadership dynamics can work differently in those congregations. (Further details about this analysis can be found in the Data Appendix.)

In our analysis, the only factor that predicts a preference for female clergyperson instead of "no preference" is the gender of a person's current congregational leader. Those who currently have a clergywoman are about 9% more likely to indicate a preference for female clergyperson, controlling for the other factors described above. Otherwise, there are no consistent predictors of preferences between these two options. There are, on the other hand, several predictors of preferences for *male* clergypeople instead of "no preference." They are:

- Gender: men are 30% more likely to want a male clergyperson in their congregation.
- Gender of congregational leadership: those who currently have a woman serving as their congregational leader are 49.7% less likely to indicate a preference for male clergy.

- Gender policy of current congregation: those in congregations that allow women to serve as the principal leader (regardless of the gender of the current leader) are 36.4% less likely to desire male clergy.
- Religious service attendance: those who attend religious services more than once a week are 71.4% more likely to indicate a preference for male clergy than those who attend religious services only seldom.
- Religious belief orthodoxy: religious traditionalists are 52.8% more likely to indicate favor for male clergy than those who say that their religion or congregation should "adopt modern beliefs and practices."
- Race: those who identify as African American are 38.7% more likely to indicate a preference for male clergy.
- Political partisanship: strong Republicans are 42.7% more likely to prefer male clergy than strong Democrats.

It is not terribly surprising that men are more likely to prefer male clergy. It also makes intuitive sense that those who are currently exposed to female clergy or belong to congregations that permit female clergy are less likely to prefer male clergy. This is in line with Lehman (1985, chaps. 6–8, 1987), who finds that exposure to female clergy increases comfort and support for gender-inclusive congregational policies and the hiring of women pastors and priests. It is interesting, though, that regardless of the policies of one's congregation and the gender of one's current leader, people who are more religiously active and doctrinally orthodox as well as Republicans are more likely to favor male religious leaders in their congregations. As we will see in coming chapters, these particular factors tend to consistently organize attitudes toward gender and religious leadership in the United States.

SUMMARY

This chapter has given a brief overview of historical development and contemporary context of women's ordination in American congregations. As would be expected given gender norms of the time, women in the pulpit were relatively rare until the middle of the twentieth century, when most Mainline Protestant denominations began to ordain women. This coincided with an expansion of the role of women in the professional and secular worlds and the context of second-wave feminism in American society. Some researchers have argued that the choice to ordain women is a key indicator of a denomination's cultural orientation and its acceptance or rejection of modernity.

Most previous research on female clergy has focused on the clergywomen them-selves. Work done in the 1980s and 1990s found that despite the door of ordina-tion being open to women in many denominations it was still more difficult for female clergy to find work, and when they did, they tended to be paid less and were more likely to be employed in supportive rather than primary leadership roles. More recent research has shown that this has not changed significantly in the last two decades. Also, the evidence is mixed on whether male and female clergy are signifi-cantly different in their leadership styles.

Right now a little over half of American churchgoers attend congregations in which women are allowed to be ordained, although only about one in every ten attends a congregation in which a woman is actually serving as the congregation's leader. These are found largely in the Mainline Protestant and Historically Black Protestant traditions. Given these traditions' more progressive approach to both theology and politics, it is perhaps no surprise that political liberals and Democrats are more likely to attend congregations led by women (or congregations that permit women to be ordained) than conservatives and Republicans. Our survey results also show that about 72% of American congregants support women being allowed to serve as clergy, including a majority of every major religious tradition.

Finally, our survey results show that about two-fifths of these same survey respondents say they have no preference as to whether their personal clergyperson is a man or a woman. Of those who do have a preference, though, the vast majority say they would prefer a man to be their personal pastor, priest, rabbi, or imam. They tend to be more religiously active and theologically and politically conservative and come from congregations that currently have male clergy and male-only leadership policies. They are also somewhat more likely to be men themselves. All in all, only about 10% of American worshipers say they would prefer a woman to be their personal congregation's spiritual leader. In the introductory chapter of this book, we note that women's advancement in America's pulpits (as well as other areas in society) has stalled over the previous few decades, and that this is to some degree puzzling given the wide-spread majority support for gender-inclusive leadership policies in congregations. That less than 10% of those who attend religious services in the United States specifically prefer a female leader, though, may help explain why this is so. It seems that Americans are fairly egalitarian on this issue in the abstract, but much less so in practice.

NOTES

1. In the survey we measured each respondent's religious identity but not the specific affiliation of the congregation they attend. Rather, we asked them to describe the "congregation they attend

most often." We assume throughout this book that the respondents who self-identify as Catholic attend Catholic congregations, Baptists in Baptist congregations, etc., but it is possible that this is not the case 100% of the time. This also affects how we might interpret findings for the "Nones" in our survey: we do not know whether they are attending a Catholic, Protestant, Jewish, Unitarian, or Buddhist congregation but rather that they themselves do not personally subscribe to a particular religious identity.

2. It is important to note that we rely on the respondents themselves to report the gender balance of each of these three aspects of religious leadership in their congregations. We were not able to independently verify the accuracy of each. We assume, then, that respondents know the gender of the head leader in their congregation as well as the approximate balance of men and women in the congregational lay leadership body. Those who said "I don't know" to these questions were excluded from the analysis. These are common and necessary assumptions in most public opinion survey research.

3. Personal correspondence between the authors and Mary Gautier, Senior Research Associate of the Center for Applied Research in the Apostolate, Dec 22, 2016, based on *The Official Catholic Directory*.

4. We suspect that this is likely due to the differing samples between the two surveys: the 2006 Faith Matters survey included those who report never attending religious services while our sample excluded them, instead looking only at those who attend at least "seldom."

I'm going to trust in the authority of the Church. I'm going to say yes. And I'm going to trust if there are things that need to be changed, that will happen in the fullness of time and I will follow where it leads. (Interview 29)

Right now I'm thinking particularly of a little girl who—her mom tells me—when she goes home, she plays church. And when she would play church and she was at a different congregation, the pastor said, "oh, how lovely. She must be . . . playing the music director." And she [the mom] goes, "oh, no, no, no she plays pastor. My son is the one that plays music director." And so then when she came here, her mom was very excited because now when she plays and she's pastor she has me in a role . . . [she knows] that she can be a pastor . . . What I like about it is she doesn't have any idea that that's not possible. So, to be able to break those barriers that once were there to say "yes, it is a possibility," and allow her to have hopes and dreams and not be told, "no, those—that can't happen." I think that's incredible. (Interview 27)

3

SUPPORT AND SKEPTICISM REGARDING

WOMEN'S ORDINATION

STORIES SUCH AS these are a large part of why we decided to talk with individuals in America's churches, synagogues, temples, and mosques. Between September and December of 2015, a research team of advanced undergraduate students interviewed more than seventy individuals from a wide range of backgrounds and experiences throughout the central Kentucky area where our college is located. Through these interviews we spoke with women and men, young and old, "cradle Catholics" and converts, pastors, priests, rabbis, imams, deacons, and parishioners in a variety of occupational fields—from students to working professionals to retirees to stay-at-home moms. We also made sure to interview individuals from each of the major religious traditions within the United States as well as from a number of minority religions both Christian (Christian Science, Jehovah's Witness, Latter-day Saints, Seventh-day Adventists) and non-Christian (Judaism, Islam, Buddhism, and Hinduism). In all, about a third of our interviews were with clergy and congregational leaders, while the remaining two-thirds were with members of the congregations themselves.

As expected, there was a wide range of views on the role of women in society and in religious organizations among such a diverse group; respondents varied from self-proclaimed "huge feminists" to those who align more closely with one woman who said, "feminism [says] . . . 'women are equal'; they're not. They're not physically, they're not spiritually, they're not mentally. And so we shouldn't pretend that they are" (Interview 52).

The key questions that we seek to answer in this chapter are these: in what ways do people think about gender and leadership in their congregations? How do they feel about women serving as pastors, priests, and rabbis in their congregations? What reasons do they give for either supporting or opposing women's ordination? In essence, this chapter seeks to question the "why" of support for female ordination. To answer these questions, we mine our interviews to see what insights they reveal. Social scientists generally use two methods to answer their research questions. The first is to review the previous research on the topic, form specific testable hypotheses about relationships between different variables, and then test those hypotheses using empirical evidence. The second approach reverses the order: gather empirical evidence, see what it says, and then use the findings to help form theories and explanations of the topic under investigation. In this book we use both approaches to learn more about the interaction of gender and leadership in congregations.

This chapter begins by analyzing our face-to-face interviews using the second method described. Our research team transcribed the interviews and then we read through those interviews several times to look for common themes and patterns as they relate to people's views on women's ordination (full technical details on our interviews and our methodological approach is explained in the Data Appendix). We refer to specific interviews when quoting directly from the interview transcripts by a unique identification number that corresponds with a table in the Data Appendix that shows the interviewee's gender, race, approximate age, religious affiliation, and whether the individual is a clergyperson or congregant.

SCRIPTURAL AUTHORITY

Scripture quickly emerged as the most commonly cited explanation behind individuals' stances on female ordination. Of those who mentioned scripture as related to their support of female ordination, some individuals support ordination *because of* scripture while others held their views *in spite of* certain passages. Individuals who support ordaining women because of scripture often referred to the creation narrative in the Bible, in which both men and women are created in the image of God. One male Jewish leader explained:

> One place we can look at is in the beginning of the Torah, the beginning of the Bible, the idea that men and women were created both in the image of god at the same time. And so you have Chapter 1 and ... Chapter 2 being this first kind of story, first kind of narrative of creation and both are created in the image of God and both kind of together. (Interview 9)

Others cite the prominence of female leaders in the Bible, such as Mary Magdalene, as influential in their support of women's leadership within their congregations today. As one older African American woman who attends a Baptist congregation describes:

> Mary Magdalene, you know, walked with him just as the twelve disciples did. You know, he loved her and taught her just as he did his twelve disciples. She preached the word, just as his twelve disciples did. So, with that I think that ... females have a role in that just as much as ... males. (Interview 45)

Other individuals expressed support in spite of certain scriptures that seem to place women in a subservient position. They view scripture as presenting two different "strains of thought": some passages promote women's submission and others highlight their leadership. Due to these conflicting themes, "everyone is picking and choosing" (Interview 8). Others see Bible passages such as those in 1 Corinthians and 1 Timothy that speak of women's submission as being "taken out of context." A female Disciples of Christ minister explained: "We've always known that those scriptures against women teaching or preaching were taken out of context. So we haven't had those theological debates" (Interview 24).

This view that scriptures have been selectively interpreted to oppose gender equality in leadership is not limited to the Judeo-Christian tradition or the Biblical text. One young Hindu woman echoed this theme when she said, referring to the Hindu Vedas, that the scriptures "show equality for men and women. But I think along the way people have somehow, sometimes, changed it up to do what they want to do" so that "the gender roles have ... evolved" (Interview 61). These individuals tend to believe they should support female ordination because scriptures once supported equality but have since been interpreted and adjusted so as to place women in subservient roles within religious traditions.

In the same way that individuals see the scripture as supportive of female ordination, others reference specific passages in explaining why they oppose it. Many

Christian respondents in this group commonly referenced Jesus's choosing twelve men as disciples as a legitimate reason for denying women the opportunity to preach. Because Jesus selected men instead of women to follow him and lead others to him, these Christians believe their churches should follow Christ's example and permit only men to lead. Several others cited passages in Ephesians, 1 Timothy, and 1 Corinthians that describe women submitting to their husbands and remaining silent in church. Specifically, these passages included:

> *Wives, be subject to your husbands as you are to the Lord. For the husband is the head of the wife just as Christ is the head of the church, the body of which he is the Savior. Just as the church is subject to Christ, so also wives ought to be, in every-thing, to their husbands.* (Ephesians 5: 22–24 NRSV)
>
> *Let a woman learn in silence with full submission. I permit no woman to teach or to have authority over a man; she is to keep silent.* (1 Timothy 2:11–12 NRSV)
>
> *Women should be silent in the churches. For they are not permitted to speak, but should be subordinate, as the law also says. If there is anything they desire to know, let them ask their husbands at home. For it is shameful for a woman to speak in church.* (1 Corinthians 14:34–35 NRSV)

A middle-aged male pastor from a nondenominational Evangelical church, for example, referenced 1 Timothy when explaining his opposition to women serving as pastors: "I believe that scripture says that a man should be the overseer in the church . . . I believe that the role that Paul is speaking of specifically in scripture is the pastoral, the leader, the elder role within the church, [which is] reserved for men" (Interview 5). Other individuals connected their opposition to female clergy to the order of creation as described in Genesis. While some of those who referenced scripture in support of female ordination cited the creation story as proof that both men and women were created in the image of God, some in opposition cite God's creation of Adam before Eve as reason for men serving in the leadership position within their congregations. One example is from a Jehovah's Witness woman in her thirties who argues that because God created Adam first, men are supposed to lead while women are to assist.

> My favorite scripture about that is with the apostle Paul and he's just like, the only reason why men are used in the leader position is because Adam was created before Eve. And he [Paul] makes it very clear that it has nothing to do with intellect, or talent, or personal strength, nothing even to do with emotion. It's just that when God created the first human it was a male and he created him with a certain purpose in mind that he didn't fulfill, so until that purpose

is fulfilled he wants anyone who is kind of looking for that position to . . . train himself in that same vein. Because Adam had certain jobs to do, and when Eve came along she was there to help him in his task, which was to make the whole earth beautiful. And even throughout the Hebrew and Greek scriptures, it's always followed that same thing, where you have all these women who are fantastic supports, even stronger supports. They're there to help them see it through, provided they agree. (Interview 71)

Several individuals said that even though their opinion was based in scripture, they would adjust it if and when their church changed its stance. In other words, they followed their church's lead. Noting that Jesus had twelve male apostles, one man who attends a Jehovah's Witness church stated: "He, the Savior, set it up this way, and if and when he changes it then we'll get in line with it" (Interview 14).

This sentiment of following God, and thereby the Church's lead, was more explicitly described in our interviews with Catholics, who frequently discussed the importance of "following Rome" or "following where the Church leads." One Catholic woman in her sixties, for example, explained the connection between scripture and church teachings this way:

I feel that the subject has been faithfully researched by those who have made the decision. . . . I don't feel that the different committees or the different individuals who have looked at it have done so with the intent of not granting the women with the ability to become priests. I think that they researched it and studied it and prayed upon it theologically and within the parameters of our faith. (Interview 32)

This trend of respondents aligning their beliefs with those of their churches did not seem to be strictly dependent on age, as both younger and older individuals described the same phenomenon. A Catholic woman in her mid-thirties, for example, explained that while she was personally opposed to female ordination, she nevertheless "believes that in the fullness of God's understanding . . . if the Church needs to welcome women as deacons or whatever in the future, [she's] going to trust the Church on that" (Interview 29).

PERSONAL EXPERIENCES

We had an older man that came up to me and, he says, "So you know we're gonna have a woman priest?"

I says, "Yeah, I do." And I says, "So?"

And he says, "Well, we've never had one."

And I says, "Does it make a difference to you whether it's a woman or a man up there?"

He says, "Well, I don't know . . ."

I says, "Well it sounds like it did. . . . I hadn't even heard her. I'd seen her once and met her and I says, "Well, give her a month and see what you think."

Well, it wasn't till the second Sunday he says, "This is a keeper." Yep. But he was set in his ways. . . . I can't think of anybody that really said anything negative, because when she first preached, or you first met her, she put you at ease. (Interview 36)

This quotation from an Episcopalian man in his seventies demonstrates the second-most prominent theme of support that emerged in our interviews with both clergy and congregants. Individuals related "experience" to support for ordaining women. This theme was manifest in two ways: individuals either related their support to direct experience with clergywomen (for example, having gone to a church with a female pastor) or to experiencing/witnessing the increased participation of women in the workforce.

As detailed in the quotation at the beginning of this section, many individuals related support of female ordination to their personal experiences with clergywomen. Those whose congregation is led by a female pastor or was in the past were more likely to support female ordination than those who had only had male religious leaders. In the instance described in the quotation, the "older man" did not initially support clergywomen because his congregation had "never had one" before. After hearing her preach he changed his mind. His initial hesitation, or even opposition, was replaced with acceptance—in his words, he realized she was "a keeper" (Interview 36).

One conversation with a Catholic priest in his late fifties further illustrates this theme. He told us that he first heard a woman preach at a community thanksgiving that brought different denominations together:

I [once] participated in a ministerial group that included several women. The interim pastor of the Methodist church for a while was a woman. And I remember when it came time for the community thanksgiving service, which was like on a Tuesday evening of Thanksgiving week, we all came together and she preached. And I remember she did an excellent job. And that was—it was when it first began to disturb me that we couldn't invite women in our own congregation to go to school and prepare to do that. So over the course of the years, I've known women in ministry who could do the job as well as, if not better than, some of the pastors we have now. So, yeah, I'd like to see it open up. I'd like to see it opened up to that. (Interview 18)

This suggests that until individuals gain an outside perspective, as this priest did, they see their own system as "perfectly natural." It is worth noting that this priest was the only clergyperson we interviewed whose beliefs regarding female ordination go against those of his church. While the congregants we spoke with do not unanimously agree with their religious tradition's stance on female ordination, disagreement is rare. This suggests that congregational context is a related factor to whether an individual supports female clergy.

A few individuals we talked with belong to denominations that permitted female clergy, but they had never had a clergywoman as their own congregation's primary religious leader. One woman in her sixties who is a member of the Assemblies of God denomination explained:

It would be strange to me to sit under a female pastor although I'm fine with it, and I guess it would be something to get used to. So I don't, I think it's just where I've always had a male as a pastor. I can't, I, I just don't know. I'm sure I would adapt but I guess ... even though I believe women can be pastors, that was my only experience. (Interview 51)

Another young man from a traditionally black Baptist denomination echoed this theme:

I feel like it would be something to get used to just like anything else in life. When you've always seen for the most part male pastors through the male leaders, to have a female tell you that this is what the Word of God is would be a little bit different. Even though I would not *not* listen to her just because she's a female, it would take me awhile to adjust. But I feel like it's the same way with presidents as far as we haven't had a female president yet because our nation's a little slow on change and the idea of a female leader in the White House kind of throws people off. It's starting to become more acceptable now but for the most 150–200 years it's always been we need a man. . . . So in the church—in the church I believe that it's possible and I believe that I would accept it, but I think it would take time just like everybody else. (Interview 47)

This theme of experiences as being connected to acceptance seems to extend past having a female pastor. Several individuals discussed how seeing women succeeding in leadership positions in other areas of society led them to question why this equality did not extend to the pulpit. One woman in her sixties related her experience "in the workplace" as leading her to think more about women's roles in the church.

> I think because I was out there and many of my friends were, we were working, we were in the workplace . . . [and] you began to say, "Hey, you know, maybe women aren't being promoted to jobs. And maybe they aren't getting the same kind of salaries." And so when you started thinking about that you started thinking about females in your church. (Interview 31)

One Evangelical Lutheran pastor in her mid-fifties described conversations with older individuals in her church who were accepting of the idea of a female pastor:

> I'd say those who are older, women and men in general, as they are aging it's become more acceptable, I believe, for them to have a woman pastor. What I hear is, "Oh, I have a woman doctor now, why can't I have a woman pastor?" Or "I have a" something else dealing with a woman or . . . "in a former city we had a woman mayor," so that was really cool. But it's nice for them to make that transition to say that it's good. (Interview 27)

These statements further demonstrate the interconnectedness of gender equality (or lack thereof) in the public and private spheres with gender equality in the religious sphere that was discussed in the introductory chapter. If individuals who witness a woman leading in the medical field as a doctor, for example, come to question why they don't see more women leading in their church, the reverse could also be true. Women's advancement in our places of worship could spill over to our businesses and government buildings as people begin to question why, if they have "a woman [pastor] now, why can't I have a woman [mayor or manager or president]?" (Interview 27).

RESISTANCE FROM MIDDLE-AGED AND OLDER WOMEN

Although the individuals we interviewed tended to emphasize their interpretation of scripture or personal experiences with women in leadership rather than their demographic characteristics as leading to their stances on female ordination, demographics did come up when clergywomen discussed those who were *least likely* to support them. Middle-aged and older women were often identified as the groups that had the most difficulty accepting women as pastors. A clergywoman in the Evangelical Lutheran Church of America stated:

> I think before, when I first became involved in ministry, the people that were the most hesitant to accept a female pastor—because that is still a relatively new thing within the Christian church—actually tended to be older women.... I suspect there's some reasons behind that based upon their identity in the Church and their role in the Church, and if they couldn't then, then why should I? But as I'm more involved in ministry, that seems to have gone away. But there's still, there's occasionally a couple individuals that I've had instances with and probably half the time they've been older women. (Interview 27)

"With women," states one female Presbyterian associate pastor, "it is, interestingly enough, more of an issue about my gender than it is anything else" (Interview 26). Four of the nine clergywomen we interviewed independently brought up this theme of opposition from middle-aged women. (Similarly, Carroll et al. [1983, 186] found that middle-aged men and women are among the groups most strongly resistant to female clergy.) When asked to elaborate, these clergywomen explained that this lack of acceptance among some women may be due to a feeling of jealousy. This same female Presbyterian associate pastor explained:

> I think, and this is just completely my theory, I think with a lot of the older women it is maybe a little jealousy because they were raised in an era where they couldn't.... You know, they legit couldn't be in ministry or be a leader in any way. So I think that's a part of it. I also think there is a competition factor of "I can do it better than you." ... And I think because we're both women there's not that difference to a man. ... We are now on legit equal footing, which is a larger conversation within the wider scope of our culture of why woman to woman, man to man, makes you on equal footing. (Interview 26)

An Evangelical Lutheran Church in America (ELCA) female pastor explained that she was initially surprised that she was not better received by the women in her congregation:

> I actually thought that it would be more women that would like having a woman pastor and for a long time I actually thought more women liked having a woman pastor than males did. And now I think it's more of a balance. ... Because, like I said, I suspect that it had to do with the church continually telling women "no, no, no," and then finally saying "it's okay." And then when

it's okay, then what about them? And why wasn't it okay for them, and why is it okay for this particular female? And I think that's really hard as a woman especially who's grown up in her church her entire life. (Interview 27)

For these laywomen, it seems as though a lack of opportunity in their youth affects their ability or willingness to accept female pastors today. This lack of acceptance from middle-aged and older women seems to extend beyond the Mainline Protestant tradition. This phenomenon also emerged in a conversation with a female Reform Jewish rabbi who explained that, "the only people I have trouble with are women my mother's age. . . . Maybe [they] have gone through their own journey and their own careers but at a time [when] it was even harder" (Interview 8).

She goes on to describe how the experiences of female clergy are comparable across traditions: "I think that what women clergy experience in Judaism, whether it's Conservative or Reform, are probably not that much different than any other clergy or any other major profession. So I think my friends who are lawyers or doctors, they run into the exact same issues" (Interview 8). The Jewish Reform tradition began ordaining in the 1970s in the United States, around the same time as many Mainline Protestant denominations, including the Episcopal Church in 1972. Women who did not have the opportunity to serve in that capacity earlier in their lives comprise the demographic that clergywomen point to as most hesitant to accept women's ordination today. This, again, relates to the wider issues of women and leadership in American society that were discussed in the introductory chapter. While no two experiences are the same, this rabbi suggests that commonalities and general trends persist not only across religious traditions but also across occupations. This suggests to us that the many of the same forces that contribute to the gender gap in various areas of American society drive the persistent disparity of women leaders in American religious congregations as well.

GENDER STEREOTYPES

Some individuals pointed to differences between men and women as related to their support for or opposition to female ordination. Respondents variously declared these differences innate, a product of socialization and societal norms, and a combination of the two. To a large extent, these perceived differences were based on typical gender stereotypes that are common in American society.

Those who relied on gender differences to justify their support for female ordination often talked about women as having specific talents that enable them to effectively serve as pastors and priests. For example, the Catholic priest mentioned earlier in this chapter, who supports female clergy, said:

> I would like to see the doors opened to women. You know, include women in every one of our ministries. I have known women over the course of the years who had the gifts that are needed in ministry. I remember one member of our congregation went to . . . seminary [and] they had a homiletics class. The class voted for her at graduation, for her to receive an award as the most gifted speaker. Now here she is, a woman with the gift for speaking, preaching, giving a homily or a sermon, and yet our church says, "You can't use that gift." Now that doesn't make any sense to me. It seems to me that if the Holy Spirit endows someone with a certain gift there should be a way that they can use it for the benefit of other people. And I think that we could do this gradually. We could first ordain women as deacons. Let people get used to the idea of seeing them, you know. We already have women as Eucharistic ministers, you know, giving out communion. We have women as lectors. We have women as altar servers. They can do an awful lot. But the door to the deaconate and priesthood is closed to them. And so, basically, yes, I'd like to see that changed. (Interview 18)

One older Presbyterian clergywoman pronounced the ministry a "logical field for women" (Interview 22). Others (both men and women) shared their perception that women have skillsets uniquely suited for ministry. The ELCA female pastor noted earlier said:

> Women are at least fifty percent of the population, if not more, and women have a variety of gifts and talents. I think we do a really good job of thinking between two different hemispheres in our brain. And we have a better ability to collaborate. We have a better ability to communicate. We have a better (usually) sense of compassion. And I think all of those things are Christ-like attributes that God wants us to share within the church and within the body of Christ that are desperately needed. Especially in times where there seems to be more fanaticism, there seems to be more of focus on what is right, . . . I think we have lots of gifts to offer. (Interview 27)

These individuals believe that women should be allowed to lead not only because they have the skillsets necessary to succeed, but also because there is a job that needs to be done. As one African American woman in a Historically Black Protestant denomination explains, "males and females not only in the black church but in all churches . . . have an equal role to play." Instead of differentiating which gender is allowed to participate in certain aspects of church leadership, she does not "think it matters which role they play, or who can do what or whatever based on their gender." According to this congregant, "the only thing that matters is where their God-given gifts lie, and they should use that for the purpose of the church." She goes on to clarify that by "church" she does not "mean the building but the group of people who get together for spirituality reasons." Through utilizing the "God-given gifts" of both men and women, the church can work "towards making sure that that institution continues on in the future, better and stronger" (Interview 45).

While some see women as having unique gifts suited to ministry, those who use differences between men and women to justify their opposition to female ordination often label women as too emotional to handle the job of pastor. One woman who attends a nondenominational Evangelical church reports that her disapproval of ordaining women is rooted in women's personality characteristics:

> I feel like I am a very independent, strong woman, but I was a teacher, and when I looked for a teaching job I looked for a male principal. . . . I love women, I love hanging out with women, I have tons of friends, but women are very emotional. Women are very moody and women make immediate, rash decisions because I do that. . . . Not every woman is like that, not every man is like that, but I think when I look at myself and a lot of my friends, our husbands are very strong. They think things through for the most part, very wise. And I make rash, immediate decisions. And so that was one of the things when I looked for a job, I was like, "I don't want to deal with all that." And . . . I found a principal that was a man and it was wonderful. (Interview 49)

A Jehovah's Witness woman in her thirties echoes this assessment of women as emotional beings: "When you stick them in a room with one hundred people dealing with spirituality, they can't keep their emotions out of it. It's a lot to carry, the burdens, and women talk, women gossip. So I can understand why there's discipline in confidential matters. Not that women aren't smart" (Interview 72).

A few individuals took a different approach in relating gender differences to ordination. They connected their opposition to female ordination to their belief that if women were permitted to lead they would naturally "take over." One woman who attends an Evangelical nondenominational church explained her belief that "if women are allowed at all levels of leadership . . . men [would] start not to do what they're supposed to do" (Interview 53). In other words, it would give men a pass on their church service, and women would step in and run everything. Others framed their opposition to female clergy as a way to balance the gender-specific talents and traits that they viewed as natural. A male branch president in the LDS Church, for instance, sees women as naturally caring for others; in his view, male-only leadership gives men a chance to develop the same caring traits that come more naturally to women:

> The current theory is—now I may get snapped by a bolt of lightning because of "theory versus doctrine"[1]—but the current theory is women have a really big heart, and you don't need to tell them how to help serve others. The guys on the other hand are more interested in video games, cars, and the football game. Somebody's gotta knock [them] on the head and tell them "Hey, somebody needs help." So that's why men are given that role. It forces them to care. You know men can't have babies and . . . it's nothing like being a mother, but it gives us at least a taste to what it's like to have a heart and love others. (Interview 17)

It is interesting to note from the above interviews that these individuals offered reasons for opposing female ordination both because women do *not* have the necessary skills for ministry and because they *already* are naturally skilled in serving and caring for others.

Although some individuals perceive differences between men and women, it is important to contrast these interview statements with the bulk of previous research that indicates no clear consensus on whether clergypersons act differently based on their gender. Some studies did find a difference in attitude or behavior (Deckman et al. 2003; Zikmund, Lummis, and Chang 1998), while others discovered limited discernible difference (Lehman 1993, 2002). Regardless of the validity of these differences between men and women, some individuals perceive such differences and allow those perceptions to influence their stance on female ordination.

SUMMARY AND CONCLUSION

A few key patterns and themes became immediately apparent as we analyzed our interview transcripts. First, our interviewees often referenced scriptural authority to justify either their support for or opposition to female clergy in their congregations. Supporters cited biblical texts that emphasized more egalitarian themes, while opponents mentioned more patriarchal passages. Since scriptural passages could be found to support a position either way, supporters and opponents tended to cite passages that bolstered their pre-existing preference on the issue.

As we noted in Chapter 1, sincerely held theological beliefs are one factor that can help explain the gender gap in religious leadership. Our conversations with individuals mentioned in this chapter, however, allow us to add a little more nuance to that claim. While many individuals in opposition to female clergy referenced scripture and their subsequent theological beliefs as motivating this opposition, a comparable number discussed their theological beliefs as leading to their support of women clergypeople. Many even rationalized their support or opposition in spite of scripture, arguing, for example, that any passage could be taken out of context. While our interviews lead us to believe that theological beliefs are a contributing factor to opposition to female clergy and thus the gender gap in female leadership, these theological beliefs cannot fully explain this phenomenon—as evidenced by the willingness of most interviewees to change their own position if their church were to announce such a change.

Second, personal experience with women pastors or priests was a major factor in explaining why someone either supported or rejected female ordination. Some of our interviewees explained that having a woman pastor in their congregation changed their views on the topic, while others cited direct interaction with a female leader from a different congregation or religious tradition as influential in driving their support for female ordination. Some of those who were more hesitant pointed out that their reluctance stemmed largely from unfamiliarity—they had never had a female pastor before, and they were not sure what it would be like.

Others explained how experiences with female leadership beyond the doors of their place of worship led them to question the lack of gender equality within their own congregations. These interviewees made a connection between women's advancement (or lack thereof) in the secular world to the state of women's equality in their individual congregation or religious tradition. They commonly linked the pursuit of women's equality in broader American society to that same quest in America's places of worship. These interviews suggest that in some cases, this connection between secular and religious gender equality has a direct and meaningful effect in shaping views on gender equality.

Third, female clergy tended to identify middle-aged and older women as the demographic that had the most difficulty accepting them in their role as pastor or priest. The clergywomen we talked to suspected that these female congregants' aversion stemmed from resentment or envy because they grew up in a time when they had fewer opportunities to serve in ministry or in the professional world. Other research has shown that while there are of course numerous exceptions and counterexamples, men generally tend to form hierarchical structures in their social interactions, while women gravitate toward egalitarian, cooperative relationships (see Baumard 2016, chap. 5; Benenson, Markovits, and Wrangham 2014; Buchanan, Warning, and Tett 2012, e.g.). This research may help explain why many clergywomen perceived more opposition from women in their congregations than men. Perhaps women in these congregations are resistant (either consciously or subconsciously) to a relationship of hierarchical authority with another woman, while men are more comfortable in these vertical arrangements of power.[2] On the whole, however, it is important to emphasize that the clergywomen we talked to reported that they experienced strong support from most women as well as men.

Fourth, both supporters and opponents used gender stereotypes to justify their preferences and beliefs about the role of women in their congregations. Supporters argued that women tend to possess traits and talents that are well suited to ministry work. Other supporters argued that both genders possess gifts and talents that enable them to be effective pastors and priests. Those who supported the male-only policies of their congregations tended to use gender stereotypes in two ways. Some argued that women's more emotional and impulsive traits would prevent them from being effective as leaders and organizers. Others, though, argued that it is the very deficiency of loving traits on the part of men that explain why they need to be the leaders in their congregations: so that they can learn the values of service and compassion that come naturally to women. These individuals reasoned that women do not need the priesthood as much as men do, so it is best to keep the priesthood reserved only for men.

When it came to the rationales of "scriptural authority" and gender stereotypes, it seemed that those we interviewed used these arguments to rationalize, post hoc, either their support or opposition, which generally aligned with the views of whatever policy their congregation had in place. (Psychologists call this "motivated reasoning"; see Kunda 1990.) In other words, they knew what they thought about the subject and looked for reasons to justify it when explaining their views on the matter to us. This suggests that it would be difficult to change their minds on the subject one way or another by using either the same authority of scripture or similar arguments. This observation leads us to interpret the effect of scriptural authority/sincere theological belief on opposition to female clergy with even greater skepticism. Although we do not doubt that sincere theological belief motivates many individuals' stances on female ordination, a deeper analysis of our interviews suggests that other factors may matter more. For example, one factor that did seem to consistently change minds was personal interaction with female clergy. Some of our interviewees who were originally hesitant or opposed became more supportive of female ordination after actually interacting with a woman priest or pastor, either in their own congregation or another.

As explained at the beginning of the chapter, one of our goals was to assess the "why" of support for female ordination. Our next chapter turns to the "who," as we continue to explore perceptions from a more quantitative perspective, broadening our sample to the United States as a whole.

NOTES

1. Here the LDS congregational leader is referring to a common discussion in the Mormon tradition as to whether a particular explanation for an institutional policy is official doctrine or a commonly accepted, but unofficial, rationalization created by either leaders or lay members. As in many traditions, the lines are often blurry on such questions.

2. Of course, there is also a host of research documenting male resistance to female authorities in the workplace. See, e.g., Netchaeva et al. (2015).

4

WHO SUPPORTS WOMEN'S ORDINATION IN AMERICA?

IN SEPTEMBER 2015, when discussing Pope Francis's upcoming visit to Congress, Virginia Democratic Senator Tim Kaine stated that "there is nothing this Pope could do that would improve the world as much as putting the Church on a path to ordain women." In saying this, Kaine situated the issue of women's ordination within the broader context of women's advancement in society. He went on to explain that "if women are not accorded equal place in the leadership of the Catholic Church and the other great world religions, they will always be treated as inferiors in earthly matters as well" (Bartel 2015). To Senator Kaine, the granting of female ordination is an essential step in working toward greater equality. This is especially noteworthy because Senator Kaine is a devout Catholic who devoted time to missionary work in his youth. Is Kaine's view of female ordination typical among his fellow Democrats? Do political liberals tend to agree on this topic even when it puts them at odds with the leaders of their faith traditions?

The Women's Ordination Conference (i.e., the "oldest and largest organization that works to ordain women as priests, deacons and bishops into an inclusive and accountable Catholic church") was one of many organizations that shared Tim Kaine's comment as a news story. Although men as well as women are involved with the Women's Ordination Conference, its leadership structure is overwhelmingly comprised of women, and it has a self-described commitment to "Feminist,

Mujerista and Womanist Thought and Action." It states that "the hierarchy must not define male and female 'roles' or perpetuate any system that defines or limits one's gifts or calling on the basis of gender" (Women's Ordination Conference 2017). Is gender, then, a defining characteristic of support for female ordination? Do women tend to support ordaining women at higher rates than men?

In Chapter 2 we saw that about three-quarters of those in our Gender and Religious Representation Survey say that they either somewhat or strongly support women being permitted to serve as the principal leader in their church or congregation, a level of support that is fairly consistent across religious denominations. Chapter 3 then turned to our face-to-face interviews with both clergy and congregants to uncover the "why" of people's preferences—what reasons do people give for their position on women's ordination? The key themes we found included scriptural proscriptions, personal experiences, envy or resentment from older women, and basic gender stereotypes. Now we will turn again to our nationwide public opinion survey data to explore this question from a different perspective. In contrast to our face-to-face interviews, our public opinion survey did not intentionally sample any clergy. We wanted instead to focus more on the "views from the pews"—what types of regular churchgoers support or oppose female ordination in their congregations? Are they political liberals like Senator Tim Kaine? Are women more likely than men to be supporters, as we might assume to be the case based on the gender representation in the Women's Ordination Conference? Are there any other trends and patterns?

The basic approach that public opinion researchers use when analyzing quantitative data is to examine the nature of the relationship between different variables: how does one variable change as another variable changes? In our case, the basic approach is to see how support for female ordination either increases or decreases in the presence or absence of other factors that we hypothesize might make a difference. The interviews from the previous chapter allowed us to examine the "why." The public opinion surveys analyzed in this chapter allow us to determine the "who"— who supports female clergy? What individual traits, behaviors, or attitudes are associated with more or less support?

Given that existing research on support for female ordination in American churches is somewhat limited, however, we also draw on scholarship that has investigated backing more broadly for societal "gender egalitarianism." This has been defined as "the underlying concept of an individual's level of support for a division of paid work and family responsibilities [between men and women] that is based on the notion of separate spheres" (Davis and Greenstein 2009, 89). It is reasonable to assume that attitudes toward the role of men and women in the family and workplace would also likely extend to religious congregations, as pastors are often considered to be in a metaphorical "parent" relationship with their congregations and also because pastoring is a full-time paid job in most religious traditions.

FACTORS THAT AFFECT SUPPORT FOR FEMALE CLERGY

Here we review the findings of previous research in terms of what sorts of factors are associated with either support of or opposition to female clergy in the United States. We will discuss each factor separately and summarize the relevant studies associated with each. This will allow us to form some preliminary expectations about what we might find in our Gender and Religious Representation Survey.

Gender. Previous research suggests that gender, perhaps the most obvious factor, would be associated with support for women clergy. Davis and Greenstein (2009) explain from a utilitarian perspective that women should be stronger proponents of gender egalitarianism as it would increase their access to power in the workplace and in society as a whole. In this case, women may be more likely to support female ordination because theoretically it would give them greater access to power and influence in their congregations. Identity theorists would argue that women may be more likely to favor female clergy as female clergy have important "symbolic" value, signaling the importance and equal status of women in their communities. Empirical evidence has found support for this relationship. For instance, Lehman (1985) surveyed laity in the Presbyterian Church USA in 1980 and finds that women are more accepting of female clergy, while Bolzendahl and Myers (2004) and Brooks and Bolzendahl (2004) find that women are more likely to promote societal gender egalitarianism in general. Sanbonmatsu (2003) also shows that women value the idea of increasing the proportion of women in elected office.

On the other hand, there are some compelling reasons to predict that female churchgoers would actually be *less* accepting of female clergy in their congregations. Jost et al. (2004), for instance, outline existing research on "system justification theory," which argues that humans implicitly internalize narratives and ideologies that support the status quo of their environments and contexts, often outside of conscious awareness. This leads to situations in which members of disadvantaged groups internalize inferiority narratives that then manifest themselves as implicit biases in favor of contexts that perpetuate these inequalities. In this case, system justification theory would predict that because churchgoing American women are often raised in Christian religious contexts that convey at least some degree of patriarchal narratives and bias, women may actually be *more* likely to embrace male-only congregational leadership than men.

There is some evidence in favor of this contrasting expectation. Glick and Fiske (2001), for example, found that women are more likely to accept religiously based ideologies of "benevolent sexism," which they define as "a subjectively favorable, chivalrous ideology that offers protection and affection to women who embrace conventional roles," than are men. Burns et al. (2001, 239) show that American women are less supportive of female ordination in their congregations than are men, especially among Protestants in denominations with male-only clergy. In such denominations, approval is as low as 15%. Putnam and Campbell (2012, 244) also found that Mormon women are less supportive of female ordination than Mormon men, a finding corroborated by Cragun et al. (2016). In all, it seems that there are compelling reasons to expect women to be *more* supportive of female ordination than men, and equally plausible reasons to expect women to be *less* supportive.

Socioeconomic status. One of the most consistent findings in previous research on gender egalitarianism is that highly educated people are less likely to prefer traditional gender roles in society. This is often attributed to the liberalizing/egalitarian attitudes that people frequently develop when exposed to higher education (Brooks and Bolzendahl 2004, 2004; Bryant 2003; Ciabattari 2001; Fan and Marini 2000). This has also been shown to be the case when it comes to ideas about women's ordination, as Lehman (1985) demonstrated that more education was associated with more support for female clergy and Cragun et al. (2016) found that education and political ideology were key predictors of support for women's ordination among Mormon respondents.

Research is mixed in terms of class and income. Some research has shown that middle- and upper-class individuals are more supportive of both gender egalitarianism (Bartkowski 2001) and female ordination in their congregations (Cragun et al. 2016). In contrast, Carroll et al. (1983) found that those employed in business and executive positions were among the most resistant to women clergy in their congregations. Lehman (1985) also found that income did not reliably predict attitudes one way or another among Presbyterian laity.

Age. Another consistent finding in the scholarly literature on this topic is that younger individuals are generally more accepting of female ordination than older individuals (Carroll, Hargrove, and Lummis 1983; Lehman 1985). Age is also a reliable predictor of gender egalitarianism (Brooks and Bolzendahl 2004, 2004; Ciabattari 2001). This is often attributed to cohort effects as younger individuals were raised and socialized in more egalitarian social environments. During and after the 1970s, for example, ordination was extended to women in many Mainline Protestant traditions in the United States, so this was the context in which younger Americans came of age.

Race/ethnicity. There is scant existing research on the link between racial or ethnic identification and support for female clergy. Lehman (1985) found that minority identification was not associated with support among Presbyterians in his sample. Others, though, have found a stronger link when it comes to more general attitudes toward gender egalitarianism. Bolzendahl and Myers (2004), Brooks and Bolzendahl (2004), and Fan and Marini (2000) all showed that African-Americans have higher levels of gender egalitarianism than whites, possibly due to the higher rate of black women employed in the work force but also very likely due to the historical rate of racial discrimination experienced by blacks. One theory is that this experience of marginalization may lead them to be especially sensitive to the situation of other groups also excluded from positions of influence or leadership, including by gender discrimination (Fetzer 1998; Knoll 2009).

On the other hand, research has found that Latinos have lower levels of gender egalitarianism than non-Latinos (Fan and Marini 2000; Kane 2000), possibly due to lingering effects of *machismo* cultural norms in many Latin American countries which may be manifested by some Latino-Americans with closer generational immigrant ties. Although this research takes religious affiliation into account, it may also be due to the strong influence of the Catholic Church and Evangelical Protestantism in Latin American culture.

Religious beliefs. Theological traditionalism across Western religious traditions (Christianity, Islam, Judaism, etc.) has been associated with more conservative gender roles for many centuries (Crandall 2012; Fisher 2006). It is accordingly no surprise that Lehman (1987) found higher levels of belief orthodoxy to be associated with lower support for female ordination among Mainline Protestant congregants. This is supported by Peek et al. (1991), Bolzendahl and Myers (2004), and Ciabattari (2001) who demonstrated a strong link between gender traditionalism and higher levels of religious belief orthodoxy. This has shown to be the case for women as well as men (Bartkowski and Hempel 2009).

Religious behavior. One of the more consistent findings in the literature is the influence of religious activity and behavior on support for women's ordination. Lehman (1985, 1987) showed consistent evidence that those who exhibit more frequent religious behaviors (attending religious services, donating money, etc.) were more opposed to female clergy than their less active counterparts in the same congregations. This is supported by Smith and Stevens (2003), who observed that increased church attendance decreases support for female clergy among Protestants (but not Catholics). Also, Brinkerhoff and MacKie (1985) and Brooks and Bolzendahl (2004) each demonstrated that higher levels of church attendance are linked with lower levels of gender egalitarianism among Americans, including women (Bolzendahl and Myers 2004). Burns et al. (2001, 241) found that both men and women (but again, especially women) who support male-only clergy have much higher levels of weekly church attendance. From the political science discipline, Dolan (1998) revealed that higher levels of religiosity were associated with a lower likelihood of voting for female political candidates. This suggests that religiosity and religious behavior affect support for women in several different areas, including religion as well as politics.

Religious belonging/context. As we know, some religious traditions in the United States permit women to serve as pastors and priests in their congregations while others do not. Institutional rules and customs can often influence the attitudes and behaviors of those who identify with and participate in those institutions and traditions. For example, researchers have learned that Protestant religious affiliation is a key predictor of individual preferences toward same-sex marriage policies (Olson, Cadge, and Harrison 2006), economic policies (Barker and Carman 2000), and other political attitudes (Wilcox 1990). Applying this theoretical framework to our current topic, we might expect those who identify as members of religious traditions that permit female clergy in their congregations to be more supportive than those who identify as members of traditions that do not. We have already seen some limited evidence for this. Chapter 2 described how American Catholics and many Evangelical Protestants—groups that maintain a male-only leadership policy—have lower levels of acceptance of female ordination than Mainline Protestants, whose denominations more widely allow for female ordination. In Chapter 3 we saw how the vast majority of our interviewees held the same view on clergywomen as did their specific congregation or place of worship.

It is important to keep in mind, though, that Chaves (1997) explained that there is a strong "decoupling" of institutional rules and practice in American congregations on this issue. Some traditions that openly allow for female clergy have low rates of *actual* congregational female leadership while some traditions that technically prohibit female clergy in *practice* have a number of congregations led by women, often for practical reasons including the absence of any ordained male clergy in the congregation's area. It is therefore reasonable to suspect that the individual policies of specific congregations "on the ground" may have a stronger impact on the attitudes of parishioners than the policies of the denomination or tradition at the regional or global level.

In addition to the influence of attending a congregation that would permit a woman clergyperson in theory, there is reason to expect that actual experience with a female pastor or priest would affect attitudes as well. Social scientists have long demonstrated support for the "social contact hypothesis," which argues that direct exposure with members of a disliked or feared group decreases negative attitudes toward members of that group. In other words, as different types of people directly interact with each other, they learn to get along and have more favorable attitudes toward one another (Forbes 1997; Jost and Sidanius 2004, chap. 6; Oliver and Wong 2003; Powers and Ellison 1995; Tolbert and Grummel 2003; Welch, Hinnant, and Moon 2005).

Lehman (1985) examined this question directly in terms of female clergy. He compared survey results from a variety of Presbyterian congregations (specifically, United Presbyterian Church, USA). He compared congregations that had recently hired female pastors in their congregations to those that had not, and used panel data to compare attitudes of those in the congregation both before and after the female pastor was hired. Lehman was also able to take advantage of a "Women-In-Ministry" project that ran from 1977 to 1982 and involved placing recent female seminary graduates as interim pastors at various congregations around the country. In surveying the congregations that received these female interim pastors he found, as expected, that attitudes toward female clergy improved among congregants that were exposed to female pastors (comparing before and after) and were also more favorable in congregations that had a female pastor compared to those that did not (Lehman 1985, chap. 6). As we discussed in Chapter 3, our conversations with religious leaders and worship attendees revealed anecdotal support for this theory as multiple interviewees described how they began to support female clergy after having a personal experience with a clergywoman.

Of course, most congregations include more than one leadership position. There are opportunities for either ordained or lay members to serve as various ministry and/or small group leaders in congregations. It is thus possible for there to be many women serving as assistant ministers or small group leaders in a congregation, even constituting a majority, while still having a male senior pastor or priest. As discussed in Chapter 2, our Gender and Religious Representation Survey revealed that women make up at least half of the ministry and small group leaders in a little over a third of the congregations attended by American churchgoers. Further analysis reveals that there is a clear relationship between the gender of the congregational leader and the gender make-up of the lay leadership. In congregations that are headed by men, women make up at least half of the lay leadership only 34% of the time compared to 57% of the time in congregations led by women.[1] It is clear that there are several ways in which gender leadership can potentially activate the social contact hypothesis to drive attitudes toward female clergy.

Political ideology/partisanship. One of the most consequential factors in American politics over the last half-century has been the gradual alignment between political and religious ideologies among the American public. As Putnam and Campbell (2012, chaps. 5, 11) described, Americans are increasingly adjusting their religious beliefs and choosing religious congregations on the basis of their political ideologies and priorities rather than the other way around. Others have demonstrated that American partisan constituencies are becoming increasingly polarized along religious lines: adults who are religiously active and devout are now identifying with and voting for the Republican party while religiously disinclined and secular individuals are gravitating strongly toward the Democratic party (Abramowitz 2012).

These factors have important implications for the link between politics and attitudes toward female clergy in the American public. When it comes to contemporary political ideologies, American liberalism continues to embody the classical Enlightenment concept of "atomistic individualism." This is the idea that the core element of society is the individual, who has rights and interests separate from and prior to the groups to which the individual belongs. This belief helps explain why American liberals have traditionally been more active in their pursuit of overcoming stereotypes and institutions that disadvantage or discriminate against individuals on the basis of their group identities (Heywood 2012, chap. 2). Others theorists have argued that the recognition and legitimization of group-based rights are necessary to preserve individual rights, as individuals exist in social groups that help form their identities (Campbell 2013; Kymlicka 1995). This has translated into support for civil rights movements of various kinds, including the women's suffrage movement, second-wave feminism, and civil rights movements of the twentieth century. More recently this has been evident in political efforts to expand rights for immigrants and LGBT individuals.

Liberals also tend to be less hesitant about the prospect of societal change. They have tended to favor structures and institutions that promote the individualistic principles described above. Conservatives, on the other hand, are generally more cautious in their approach to major changes in society or political institutions. This caution has theoretical roots in pragmatic objections to the radical political changes in Europe during the eighteenth and nineteenth centuries (Burke 2009). The idea is that fast and far-reaching change is very difficult for societies to manage and more often than not results in chaos and anarchy. Thus, conservatives prefer cautious and incremental change that favors tradition and the status quo as guides.

More recently researchers have shown that whether humans embrace or resist change in general has some degree of neurological and psychological roots as well. This is because our personality traits are to a moderate extent genetically hereditable and give us a propensity to prefer predictability and routine or to prefer spontaneity and change (Amodio et al. 2007; Jost et al. 2003, 2007; Jost, Nosek, and Gosling 2008). The link between female ordination and a cautious approach to change is supported anecdotally by an interview conducted by Sentilles (2009, 114) in which a female associate pastor was asked to leave a congregation on several grounds that all "had to do with change—theological change, political change, and relational change. They wanted change to stop, so they needed the person they perceived as engineering it to leave."

As would be expected, research has shown basic political and ideological orientation to be one of the strongest predictors of societal gender egalitarianism (Bolzendahl and Myers 2004; Brooks and Bolzendahl 2004; Reingold and Foust 1998). There has been less research on the link between political ideologies and support for female clergy specifically, although Martínez et al. (2012) showed that ideology mattered in predicting acceptance of female clergy among Spanish college students; and Cragun et al. (2016) observed that politically liberal Mormons are more supportive of female clergy in their congregations than are Mormon conservatives. Burns et al. (2001, 241) found that conservative political ideology is associated with higher levels of support for male-only clergy. Anecdotally, Sentilles (2009) opines that views on female ordination in American congregations are essentially a matter of willingness to either embrace or resist change, specifically in religious institutions but also society at large.

Political party identification may also play a role. Political science research has demonstrated that partisans are often responsive to cues from party elites (Brader, Tucker, and Duell 2013; Goren, Federico, and Kittilson 2009; Kam 2005; Miller and Shanks 1996; Zaller 1992). In other words, individuals with partisan identities but with less stable attitudes on a particular issue will often look to their party's elected officials, political candidates, and party platforms for cues on how to think about that issue. The logic is that these cues serve as mental shortcuts (cognitive heuristics) to help make decisions in the absence of full information. Partisans are also often motivated to internalize the priorities and opinions of their party leaders so as to avoid cognitive dissonance (Elliot and Devine 1994; Lodge, Steenbergen, and Brau 1995; Lodge and Taber 2013; Redlawsk 2002) and to conform to the norms of their salient political in-group (Tajfel and Turner 1986).

Given that the Democratic Party in the United States has more vocally positioned itself as promoting gender equality since at least the mid-twentieth century (Gilmore 2008; MacLean 2008), we might expect Democratic partisans to internalize their party's position on gender equality issues in secular society and then transfer those opinions into their religious communities. Deckman et al. (2003) and Olson et al. (2005) also found that clergywomen tend to be more ideologically left leaning, Democratic, and politically active than clergymen. Thus, there is good reason to expect that Democratic partisans would be more supportive of female clergy in their congregations than Republican partisans.

Moral Foundations Theory. Over the last decade, social psychologist Jonathan Haidt and his colleagues have published a voluminous amount of research on his Moral Foundations Theory. This argues that humans perceive five basic "flavors" of morality: care/harm, fairness/cheating, loyalty/betrayal, authority/subversion, and sanctity/degradation. While most people are sensitive to each of these aspects of moral thinking to one degree or another, Haidt shows that liberals tend to be most sensitive to care/harm and fairness/cheating but less sensitive to the other three, while conservatives tend to be about equally sensitive to all five. According to Haidt, this helps explain why it is very difficult for contemporary liberals and conservatives to find common ground on many issues: they are speaking and feeling different "moral languages" (Graham, Haidt, and Nosek 2009; Haidt 2012; Haidt and Graham 2007; Koleva et al. 2012).

This framework may also help explain variation in ideas about female clergy. Those who have stronger sensitivity to fairness/cheating may be more aware of and concerned about equal opportunity and fair access to positions of power or employment, thus increasing support for women to work as clergy in religious congregations. On the other hand, those who are more sensitive to authority/subversion may be *less* supportive, as they are more apt to defer to societal traditions (including traditional gender roles). Alternatively, they may feel more constrained by the authority of a literal interpretation of their religious texts, which across Abrahamic traditions contain fairly clear delineations of gender roles both in society and in religious congregations.

Summary. Previous research suggests that those who would be more inclined to welcome female clergy in American religious congregations are: women, those with more education, younger individuals, African Americans, non-Latinos, traditionally orthodox believers, those who are less active in religious behaviors, those who attend congregations in which women are permitted to serve as clergy, those who are politically liberal, and finally those who are more sensitive to the care/harm aspect of morality and less sensitive to authority/subversion. We will now test each of those factors with data from Waves 1–3 of our quantitative public opinion survey. Technical details on the variable coding and specific methods of analysis can be found in the Data Appendix.

WHO SUPPORTS FEMALE CLERGY?

We begin the analysis by examining Table 4.1, which indicates the proportion of each demographic, religious, or political subgroup that that either somewhat or strongly supports female clergy being permitted to serve in their congregations. While the overall average of support is 69.5%[2] across all churchgoers in our survey, the groups with the highest levels are theological modernists (i.e., those who say that their religion or church should "adopt modern beliefs and practices"), political liberals and

TABLE 4.1

Stated support (%) for permitting female clergy in respondent's congregation, by demographic subgroup[a]

Theological modernists	89.6
Political liberals	88.2
Currently have a female pastor/priest	88.0
Currently attend a congregation that permits female clergy	87.4
Democrats	85.7
Theological moderates	81.7
African Americans	81.1
Low religious behavior	80.0
College education or more	76.4
Age 18–34	74.3
Political moderates	73.8
Currently attend a congregation in which women make up 50% or more of lay leadership	73.7
Income above $50K/year	72.3
Latinos	70.8
Women	69.8
OVERALL	**69.5**
Age 35–49	69.3
Men	69.1
Currently have a male pastor/priest	67.2
Age 50–64	65.9
Age 65 or older	65.8
Currently attend a congregation in which women make up less than 50% of lay leadership	65.8
Whites	65.3
Income less than $50K/year	65.2
Less than high school education	63.7
High religious behavior	61.3
Political Independents	59.3
Political conservatives	53.5
Theological traditionalists	52.8
Republicans	50.5
Currently attend a congregation that does not permit female clergy	48.6

[a] *Source:* Gender and Religious Representation Survey.

Democrats, those who are currently in a congregation that permits female clergy, and those who currently have a woman serving as their congregation's pastor or priest. Acceptance is above 85% for female ordination for each of these groups.

Conversely, those with the lowest levels of support include political conservatives, Republicans, Independents, and theological traditionalists ("my religion or church should maintain traditional beliefs and practices"). These groups have support between 50% and 60%. That said, the only group for which acceptance is *below* 50% is comprised of those in congregations whose policies do not permit women to serve in the pulpit, although the rate for that group is nearly 49%. In other words, nearly half of those in congregations that do not ordain women are still supportive as are a majority of every other demographic, religious, contextual, and political group that we examined. This evidence indicates that support for ordaining women appears to be widespread indeed.

We can also observe in Figure 4.1 the groups that have the widest degree of opinion polarization on the subject. Congregational policy makes the largest difference, with those in congregations that permit female clergy 38.7% more supportive than those in congregations with male-only policies in place. For comparison, the correlation coefficient between congregational policy and support is a statistically significant +0.42, a strong degree of correlation for social science relationships.[3] We also see

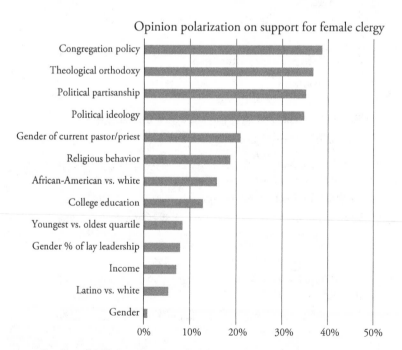

Opinion polarization on support for female clergy

FIGURE 4.1 Gender and Religious Representation Survey

that theological modernists are 36.8% more inclined to favor female ordination than theological traditionalists (+0.32 correlation). Democrats are 35.2% more supportive than Republicans (+0.36 correlation) and liberals are 34.8% more supportive than conservatives (+0.35 correlation). Interestingly, we see that individual demographics and socioeconomic status matters less, as there is a difference of 15% or less among various age, income, and race/ethnicity groups.

Perhaps most interestingly, there appears to be almost no difference between women and men on this issue: 69.8% of women support female clergy compared to 69.1% of men, a statistically insignificant difference of 0.8% (and a statistically insignificant correlation of +0.01). On what is perhaps the most obvious factor in predicting preferences for gender and religious leadership, women are no more likely than men to express support for female clergy.

A DEEPER LOOK

While these percentages are instructive, there is also a great deal of overlap among many of these groups, making it difficult to sort out which factors are more responsible for driving support for female clergy. For example, we can see that theological modernists and Democrats are more supportive than theological traditionalists and Republicans, but many Democrats are *also* theological modernists. Do Democrats accept female clergy because they are theological modernists or do modernists accept female clergy because they are Democrats? Or is it the case that each variable makes a difference independent of the other? If so, which factor is more important in predicting attitudes?

A multivariate regression analysis can tease apart the independent effect of each variable while statistically controlling for all the other variables. In the scenario above, for instance, we can hypothetically examine two individuals who are exactly the same with regard to age, gender, race, education, and religious activity. However, one is a theological modernist and the other is a theological traditionalist, making it possible for us to then observe differences in their views on female clergy. This allows us to scrutinize each variable *in isolation* from the others and thus understand which variables are ultimately more important in driving acceptance. The variables we tested against each other include all of the ones discussed above: gender, education, income, age, race/ethnicity, theological orthodoxy, religiosity, political partisanship, political ideology, and our three congregational gender leadership variables.[4]

This statistical test then gives us the unique and independent effect of each variable on the outcome (support for women's ordination) while all other variables are held constant at their means. Those that are statistically significant are those that the test shows to have a strong probability of having a unique effect independent of the other factors.[5] (This is the same analytical tool that was used in Chapter 2 to determine which groups were more likely to prefer a man or woman as their own congregation's personal pastor or priest.)

Figure 4.2 displays the key results of our first test.[6] Only four variables were found to be significant: theological orthodoxy, religiosity, political partisanship, and congregational policies. The graph shows the level of support for a hypothetical "average" person in our data sample and how the probability of support for female clergy changes as this hypothetical person moves from the minimum to the maximum value on each of these four factors.

What Figure 4.2 shows us is that Democratic political partisanship and being a member of a congregation that allows women to serve as clergy drive the likelihood of support up while high levels of theological traditionalism and religiosity drive it down, all other factors being constant. Specifically, this shows that political partisanship can change acceptance levels by nearly 30%: a strong Republican compared to a strong Democrat, both identical and average in all other factors, support female ordination at a rate of 59.6% and 89.3%, respectively. The influence of congregational policy is even stronger: those in congregations that have male-only leadership

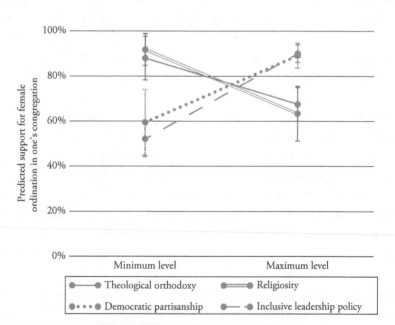

FIGURE 4.2 Gender and Religious Representation Survey; Note: the figure displays the average change in the predicted probability of stating support for female clergy in one's congregation as the variable in question moves from its minimum to maximum value, holding all other variables constant at their means.; Error bars are 95% confidence intervals for each statistical estimate.

policies are 52.2% likely to approve of female ordination compared to 90.2% for those in congregations with inclusive leadership policies (again, holding all other factors constant). Conversely, those who are theological traditionalists are 67.6% likely to support female ordination while those who are theological modernists are 88.1% likely. Finally, those with the highest levels of religious activity (worship service attendance, volunteering, prayer, etc.) are 63.5% likely to support female ordination, while those with the lowest levels of religiosity are 91.9% likely.

In sum, our public opinion data reveal a portrait of someone likely to be a strong supporter of female ordination: he or she is a theologically progressive Democrat who sporadically attends a congregation that allows women to serve as pastors or priests. In our data, there is a 99.4% chance this person will approve of female ordination. On the other hand, the portrait of someone who is likely to strongly oppose women's ordination is a theologically traditional Republican who frequently attends a congregation with a male-only leadership policy. In our survey, this person is only about 13% likely to support female ordination.[7] As we observed before, basic demographic factors such as race/ethnicity, age, education, and income seem to make little difference. Even gender does not make a difference. At this point, the evidence indicates that the key factors predicting support for female ordination are political, religious, and contextual, not demographic or socioeconomic.

THE EFFECT OF ORTHODOXY AND CONGREGATIONAL POLICIES

At this point we can examine some possible interactive effects for these findings, and explore whether a particular factor might influence outcomes differently for people at various levels of another factor. For instance, political partisanship or theological orthodoxy may matter more (or less) for women than it does for men. Alternatively, men may respond differently than women in their views on women's ordination when they are in a congregation that allows for it, compared to when they are in congregations with male-only leadership policies.

Figure 4.3 shows some interesting results that add nuance to those presented earlier: the relationship between belief orthodoxy and opposition to female clergy is stronger for women than it is for men. Specifically, women who are theologically modernist are 96.1% likely to support female ordination (holding all other variables constant at their means), while women who are theologically traditionalist are 67.2% likely to approve, an increase of about 29%. Men, on the other hand, are similarly less likely to support female ordination when they are theological traditionalists compared to men who are moderates, although there is no statistically significant increase for men who are theologically modernist.

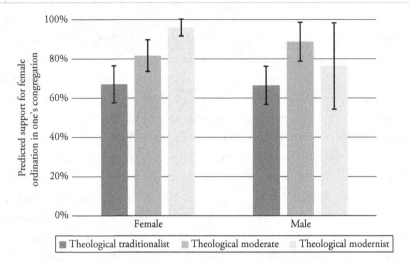

FIGURE 4.3 Gender and Religious Representation Survey; Note: the figure displays the predicted probability of stating support for female clergy in one's congregation for the indicated factors, holding all other variables in the multivariate analysis constant at their means.; Error bars are 95% confidence intervals for each statistical estimate.

Otherwise, we see no significant effect of the interactions between gender and religious behavior, political partisanship, or congregational policies on gender leadership. For the most part, gender is not a significant predictor of positive views on female ordination among these different relevant subgroups *except* for belief orthodoxy, where we see that modern orthodoxies lead women (but not men) to be more accepting than those with traditional orthodoxies.

Are there other factors that might make more of a difference? It is likely that congregational context plays an important role in influencing how these factors interact with one another. Given the strong effect of religious environment on behavior (Ellison 1995; Finke and Adamczyk 2008; Mowday and Sutton 1993; Stroope 2011), the factors uncovered above may work differently depending on the context, specifically the congregational norms and expectations regarding female clergy. This is especially true given that differences in congregational policy produced the highest level of opinion polarization on attitudes toward female clergy (see Figure 2.1). Also, psychological research has shown that "motivated reasoning" is a strong factor in the influencing of individual opinions and beliefs (Kunda 1990). Those who attend congregations with male-only policies could very well be motivated to defend the practices, policies, and traditions of those congregations so as to avoid the cognitive dissonance of associating with a congregation with whose policies they disagree.

Figures 4.4, 4.5 and 4.6 tell a fairly consistent story: an individual's congregational policies matter, but they matter *more* for theological traditionalists, political

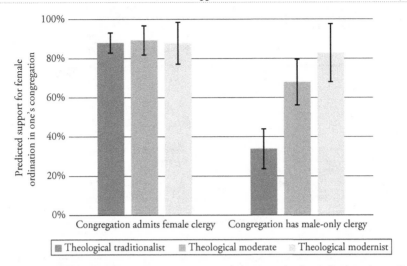

FIGURE 4.4 Gender and Religious Representation Survey; Note: the figure displays the predicted probability of stating support for female clergy in one's congregation for the indicated factors, holding all other variables in the multivariate analysis constant at their means.; Error bars are 95% confidence intervals for each statistical estimate.

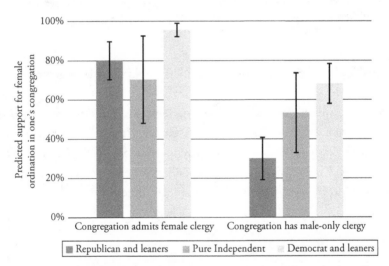

FIGURE 4.5 Gender and Religious Representation Survey; Note: the figure displays the predicted probability of stating support for female clergy in one's congregation for the indicated factors, holding all other variables in the multivariate analysis constant at their means.; Error bars are 95% confidence intervals for each statistical estimate.

Republicans, and those with higher levels of religious behavior. In each of these cases, those with more traditional/conservative/observant behaviors and attitudes are less supportive of female ordination—but only when they are in congregations with male-only leadership policies. When those same individuals are in congregations that allow women to serve as head clergy, they are generally about as open to women's

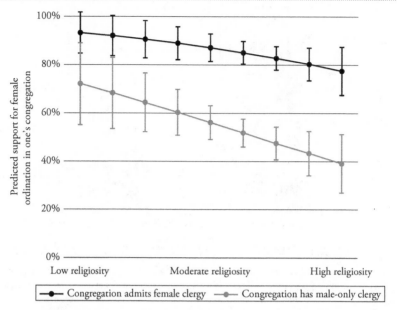

FIGURE 4.6 Gender and Religious Representation Survey; Note: the figure displays the predicted probability of stating support for female clergy in one's congregation for the indicated factors, holding all other variables in the multivariate analysis constant at their means.; Error bars are 95% confidence intervals for each statistical estimate.

ordination as theological modernists, Democrats, and those with lower levels of religious behaviors.

Collectively, this evidence shows that congregational policies matter in affecting parishioner support for female ordination. Congregations that permit women to serve as head clergy generate widespread support across theological, political, and behavior lines. Congregations with male-only policies, however, tend to polarize levels of support for female clergy along these same lines.

MORAL FOUNDATIONS THEORY

As discussed earlier, another possible source of attitudes regarding women priests and pastors may include basic morality orientations. Those who are sensitive to situations that involve fairness may be more likely to support female clergy as a basic issue of gender equality. Alternatively, those who are sensitive—and especially submissive—to authority may be, as an expression of deference to authority, more likely to oppose women serving as congregational leaders. Specifically, they may be attuned to the authority of religious texts, such as the Bible, that strongly prescribe traditional family gender roles, or to the guidance of religious institutions or leaders who have often played an influential role in promoting such roles.

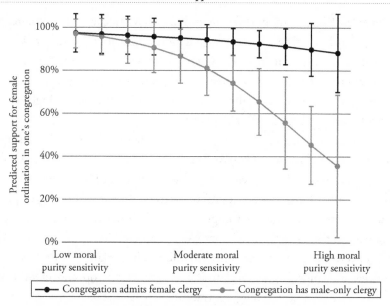

FIGURE 4.7 Gender and Religious Representation Survey, Wave 3; Note: the figure displays the predicted probability of stating support for female clergy in one's congregation for the indicated factors, holding all other variables in the multivariate analysis constant at their means.; Error bars are 95% confidence intervals for each statistical estimate.

To test whether the moral foundations traits influence support for female clergy, we included survey measures[8] in Wave 3 of the five different factors (harm/care, fairness/cheating, loyalty/betrayal, authority/subversion, and sanctity/degradation), along with all of the factors included in the previous analyses.[9] Contrary to our expectations, neither fairness/cheating nor authority/subversion makes a difference once we control for the other factors discussed earlier in this chapter. One moral foundations trait, however, is statistically significant at the 95% confidence level: sanctity/degradation. Individuals with higher levels of sensitivity to sanctity/degradation are more prone to view questions of morality in terms of "purity" vs. "contamination." They are more likely to avoid, for themselves and their communities, influences that they perceive to be defiling or desecrating.

Further analysis reveals an important, but at this point not surprising, caveat to this finding: the effect of sanctity/degradation on approval of female clergy matters only for those in congregations with male-only leadership policies in place. The effect, displayed in Figure 4.7, is large: those in male-only clerical congregations with the lowest levels of sanctity/degradation sensitivity are 97.7% likely to support female clergy, while those with the highest levels are 27.1% likely to support, a difference of nearly 71%. In other words, individuals who strongly perceive moral questions in terms of protection against contamination and impurity are more than *three times* less likely to support female ordination when they are in congregations with male-only leadership. Sanctity/degradation sensitivity more than *triples* opposition to female clergy for those in congregations with male-only leadership. For those in congregations that allow female clergy, however, sanctity/degradation sensitivity has no impact on views about female ordination: support is high regardless of a person's sensitivity to sanctity/degradation.

While we can only speculate as to the precise reasons for this relationship, it is possible that individuals who are more sensitive to the sanctity/degradation factor, having internalized their congregation's policies on gender leadership, view patriarchal religious customs as more "pure" or "sacred." This would make the prospect of female leaders undesirable as it might "defile" their understanding of the proper arrangement of things in their religious worldview. Nesbitt (1997, 176) provides an alternative intriguing perspective that may also help explain this finding: "Given the linkage of women's biological functions—menstruation and childbirth—to concerns of purity in various religious traditions . . . it's not unrealistic that women's full inclusion [in religious leadership positions] might either radically reconstitute notions of purity or diminish their traditional importance, with a consequent reconfiguration of the meaning of 'sacred' or 'holy.'"

COMPARING OUR FACE-TO-FACE INTERVIEWS AND PUBLIC OPINION SURVEY RESULTS

When we compare the previous chapter's face-to-face interviews and the public opinion survey results from this chapter, a few common themes that help us better understand each perspective immediately emerge. One of the key quantitative findings of this chapter is that congregational policies on female ordination tend to structure the other factors that also make a difference. The theme from the qualitative interviews about the strong scriptural basis for support or opposition helps us understand why: prevailing interpretations of scripture are often internalized by devoted members of those congregations. As one individual described, she "understands completely why people think different things because . . . what [she] reads is different from what you're going to read or someone else is going to read" (Interview 49). Because the sacred texts can be interpreted in so many different ways, readers' understanding of texts that speak to gender roles is largely driven by congregational context. An individual whose congregation emphasizes equality in the Biblical creation story, for instance (i.e., men and women both being created in the image of God), may have a more affirming stance on female ordination than someone who attends a congregation that focuses on the order of creation ("For Adam was formed first, then Eve" [1 Tim. 2:13 NRSV]).

This also helps us understand the quantitative finding that traditional belief orthodoxy and higher levels of religiosity are associated with lower levels of support for female ordination. Those who believe that their church or congregation should "preserve traditional beliefs and practices" also tend to interpret scriptural texts in a more literal way. They view the authority and interpretation of their sacred texts as much more rigid as compared to those with more progressive approaches to theology and scripture. These individuals are thus more likely to take seriously the many passages that reinforce traditional gender spheres that place men in leadership positions and women in subordinate positions. When they have higher levels of religious behaviors such as church attendance and regular reading of their sacred text, they are more frequently exposed to that scriptural approach, which only strengthens its impact on their attitudes. On the whole, it seems that scripture, orientation toward theology, level of religious activity, and congregational policies all strongly reinforce one another to influence people's position on female ordination.

Our public opinion survey results show that while congregational policies that allow female ordination are related to support for female ordination, the actual presence of a man or woman currently serving as the principal leader in an individual's congregation does not necessarily matter. Our face-to-face interviews provide some evidence that helps explain why this might be the case. Several people in our interviews explained that seeing women in positions of leadership in the workplace or the secular world influenced their attitudes toward female leaders in their religious communities. Some also reported that their attitudes became more positive once they experienced a female pastor or priest in their congregation, even if it occurred some time ago. Those who attend congregations in which women are able to serve as clergy are more likely to have encountered a woman priest at some point along the way, whether as a previous leader in their own congregation or in other congregations within their religious traditions. As one interviewee put it: "I think our church now would accept that without any problem, because they've had a female pastor before, and they see that, oh, female pastors are just as good as male pastors" (Interview 34). This helps explain why *currently* having a female pastor does not affect attitudes on female clergy beyond the overall policies of the individual's congregation on the subject.

As explained in Chapter 3, our face-to-face interviews also showed that middle-aged and older women tended to be the most resistant to female clergy, often due to feelings of resentment or envy (at least, as perceived by their female pastors and priests). This is one finding that we were not able to independently confirm at the national level with our public opinion survey. We were unable to find any evidence in our telephone and internet surveys that either gender or age made a difference in explaining support for female clergy once we statistically controlled for the other factors we described earlier. It may be the case that middle-aged and older women do not differ greatly in terms of their support for women serving as clergy *in the abstract*, but have a more difficult time interacting with actual women pastors and priests when they are part of their congregations for the reasons discussed in the previous chapter.

SUMMARY AND CONCLUSION

The goal of this chapter has been to explain the "who" of support for women's ordination—which groups of people tend to support it and which tend to oppose it? To that end, we analyzed responses from hundreds of public opinion surveys on the subject. Our results found that support for female ordination is associated with a few key religious and political factors: religious belief orthodoxy, religious behavior, political partisanship, and congregational context, specifically policies regarding gender and the chief leadership position. We also found that congregational context is key: even highly religious and theologically traditionalist folks will get behind female ordination when they attend congregations whose policies allow for it. Indeed, our results show that pretty much everyone says that they support female clergy when they attend congregations in which women are permitted to serve as clergy. Opinions tend only to diverge in congregations that do *not* allow for it. In those instances, those who are theologically and politically conservative, or who have higher levels of sensitivity to sanctity/degradation flavors of morality, follow the cues of their congregations' leaders and decrease support for female ordination. Those who are more theologically and politically progressive, though, maintain high levels of support regardless of their congregations' policy on the matter.

This key finding dovetails with other recent research by Cragun et al., (2016) who show that devout Mormons are more opposed to female ordination in their religious tradition than less devout members but become even more supportive than those less devout members when presented with a hypothetical scenario in which the decision to ordain women came from top church leadership. We find evidence of a similar effect among all Americans who attend religious services. Higher levels of religious orthodoxy and stronger religious orientation in general lead individuals to support whatever policies on female ordination are currently in place in their congregations. This suggests that the leadership and decision-makers in religious organizations have a good deal of influence on how their congregants and parishioners view the subject of female ordination. In many ways they are in the driver's seat on this issue. Devout members of their congregation tend to follow their lead.

It is also noteworthy that there is a strong effect when it comes to political partisanship: Republicans are more likely to reject female ordination, while Democrats are more likely to embrace it. This is important because it provides further evidence of the strong link between political and religious attitudes in contemporary American society (Putnam and Campbell 2012). Identification with political parties that are more receptive to women's identity issues in the political sphere increases personal support for women's equal access to the pulpit. We are accustomed to hearing about how religion drives political attitudes and voting behavior. Here we see an example of how it can work the other way around: political identity drives religious attitudes.

Perhaps most surprisingly, there is very little evidence that an individual's gender matters on this question. Our quantitative results demonstrated that women are no more or less likely to support female clergy than are men. Moreover, our qualitative interviews showed that from the perspective of women pastors and priests themselves, the most resistance they encounter tends to be from middle-aged and older women. The fault line of support for female ordination in American congregations is not male versus female, but rather progressive versus traditionalist.

Looking to the larger questions posed at the outset of the book, this chapter provides a number of insights to help us better understand the persistence of a gender gap in leadership in American religious traditions. In the introductory chapter, we proposed sincere theological belief as a contributing factor that explains why some individuals oppose female clergy, thus contributing to the lack of equality seen in America's places of worship. As we saw in this chapter, theological traditionalists—in particular those who frequently attend a congregation with a male-only leadership policy—are more likely than theological modernists to oppose female clergy. As theological beliefs tend to be shaped by one's religious community, it is no wonder that those who attend churches that hold male-only leadership policies would likewise hold personal theological beliefs that oppose female ordination. As we saw in Chapter 3, however, congregational context seems to make a greater difference than "sincere theological belief" (either expressed in scriptural interpretation or belief orthodoxy) in predicting support for female clergy. In this chapter we saw that belief orthodoxy predicts support *only* in congregations with male-only leadership policies. In congregations that were currently led by a woman, both theological traditionalists and modernists were generally supportive of female ordination.

The results regarding political partisanship provide further insight into the persisting gender gap in American places of worship. As we discussed in Chapter 1, there is reason to believe that partisanship may be a contributing factor to a lack of support for gender equality in religious leadership. Because a congregation's stance on female ordination serves as a signal of where it stands on the ideological spectrum (Chaves 1997), and because female clergy tend to be left leaning and politically active Democrats (Deckman et al. 2003; Olson, Crawford, and Deckman 2005), we proposed in Chapter 1 that Republicans may be hesitant to support female clergy and that this opposition may help explain the gender gap in religious leadership. Analysis of our survey data provides support for that prediction, as we found Democratic political partisanship to be one of the leading predictors of support for female clergy. This suggests that a gender gap persists in the leadership of American religious congregations because the issue has become politicized to a large extent, meaning that political partisanship drives opinions on the matter. So long as this is the case, resistance to more inclusive leadership may continue among many American religious congregations because somewhere between 40% and 50% of those who regularly attend religious services identify as Republican partisans, according to our survey data.

Thus far, we have seen some of the ways in which theological belief and political partisanship relate to support for clergywomen and the tenacious gap in female leadership. In the next chapter we will take a different approach to analyzing this survey data. In doing so, we will refer to another question posed in the introductory chapter and another possible contributing factor to the prevailing gender gap in religious leadership: is there reason to question individuals' claims of support for equality? Is support for clergywomen really as widespread as the survey results suggest?

NOTES

1. These figures remain virtually unchanged if we limit the analysis to only those congregations that ordain women.

2. This is slightly different from the 72.3% reported in Chapter 2 because we exclude Wave 4 here given that several of the questions needed for this analysis were not included in Wave 4 of the survey.

3. These "bivariate correlations" are another way of examining the strength of a relationship between two variables—the higher the number means the stronger the relationship. In social science research, a standard "rule of thumb" is that a correlation of about 0.4 or higher is generally considered to be substantial/strong, 0.2 to 0.4 is considered moderate, and lower than 0.2 is considered low/weak.

4. They also include controls for non-Christian religions (Judaism and "other non-Christian" including Buddhism, Islam, etc.) due to the difference of cultural, congregational, and theological structures that may influence support for female religious leaders in those traditions.

5. By default we use a standard 95% degree of confidence in measuring statistical significance. Whenever a sample is taken from a wider population there is always a degree of random sampling error present, even if the sample is completely randomized. Relationships that are "statistically significant" are those where there is a relationship in the sample which, due the results of a statistical test, we can be 95% confident accurately reflects an existing relationship in the wider population

from which it is drawn. In other words, if we were to draw 20 samples from a population in which a relationship exists, 19 times out of 20 the relationship will be accurately reflected in the sample.

6. For the sake of simplicity in presentation we generally do not include full multivariate regression output tables throughout the book. Rather, we explain the methodology, variables, and tests that we perform and then highlight the substantive effect of the key variables and display them graphically when helpful. Full details are available in the Data Appendix.

7. These are predicted probability estimates generated with Stata's "margins" command.

8. Given the length of time necessary to collect such data, measures of the Haidt (2012) moral foundations orientations were included only in Wave 3 of our survey: a questionnaire administered exclusively to an online audience recruited by the Qualtrics organization. This sample deliberately skewed heavily toward younger and racial/ethnic minority respondents in an attempt to balance the undersampling of those groups in our telephone surveys. While a demographic weighting variable is applied to make this sample more representative, it is also the case that there is no one over the age of 65 represented in this sample. Thus, these results should be interpreted with caution.

9. Specifically, gender, education, income, age, race/ethnicity, belief orthodoxy, religiosity, political partisanship, political ideology, Jewish, non-Christian, and the three gender leadership context variables.

5

A SECOND LOOK AT VIEWS ON WOMEN'S ORDINATION

THE 1982 CALIFORNIA gubernatorial election featured two candidates vying for the state's top elected position. The Democrat was Tom Bradley, an African American who at the time was serving as mayor of Los Angeles. The Republican was the state Attorney General George Deukmejian, a man of Armenian descent. Bradley led in the pre-election polls throughout the majority of the campaign season but lost unexpectedly on Election Day by a single percentage point. The widely speculated explanation was that many white voters who were planning on voting for Deukmejian all along instead reported on the telephone to pollsters that they would be voting for Bradley. The theory was that they did this because they did not want to appear to be supporting Deukmejian out of racial prejudice against Bradley, so they opted for Bradley on the phone but Deukmejian in the voting booth. This explanation came be known as the Bradley Effect, although it has received only mixed support in later research (Citrin, Green, and Sears 1990; Hopkins 2009).

Could there be a type of Bradley Effect at play when it comes to expressed approval for women clergy in American congregations? Might some churchgoers say that they support female clergy when in reality they would prefer that only men be allowed to preach in their congregation's pulpit? Alternatively, is it also possible that some people might feel pressure to report being *opposed* to female clergy when in actuality they are more supportive? There are compelling reasons to suspect a basis for these hypothetical scenarios. People are often reluctant to express their true attitudes on a particular topic, especially if they expect that their honest opinions would be disapproved of by another person—even a telephone surveyor who they have never met and never will.

In the introductory chapter, we questioned the sharp incongruity between overarching support for gender equality in the abstract and the severe lack of female representation in America's places of worship. In the previous chapter, we found factors such as religious traditionalism, male-only leadership policies, and Republican partisanship to be associated with *opposition* to female clergy, but there is more to learn about those who say they favor female ordination. If support is as widespread as the survey suggests, why is the gender gap so broad? Is the discrepancy between support of equality in theory (about three-quarters of American congregants) and the realization of equality in practice (women fill only about one in every ten clergy positions in America) really as large as the survey suggests, or might there be something akin to the Bradley Effect at play?

In the last two chapters we saw that nearly three of every four Americans who attend religious services express support for women being permitted to serve as their congregation's principal religious leaders. We also saw that this endorsement is influenced by some key factors, including interpretations of scripture, levels of religious orthodoxy, gender stereotypes, personal experiences with female clergy, political partisanship, and congregational context. This chapter will take a more critical look at this stated level of support. The key question we seek to answer now is whether there is any evidence that support for female clergy in American congregations is either weaker or stronger than is suggested by public opinion surveys.

THE "SOCIAL DESIRABILITY EFFECT" AND SUPPORT FOR WOMEN'S ORDINATION

Social scientists have found that "social desirability" can influence survey responses on a variety of topics. It can manifest itself any time there is a reason for respondents to suspect that they will be judged negatively by the interviewer with whom they are talking, either in person or on the other end of the telephone. This can also occur when the person being interviewed wants to avoid an embarrassing social situation by saying something that could cause disagreement or conflict (Krumpal 2011; Marlowe and Crowne 1961). This calls into question the reliability of explicit answers to survey questions on topics that are socially sensitive (Berinsky 1999; Bishop, Tuchfarber, and Oldendick 1986, 1986; Phillips and Clancy 1972).

For example, research has routinely shown that people are likely to overreport behaviors such as voting (Clausen 1968; Comşa and Postelnicu 2013; Karp and Brockington 2005; Katosh and Traugott 1981; Silver, Anderson, and Abramson 1986; Traugott and Katosh 1979), frequency of attendance at religious services (Hadaway, Marler, and Chaves 1993; Smith 1998), and time spent on household chores (Kamo 2000; Press and Townsley 1998). In contrast, things such as drug and alcohol use (Druckman 2015) and sexual activities (Catania et al. 1990) tend to be underreported in survey research. Social desirability has also shown to influence survey responses to political and social values such as same-sex marriage (Powell 2013) and immigration (Janus 2010; Knoll 2013).

A common topic on which social desirability exerts an influence is that of racial/ethnic attitudes (Krysan 1998; Kuklinski, Cobb, and Gilens 1997; Redlawsk, Tolbert, and Franko 2010; Sniderman and Carmines 1999). In each instance, researchers have found evidence that people are often motivated to "self-present" more positively than would be the case if they were completely candid or honest with the interviewers. One example is Redlawsk et al. (2010), who find that approximately one-third of the population possessed some degree of reservation about voting for an African American for president despite the fact that more than 90% of the public claims willingness to do so when asked explicitly.

These effects are often not constant across social and demographic subgroups. Silver et al. (1986), Bernstein et al. (2001), and Karp and Brockington (2005), for example, all show that overreporting of voting rates is much more common among highly educated people compared to less-educated people. Those with higher levels of education, who self-report voting at higher rates than those with less education, apparently are more sensitive to the perception that educated persons such as themselves "should" be regular voters. These groups are thus more likely to misrepresent themselves when asked about voting, if they had failed to cast their ballots. This is similar to Kuklinski et al. (1997) and Gilens (1998), who found that progressive attitudes on race and racial policies are more likely to be overreported in surveys by white liberals, who are also the ones who report the most progressive attitudes on racial policies in the first place.

There is less consistent evidence when it comes to social desirability and attitudes toward support for women in leadership positions. Streb et al. (2008) find that while explicit support for a hypothetical female presidential candidate is nearly universal, nearly a quarter of the public is "angry or upset" about the prospect of a female president. In contrast, Stout and Kline (2011) find that more people actually vote for female candidates than pre-election polls would suggest, showing that support is broader than polls might lead us to believe. Hopkins (2009) finds little evidence either way: people are about as likely to vote for female candidates as support them in public opinion surveys.

All told, then, there is precedent for diverging expectations regarding survey measures of support for female clergy in the United States. A plethora of sociological and political science evidence would suggest that support for female clergy may be overstated in public opinion surveys (including our own), similar to patterns involving attitudes toward other minority groups. We may also expect that those most supportive of female clergy may also be the most likely to be overreporting their support. On the other hand, there has been less evidence directly measuring the effect of social desirability on gender and leadership specifically, and what evidence we have presents a mixed bag. Thus, we will approach these questions from a variety of angles as we investigate the extent to which support for female clergy is accurately measured by the public opinion surveys analyzed in the previous chapter. Our evidence from the last two chapters showed that almost three-quarters of American churchgoers are supportive of women serving as the principal leaders in their congregations, but is there any evidence of a social desirability effect going on our surveys? Might support be actually lower or higher than our surveys would suggest?

SOCIAL DESIRABILITY ON THE TELEPHONE

We begin our investigation of this question by examining results from Waves 1 and 2 of our Gender and Religious Representation Survey, which we described in previous chapters. We look only at these waves because they were conducted over the telephone, and theoretically the social desirability effect is stronger when individuals are answering questions in a telephone survey compared to an anonymous online survey (Wave 3). Indeed, Lelkes et al. (2012) and Kreuter et al. (2008) show evidence that the impact of social desirability is decreased when surveys are administered electronically and anonymously.[1]

We asked respondents in our live telephone surveys whether they strongly prefer, somewhat prefer, somewhat not prefer, or strongly not prefer that the congregation they attend most often "permit women to serve as the principal religious leader." If asked, the interviewers specified that this would be the pastor or priest of most congregations. The responses were ranked on a one-to-four scale, one being "strongly not prefer" and four being "strongly prefer." We also recorded whether the *interviewer* was a man or a woman. This is important because a good deal of research has shown that gender factors can influence interview dynamics, especially when the interview contains gender-related issues (Huddy et al. 1997; Kane and Macaulay 1993; Williams and Heikes 1993). Theoretically, respondents may be more likely to express support for female clergy when they are talking to a woman.

In our telephone survey, the average level of support for all respondents (both men and women) on the one-to-four scale was 2.98 when speaking to women interviewers and 2.92 when speaking to male interviewers, a small and statistically insignificant result (p=0.54).[2] While this might suggest that the gender of the interviewer did not produce a social desirability effect, we can examine further differences between men and women *respondents* while speaking to men or women *interviewers*. When *male respondents* were speaking to *male interviewers*, for instance, the average level of support was 2.76 compared to 3.05 when *male respondents* were speaking to *female interviewers* (p=0.06). This indicates that men felt pressure to give supportive answers to women or less supportive answers to men. (In contrast, there was no statistically significant difference when it came to female respondents and the gender of their interviewer.) This preliminary evidence suggests that in our survey social desirability factors influenced levels of stated support for female clergy among our respondents.

SOCIAL DESIRABILITY ON THE INTERNET

We can look at this question from another perspective as well. Our internet-only Wave 3 respondents were also asked their support for female clergy but may not have been subject to the same social desirability issues as those in Waves 1 and 2 who were interviewed on the telephone. As described previously, those completing the survey privately at home or on a mobile device would likely not feel as much pressure to self-present in a positive way if they would be embarrassed by candid answers that they might give to a person on the telephone. By comparing responses between the telephone and internet surveys, we examine whether there is any support for this possibility.

Table 5.1 summarizes levels of support for female clergy in both the internet and telephone samples and among various political and religious subgroups. These results reveal further evidence of a possible social desirability effect. The groups that give more supportive answers on the telephone than on the internet include theological modernists, those with low levels of religious behavior, Democratic women, and women in congregations that allow for female clergy. In contrast, the groups that give *less* supportive answers over the telephone than on the internet include theological traditionalists, those with high levels of religious behaviors, and men in congregations with male-only leadership policies. In both cases, respondents from those groups were adhering to the social desirability bias of their respective groups when speaking to a live interviewer.

These results are especially interesting in that they suggest that the groups shown in the previous chapter to be some of the most explicitly supportive of female

TABLE 5.1

Average (mean) support for female ordination by subgroup, telephone vs. internet[a]

	Telephone mean	Telephone N	Internet mean	Internet N	Difference of means p-value
Full sample	2.85	553	2.87	363	0.81
Women	2.89	312	2.84	197	0.56
Men	2.80	241	2.91	166	0.31
Theological traditionalists	2.24	221	2.74	189	<0.01
Women	2.28	125	2.72	102	<0.01
Men	2.17	96	2.77	88	<0.01
Theological moderates or modernists	3.30	237	3.02	155	<0.01
Women	3.30	136	3.02	86	0.03
Men	3.31	101	3.02	69	<0.01
High religious behavior	2.60	310	2.86	258	0.01
Women	2.56	159	2.84	123	0.04
Men	2.39	109	2.93	112	<0.01
Low religious behavior	3.20	221	2.88	105	<0.01
Women	3.27	138	2.83	75	<0.01
Men	3.16	125	2.86	54	0.06
Democrats	3.35	252	3.15	215	0.01
Women	3.38	166	3.18	114	0.04
Men	3.29	87	3.13	101	0.22
Republicans	2.38	239	2.43	106	0.68
Women	2.27	117	2.36	62	0.63
Men	2.49	122	2.54	44	0.79
In a congregation that permits female clergy	3.41	263	3.17	202	<0.01
Women	3.54	141	3.15	101	<0.01
Men	3.26	122	3.18	100	0.47
In a congregation that does not permit female clergy	2.23	243	2.50	161	0.02
Women	2.28	151	2.50	96	0.12
Men	2.15	92	2.48	65	0.06

[a] *Source:* Gender and Religious Representation Survey; means are calculated from responses coded on a 1–4 scale,
1 = "strongly not prefer" respondent's congregation to allow female clergy and 4 = "strongly prefer."

clergy (theological modernists, those with low levels of religious behaviors, those in gender-inclusive congregations) are also more likely to overstate their support for female clergy when asked on the telephone compared to online. Similarly, those who are explicitly less supportive (theological traditionalists, those with high religious behaviors, those in congregations with male-only leadership policies) are also more likely to understate support on the telephone. This suggests that support for women's ordination can be somewhat tepid among its strongest would-be advocates as well as stronger than we would expect among its opponents.

In sum, it seems that there is good reason to suspect that social desirability may indeed be relevant on this issue. Some groups seem more or less inclined to moderate their expressed levels of support for female clergy depending on the context and situation. While this evidence is only suggestive, we can analyze this question with an even more precise survey tool: a list experiment.

LEARNING FROM THE LIST EXPERIMENT

A list experiment (also known as the item count technique or ICT) is a survey tool designed to indirectly measure socially undesirable opinions in a given population. It works like this: survey respondents are randomly sorted into two different groups, a control group and a treatment group. In this instance, the control group is given a list of four statements and asked how many of those statements they agree with. They are specifically instructed *not* to reveal to the interviewer *which* of the items they have in mind specifically, but only to tell the interviewer the final number: zero, one, two, three, or four. The interviewer thus knows only the final result: the number of statements the respondent agrees with, but not which particular statements.

The treatment group is given a list identical to that of the control group but with the addition of one extra item: a statement reflecting the socially undesirable opinion under investigation. They receive the same instructions as the control group to report *only* the number of statements that they agree with, not which statements specifically. For this group, those who would agree with the socially undesirable attitude but might hesitate to say so explicitly in a live interview are free to express support by mentally including it in their list of statements adding up to the final number they state to the interviewer. In this way the respondent theoretically should be free to express his or her candid opinion regarding the socially undesirable item in the list without the interviewer knowing that the item in question was included in the final number that the respondent reported. This theoretically allows the respondent to be candid without fear of social pressure or judgment from the interviewer.

Afterward, we compare the average number of "agree" statements between the control and treatment groups. If the treatment average is higher than the control average, there were likely some in the treatment group who agreed with the socially undesirable statement that the control group did not receive (as the two groups theoretically were otherwise identical due to random assignment). The difference in numerical means between the two groups, then, is the proportion of the sample interviewed that agrees with the statement. We can conduct a test for statistical significance to determine whether the difference in the wider population is likely to be real or whether the difference appeared due to random sampling error.

Surveys can also include a direct measure of support for something. For example, the same survey could ask respondents directly whether they support same-sex marriage and also ask respondents the same thing indirectly with a list experiment. The researcher could then compare levels of direct support with levels of indirect support indicated with the list experiment. If support were higher among those asked directly with the explicit question than among those asked indirectly with the list experiment, it would mean that there were some who said explicitly that they agreed with the statement but who did not include it in the number of list experiment statements that they agreed with. This would indicate that there is social pressure to indicate more agreement than actually is the case. The reverse is also true. If indirect support for the socially undesirable statement in the list experiment is higher than with the direct measure, it indicates that some individuals feel pressure to indicate disapproval of something when they actually agree with it.

List experiments like this have been used to study attitudes toward race/ethnicity (Gilens 1998; Kuklinski, Cobb, and Gilens 1997; Martinez and Craig 2010; Redlawsk, Tolbert, and Franko 2010; Sniderman and Carmines 1999), religious groups (Kane, Craig, and Wald 2004), immigration and nativism (Janus 2010; Knoll 2013), female politicians (Streb et al. 2008), voting (Holbrook and Krosnick 2010), sexual behavior (LaBrie and Earleywine 2000), and employee theft (Wimbush and Dalton 1997). A more comprehensive treatment of the methodology can be found in Kuklinski et al. (1997), Imai (2011), and Blair and Imai (2012).

A word of caution is in order before we proceed. No research methodology is flawless and list experiments are no exception. This approach to studying socially undesirable attitudes has been in practice only since the 1990s or so and continues to be studied and debated among statisticians and methodologists (Holbrook and Krosnick 2010; Imai 2011; Martinez and Craig 2010; Thomas et al. 2017; Zigerell 2011). While we have made every effort to design our list experiment in such a way as to be sensitive to these various criticisms and recommendations, public opinion researchers have yet to arrive at a strong consensus about whether list experiments are accurate and reliable. That said, we believe we can safely say that there is a moderate degree of consensus among researchers that list experiments give generally reliable results, so long as the various limitations are kept in mind as the results are interpreted.

One shortcoming that is particularly relevant to our study is that list experiments tend to underestimate rates of attitudes and behaviors that are widespread in the sample population (Jonge and Nickerson 2013; Thomas et al. 2017). In our case, the findings from previous chapters showed that support for female clergy is strong among a variety of social and religious subgroups, with somewhere around 72% of the churchgoing population in favor of women serving as pastors or priests in their congregations. Given that this is a widespread attitude, our list experiment may show results biased in a downward direction, that is, that underestimates indirect support for female clergy among our respondents.

It is also the case that our subgroup sample sizes get very small (sometimes less than one hundred) and thus the associated margins of error increase substantially (Glynn 2013). Given this reality, the list experiment is more reliable when looking at the broader trends we present in this chapter than when digging into the subsamples (which is often). While we present the exact statistics, it is very important that the reader keep in mind that we do not claim that they represent more than a ballpark estimate of the levels of indirect support for female ordination among the various subgroups that we analyze in this chapter.

MEASURING SUPPORT FOR WOMEN'S ORDINATION WITH
A LIST EXPERIMENT

In Waves 1 and 2 of our Gender and Religious Representation Survey, we presented respondents with the following list experiment prompt: *"Now I'm going to read you a list of statements. Please tell us how many of the following things you would support in the church or religious congregation that you attend most often. We do not need to know which ones, just how many."* The control group then received the following list, the order of which was randomized for each respondent:

- Encouraging religious leaders to openly discuss political matters over the pulpit during campaign season
- Offering marriage ceremonies to gay and lesbian couples
- Discouraging members of other faiths to visit and participate in religious services
- Focusing more on interfaith and outreach programs in your community

The treatment group received an identical prompt and list of statement, with the exception of an additional list item (the order of which was also randomized for the treatment group list):

- Permitting women to serve as the pastor, priest, or principal leader of the congregation

As explained, those in the control group gave the interviewer a number between zero and four, while those in the treatment group gave the interviewer a number between zero and five. Note also that we included a variety of statements in the expanded list that were designed in such a way so that many people would agree with some of them as well as disagree with others. This is to prevent "ceiling effects," in which almost everyone agrees with all the options, as well as to prevent the female clergy statement from obviously standing out from the rest (Kane, Craig, and Wald 2004).

The distribution of answers between the control and treatment group is found in Table 5.2.[3] The mean number of responses given by everyone in the control group was 1.97 (N=335)[4] compared to a mean of 2.52 (N=356) for those in the treatment group.[5] Recall that if every person in the survey supported the fifth statement (about female clergy) and included it in the list of statements that the person indicated agreement with, the difference of means between the two groups should be 1.0. The difference between the two means in our list experiment is 0.55 (difference of means t-test p<0.0001), though, meaning that 55% of our interview sample indicated

TABLE 5.2

Distribution of responses to list experiment prompt[a]

	Control (%)	Treatment (%)
0	6.5	4.8
1	20.8	16.8
2	47.6	26.1
3	19.0	31.1
4	6.0	16.5
5		4.8
Mean	1.97	2.52
N	335	356

[a] *Source:* Gender and Religious Representation Survey.

support for "permitting women to serve as the pastor, priest, or principal leader of the congregation" that they attend most often. Compare this to the 72% who indicated support when asked directly. This difference of 16% means that about one in six people in our survey indicated support for female clergy in their congregations when asked directly but not when asked indirectly with the list experiment, suggesting that actual support for female clergy among American churchgoers is somewhat lower than indicated in the previous chapters. Instead of three-quarters of parishioners supporting female clergy, this would seem to indicate that a more accurate estimate is a little over half.

We can investigate this gender effect further by limiting our analysis to only those 72% who explicitly indicated support for female clergy when asked directly. Figure 5.1 shows that among explicit advocates of female clergy, only 68% indicated the same preference when asked indirectly in the list experiment.[6] We can infer that the other 32% felt pressure to indicate agreement when asked directly but shied away when asked in the list experiment. In other words, this suggests that about a third of people who say they favor having female clergy are not as supportive as they claim. In contrast, among those who explicitly indicated *not* being in favor of female clergy, the list experiment revealed no statistically significant level of support; the findings of the list experiment were consistent with this group's responses to the direct question. It seems that those who do not support female ordination are more forthcoming with their frank opinions on the matter when asked by telephone surveyors.

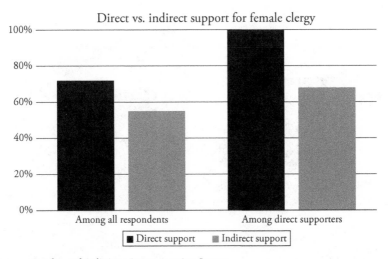

FIGURE 5.1 Gender and Religious Representation Survey

LIST EXPERIMENT RESULTS: GENDER

Because we collected information on the gender of our telephone respondents, we can analyze direct and indirect support among both men and women. Figure 5.2 shows that among men, indirect support is 73% compared to 68% when they were asked directly.[7] This suggests that men are actually slightly *more* approving of female ordination than they let on when asked directly in the telephone surveys. On the other hand, our list experiment revealed that women have only a 40% level of indirect support for female ordination,[8] compared to 74% when asked directly—a substantial difference of 34%!

Digging a little deeper, we see that among men who directly endorse female clergy, 92% also indicated support when asked indirectly in the list experiment.[9] Again, men who say they uphold female ordination seem to be sincere. Among women who say that they support female clergy when asked directly, however, their indirect level of support is almost exactly half: 51%.[10] In other words, this suggests that only about half of all women who say that they support female clergy in their congregations are genuinely supportive. We can infer that the other half may feel pressure to say "yes" when deep down they may really mean "no." It seems that most of the 17% difference between direct and indirect support for female clergy in the aggregate that we reported earlier comes almost exclusively from women.[11]

In sum, about two-thirds of churchgoing men in the U.S. agree with having women in their pulpits, and there is little reason from our list experiment to think that they are misrepresenting these preferences to appear "politically correct." If anything, it

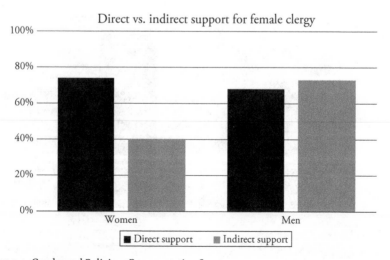

FIGURE 5.2 Gender and Religious Representation Survey

seems that men are slightly more likely to *depress* their stated support for female clergy, as indirect support among men is about 5% higher than direct support. For their part, two-thirds of women say they would like to see other women serving as their principal religious leader, but only half of those proponents appear to be sincere in their advocacy.

LIST EXPERIMENT RESULTS: RELIGIOUS TRADITION

Turning now to religious traditions, Figure 5.3 displays the breakdown of direct and indirect support for female clergy among the various major religious traditions as well as the gender subgroups within each tradition.[12] Let us here issue another reminder that due to small sample sizes with the various subgroups, the results should be considered as ballpark rather than precise estimates.

As was seen in the previous chapters, explicit support for female clergy is lowest among Evangelical Protestants, with about 63% expressing support when asked directly. What is interesting here is that we see roughly the same proportion expressing support indirectly through the list experiment. Broken down by gender, Evangelical women are slightly more likely to overstate their support for female clergy by about 9%, while men are about 3% likely to understate it. Overall, though, these differences

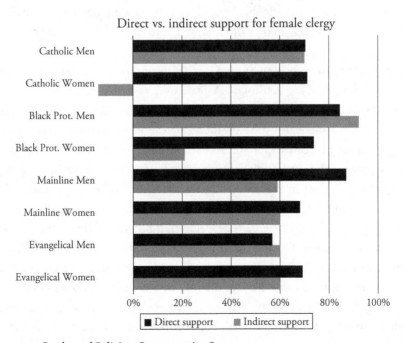

FIGURE 5.3 Gender and Religious Representation Survey

are small. It seems that Evangelicals in general are no more likely to over- or under-report their level of support for female clergy. Apparently, they seem happy to tell us what they really think on the issue.

In contrast, Mainline Protestants overstate support for female clergy by 22%. When asked directly, 80% said they approved of it, but only 58% did so when asked indirectly. It seems that in the Christian tradition in which support is ostensibly highest and in which actual rates of women serving as pastors or priests is also highest, indirect levels of support are slightly lower than those among Evangelical Protestants. In other words, our list experiment seems to show that Mainline Protestants are about as likely to back female clergy as Evangelical Protestants (58% versus 62%, respectively, in the list experiment), but Mainline Protestants are more likely than Evangelicals to say directly that they favor female ordination (80% versus 63%, respectively). It is interesting to see in Figure 5.3 that Mainline men are more likely to overstate support (29% overreport) than are Mainline women, who overreport by only about 8%.

We tend to see opposite effects among Black Protestants, though. In this tradition, men and women have similarly high levels of support for female ordination, 84% and 74% respectively. The list experiment results reveal, however, that indirect support for female ordination is 21% (and statistically insignificant, meaning we cannot be at least 95% certain it is not zero) among Black Protestant women but a solid 92% among Black Protestant men! We should emphasize again at this point, though, that due to the small sample sizes for these subgroups the margin of error is high and so these figures should not be interpreted as more than a general estimate.

Perhaps the most surprising finding is in levels of direct versus indirect support for female clergy among Catholics. A little over two-thirds (71%) of Catholics expressed support when asked directly, virtually unchanged from the 68% level of support among American Catholics found by the Pew Research Center in 2014 (Cooperman et al. 2014). Our indirect list experiment measure of support for female clergy among Catholics, however, is only 15% and not statistically significant (p=0.52). We see in Figure 5.2 that this effect is attributable almost entirely to Catholic women. Catholic men and women both have nearly identical rates of explicit support (71.1% and 70.4%, respectively), but very different rates of indirect support. Whereas Catholic men have virtually the same level of indirect as direct support, there is no statistically significant level of support among Catholic women.[13] This is to say that despite the fact that around two-thirds of Catholic women say that they favor women being permitted to serve as priests in their parishes, our survey list experiment could uncover no reliable evidence that *any* Catholic women are actually supportive.

This is especially significant given that the Catholic Church is the largest religious tradition in the United States that currently has a male-only priesthood. It seems that Pope Francis's hesitancy toward the possibility of women's ordination in the Catholic Church (Allen 2015; Povoledo and Goodstein 2016) may meet less resistance among American Catholics than might otherwise be assumed, at least among the group that would be most affected by such a change: Catholic women.

LIST EXPERIMENT RESULTS: DEMOGRAPHICS AND SOCIOECONOMIC STATUS

Table 5.3 displays the results of the list experiment for various demographic and socioeconomic subgroups. It continues the general patterns as reported in the previous section: women in a variety of demographic categories are consistently more likely to overreport their support for female clergy in their congregations than are men. As one example, it seems to be younger, not older, women who are less approving of female clergy when asked indirectly. While 77% of women under fifty are supportive of female clergy when asked directly, only 29% express this positive feeling when asked indirectly—a difference of 48%. There are similar gaps among both high-income women and less-educated women: both groups are much less likely to approve of female clergy when asked indirectly through the list experiment than they are when asked directly. In contrast, it seems that some men are more likely to underreport their preferences for female clergy, especially highly educated men who underreport support by approximately 31% (74% explicit versus 105% indirect).[14] Younger men and high-income men are also more likely to underreport support for female clergy.

Another interesting pattern occurs in terms of race/ethnicity. Both whites and blacks are more likely to overreport support for female ordination in their congregations—by 18% and 26%, respectively. In contrast, Latinos have approximately identical levels of support whether asked directly or indirectly (84% and 86%, respectively). Unfortunately, the sample sizes for our racial/ethnic minority groups are too small for us to be able to break down these groups further by gender.

LIST EXPERIMENT RESULTS: RELIGIOUS AND POLITICAL FACTORS

Table 5.4 reports the comparative level of support for female clergy between our direct and indirect list experiment measures among various religious and political subgroups. Once again we see that women in a variety of subgroups are the most likely to overreport support, while various types of men are most likely to underreport it.

TABLE 5.3

Direct vs. indirect support for female clergy, by demographic subgroup[a]

	Control mean	Control N	Treatment mean	Treatment N	Indirect support (%)	Direct support (%)	Difference of means p-value	% over-report
Under 50	1.95	183	2.51	202	56	76	<0.01	20
Women	2.15	91	2.44	107	29	77	0.05	48
Men	1.75	92	2.60	95	85	74	<0.01	-11
50 and over	1.99	152	2.53	155	54	66	<0.01	12
Women	2.05	92	2.59	84	54	70	<0.01	16
Men	1.90	60	2.47	71	57	61	0.01	4
College educated	1.98	149	2.71	163	73	76	<0.01	3
Women	2.17	85	2.66	96	49	78	<0.01	29
Men	1.72	64	2.78	67	106	74	<0.01	-32
Less than college	1.96	183	2.36	192	40	68	<0.01	28
Women	2.04	97	2.33	94	29	71	0.06	42
Men	1.86	86	2.38	98	52	64	<0.01	12
High income ($50K+)	1.99	169	2.53	169	54	73	<0.01	19
Women	2.15	87	2.45	98	30	75	0.04	45
Men	1.82	82	2.65	70	83	71	<0.01	-12
Low income (<$50K)	1.95	115	2.46	131	51	67	<0.01	16
Women	2.05	70	2.52	62	47	73	0.03	26
Men	1.79	46	2.39	68	60	61	0.01	1
White	1.97	226	2.44	223	47	65	<0.01	18
Black	1.89	36	2.46	51	57	83	0.03	26
Latino	1.89	34	2.75	46	86	84	<0.01	-2

[a] *Source:* Gender and Religious Representation Survey; means are calculated from responses to survey list experiment.

Liberal women, less religious women, Democratic women, and theologically moderate/modernist women overreport their approval of female clergy by 58%, 53%, 49%, and 48%, respectively. In each of these cases, explicit support is in the high 80s or over 90%, while indirect list experiment support is 40% or less. This is especially noteworthy given that our previous chapter identified liberals, Democrats, those that are less religious, and theological modernists to be the strongest supporters of female clergy.

In contrast, the groups with the most similar levels of direct and indirect support (indicating the highest level of "frankness" in answering the question on the survey) are men of various stripes: liberal men, Democratic men, highly religious and theologically traditionalist men, as well as *less* religious and theologically traditionalist men. In fact, politically and theologically liberal men and Democratic men have the highest level of support for female clergy of all the groups in the indirect list experiment shown in Table 5.4.

LIST EXPERIMENT RESULTS: CONGREGATIONAL CONTEXT

The findings displayed in Figure 5.4 reveal some additional intriguing patterns. Support for female clergy is fairly consistent among those who currently have a female pastor or priest in their congregation. More than nine out of ten of those with female religious leaders currently serving in their congregations say they approve of female clergy and give no reason to suspect otherwise by their responses to the list experiment (93% direct versus 96% indirect support).[15] Among those who currently have male clergypeople in their congregations, results are similar to those among the broader sample: there is a 21% rate of overreporting of support for female clergy, which comes primarily from women who overreport support by 42% (72% direct versus 30% indirect).

The second relevant finding from these results is that social desirability seems to have a major effect when it comes to congregational policies regarding women serving as the principal religious leader. As shown in Figure 5.5, among those in congregations that do *not* allow women to serve in their pulpits, direct support is a little under half (47%). In the list experiment results, however, we see that support is a very low 11%, which does not even attain statistical significance. This means that we cannot be confident from these results that there is *anyone* in congregations that forbid female clergy who privately supports women's ordination. This applies to men and women, both of whom are very likely to overreport support (42% direct versus a statistically insignificant 14% indirect for men, and 49% direct versus a statistically insignificant 6% for women).

TABLE 5.4

Direct vs. indirect support for female clergy, by religious and political subgroup[a]

	Control mean	Control N	Treatment mean	Treatment N	Indirect support (%)	Direct support (%)	Difference of means p-value	% over-report
Theological traditionalists	1.76	124	2.25	138	49	46	<0.00	-3
Women	1.77	63	2.24	75	47	47	0.01	0
Men	1.76	61	2.27	63	51	45	0.01	-6
Theological modernists	2.26	144	2.83	147	57	88	<0.01	31
Women	2.37	92	2.76	77	39	87	0.01	48
Men	2.07	53	2.90	70	83	89	<0.01	6
High religious behavior	1.90	144	2.37	181	47	55	<0.01	8
Women	1.98	86	2.37	101	39	58	0.02	19
Men	1.78	58	2.38	80	60	51	<0.01	-9
Low religious behavior	2.02	181	2.65	166	63	87	<0.01	24
Women	2.22	91	2.58	84	36	89	0.02	53
Men	1.82	90	2.71	82	89	84	<0.01	-5

Political conservatives	1.86	122	2.20	123	34	49	0.01	15
Women	1.87	61	2.12	52	25	46	0.15	21
Men	1.86	61	2.26	71	40	51	0.02	11
Political liberals	2.04	120	2.77	110	73	90	<0.01	17
Women	2.30	67	2.63	69	33	91	0.08	58
Men	1.72	53	2.99	41	127	90	<0.01	-37
Republicans	1.92	133	2.32	140	40	49	0.01	9
Women	1.92	62	2.18	62	26	45	0.13	19
Men	1.92	67	2.43	78	51	53	<0.01	2
Democrats	2.03	171	2.73	165	70	89	<0.01	19
Women	2.22	105	2.63	98	41	90	0.02	49
Men	1.73	66	2.87	66	114	88	<0.01	-26

[a] *Source:* Gender and Religious Representation Survey; means are calculated from responses to survey list experiment.

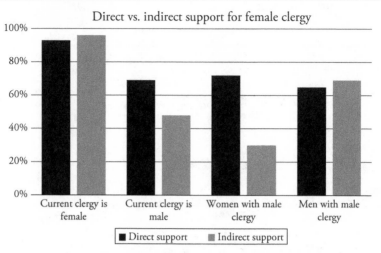

FIGURE 5.4 Gender and Religious Representation Survey

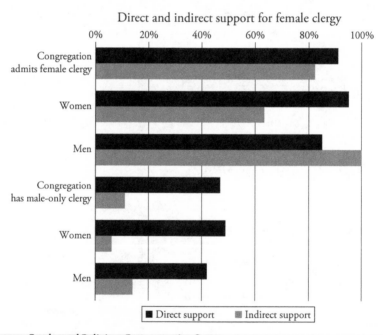

FIGURE 5.5 Gender and Religious Representation Survey

A common pattern emerges among the other various subgroups shown in Table 5.5 who attend congregations with male-only clerical policies. Those on the liberal end of the theological and political spectrum, who attend congregations in which women are not permitted to serve as pastor or priest, have consistently high rates of explicit support for female clergy: 78%, 73%, 75%, and 75% for theological

TABLE 5.5

Direct vs. indirect support for female clergy, by congregational leader gender and policy[a]

	Control mean	Control N	Treatment mean	Treatment N	Indirect support (%)	Direct support (%)	Difference of means p-value	% overreport
Clergy of current congregation is female	1.83	23	2.79	33	96	93	<0.01	-3
Clergy of current congregation is male	1.99	295	2.47	301	48	69	<0.01	21
Women	2.14	159	2.44	170	30	72	0.01	42
Men	1.81	136	2.50	130	69	65	<0.01	-4
Congregation policy permits female clergy	1.98	166	2.81	187	83	91	<0.01	8
Women	2.02	91	2.66	90	64	95	<0.01	31
Men	1.93	76	2.94	97	101	85	<0.01	-16
Theological traditional	1.77	53	2.73	61	96	83	<0.01	-13
Theological modernist	2.21	83	2.97	93	76	95	<0.01	19
High religious behavior	1.99	72	2.80	85	81	84	<0.01	3
Low religious behavior	1.98	91	2.81	98	83	95	<0.01	12
Political conservatives	1.91	51	2.49	54	58	80	<0.01	22
Politically liberal	2.09	74	2.89	69	80	96	<0.01	16
Republican	2.03	56	2.68	62	65	80	<0.01	15
Democrat	2.01	96	2.85	105	84	95	<0.01	11

(continued)

TABLE 5.5

Continued

	Control mean	Control N	Treatment mean	Treatment N	Indirect support (%)	Direct support (%)	Difference of means p-value	% overreport
Congregation has male-only clergy policy	2.03	122	2.14	135	11	47	0.44	36
Women	2.23	76	2.29	88	6	49	0.73	43
Men	1.70	47	1.84	47	14	42	0.50	28
Theological traditional	1.66	57	1.86	68	20	16	0.23	-4
Theological modernist	2.35	50	2.50	45	15	78	0.60	63
High religious behavior	1.75	65	1.95	85	20	30	0.25	10
Low religious behavior	2.36	52	2.35	47	-1	73	0.97	74
Politically conservative	1.75	56	1.88	54	13	24	0.46	11
Politically liberal	2.35	25	2.45	34	10	75	0.77	65
Republican	1.77	63	1.95	62	18	27	0.27	9
Democrat	2.37	47	2.44	49	7	75	0.79	68

[a] *Source*: Gender and Religious Representation Survey; means are calculated from responses to survey list experiment.

modernists, those with lower levels of religious behaviors, political liberals, and Democrats, respectively (the same groups identified in the previous chapter as being most open to female clergy in their congregations). Levels of indirect support for female clergy among each of these groups, however, fails to achieve statistical signif-icance, meaning we cannot be at least 95% confident that their low rates of indirect approval (15%, -1%, 10%, and 7%, respectively) are not simply due to random sam-pling error. In other words, those most likely to voice support for female clergy in congregations with male-only policies also seem to be the most likely to overstate that support.

We can compare these findings with those on the conservative end of the theolog-ical and political spectrum. For theological traditionalists, those with high levels of religious behaviors, political conservatives, and Republicans in congregations with male-only leadership policies, stated direct approval for female ordination is rela-tively low (16%, 30%, 24%, and 27%, respectively). Indirect list experiment support for female clergy among each of these groups is a statistically insignificant 20%, 20%, 13%, and 7%, respectively, meaning that once again we are not 95% confident that in-direct support for female clergy is not actually zero for any of these groups. It seems that the groups most likely to state opposition to female ordination are also the most sincere about their opinions.

The results shown in Figure 5.4 and Table 5.5 reveal quite a contrast when it comes to those in congregations that *do* have policies that allow for women to serve as the congregation's leader. Support for female ordination in those congregations is consistently high both in direct measures (91%) and indirect list experiments (83%). Even here, though, we see that the group most likely to overreport support is women, with a discrepancy of about 31% (95% direct versus 64% indirect support). If anything, we observe some evidence that men in these congregations are likely to *under*state support by about 16%. This suggests that there are a handful of men in these more gender-inclusive congregations who, for whatever reason, feel pressure to say that they do not support female ordination when they actually do. Otherwise, the results show fairly consistent direct and indirect support among both liberal and conservative theological, religious, and political subgroups in congregations that allow for female clergy, with an average direct support rate of about 89% and an av-erage indirect support rate of about 78%.

SUMMARY AND CONCLUSION

There is reason to suspect that individuals might not give completely frank answers to telephone survey questions about female clergy in their religious congregations.

Given that gender-related issues are often controversial in society, some people may feel pressure to give a socially desirable answer on the telephone when speaking to a person whom they fear may judge them if they were to give an honest but "politically incorrect" response. To investigate this possibility we used a survey tool called a list experiment (also called an item count technique) that allows people the freedom to give more candid answers than they otherwise might due to self-presentation concerns.

Our list experiment approach revealed widespread evidence that support for women leaders in American religious congregations is substantially lower than is indicated using more direct and traditional survey measures. For example, while about 72% of respondents said that they would prefer that their congregations allow women to serve as the principal religious leader, only 55% of respondents indicated the same preference when the list experiment survey tool was employed. This suggests that while nearly three-quarters of American churchgoers say that they would like to see female clergy in their congregations, the evidence generated by the indirect list experiment approach suggests that support may in actuality be a little over half.

This finding provides insight into the incongruity that we identified in the introductory chapter. The results of the list experiment give us reason to believe that the gap between support for equality in the abstract and the current state of inequality in America's places of worship is not quite as pronounced as the direct survey results suggest. While the results outlined in this chapter cannot fully explain the depth of the gender gap in religious leadership, actual support is closer to half than three-quarters of all American worshipers, which makes the gap less pronounced. Moreover, the list results indicate that support for women's ordination is actually much lower among women than it is among men. If in fact less than half of female worshipers think that women should be ordained, there may be a much smaller pool of women who feel motivated to enter seminary or pursue careers in ministry.

The list experiment tool was also able to investigate which groups were more or less forthcoming with their candid preferences on the matter. One of the most striking findings from the list experiment approach is that women are consistently more likely to overreport their approval for female clergy than are men—and often by wide margins. Only about half of the women who say they support female clergy in their congregations when asked directly indicated that backing when asked indirectly. This same pattern held for a variety of demographic, religious, and political subgroups.

It is a common stereotype that men are more direct than women in their verbal communication patterns. Communications research, however, has frequently confirmed that this stereotype is often true in situations in which gender identities are emphasized (LaFrance and Harris 2004, 149). Gender is certainly a salient factor when taking a public opinion survey on women's ordination, and so we might expect men in our sample to be more direct when discussing their feelings on the topic than women, especially as women are the focus of the discussion. The results shown in this chapter corroborate these predictions. Women seem to be more reluctant to discuss their true feelings on the topic of female ordination than men, who, for their part, generally seem to be more frank with their opinions. Also, particular subgroups of men were more likely to *under*report their support for female clergy, although not to the same extent that women were likely to overreport theirs.

These findings are all the more notable given that the analysis in our previous chapter was unable to uncover any significant difference in how men and women express support for female clergy when asked directly. In contrast, our list experiment evidence suggests that it is primarily men, not women, who are likely to give female ordination their blessing. This finding adds further ballast to the argument based on research by Jost et al. (2004) and Glick and Fiske (2001) that suggests that women are often less egalitarian than men in religious contexts, as they either consciously or unconsciously internalize the traditionalist gender narratives espoused by some contemporary religious institutions.

This evidence also adds a quantitative demonstration of our qualitative finding from Chapter 3 that middle-aged women are more likely than men to oppose female clergy. Although the resistance from women that many female pastors and rabbis described did not appear in our initial analysis of the surveys, the list experiment suggests that many women may outwardly state enthusiasm about female ordination when asked directly while harboring reservations in private. Perhaps this is part of the answer: middle-age women who are more opposed to female clergy may have a more difficult time hiding their views when interacting with their woman pastor than they are when sharing their views over the phone or in an internet survey.

Another important finding is that the groups who are most approving of female clergy when asked directly are also most likely to overreport those levels of support. These include political and theological liberals as well as Democrats. This has parallels with the research discussed at the outset of the chapter, namely that those most likely to report behaviors such as voting are also the most likely to overreport those same behaviors (Bernstein, Chadha, and Montjoy 2001; Karp and Brockington 2005; Silver, Anderson, and Abramson 1986) and those most likely to underreport racial attitudes are often white liberals (Gilens 1998; Kuklinski, Cobb, and Gilens 1997). In this case, the evidence suggests that those who are typically considered "likely candidates" for egalitarian gender attitudes—political/theological liberals, Democrats, and the women in each of those groups—are the most likely to paint an overly rosy picture of their own views. These individuals are those who are "expected" to champion female ordination and thus may be most likely to feel pressure to do so even if they are, in reality, not as supportive.

There were also some interesting findings when it came to specific religious traditions. Mainline Protestants, for example, were the pioneers of widening access to clerical positions for women throughout the twentieth century. However, our list experiment showed that they are not quite as well disposed toward female clergy as traditional survey results would lead us to believe. Much to our surprise as well, our list experiment results could not with any degree of confidence confirm that any female Catholics in our sample were encouraging of women serving as priests in their parishes even though more than two-thirds of Catholic women say they are supportive, when asked directly. Catholic men, for their part, gave consistent answers whether asked directly or indirectly, backing female ordination at a rate of about 70%.

Another of this chapter's most consistent findings authenticates those found in previous chapters: congregational context makes a key difference in driving acceptance of female clergy, both direct as well as indirect. Our list experiment results confirmed that those in congregations that permit female clergy are generally open to women serving in that capacity whether measured by direct or indirect measures. On the other hand, the list experiment also showed that those in congregations that do *not* allow for female clergy are generally not supportive when measured indirectly, even though roughly half or so of these same individuals claim they are supportive when they are asked directly. This may be at least partially attributable to motivated reasoning theory as discussed in the previous chapter. Humans are strongly motivated to adopt beliefs and opinions that match their behaviors because it is unpleasant to deal with cognitive dissonance (Kunda 1990). While many who attend congregations with male-only policies for clergy may claim to welcome more gender-inclusive practices in their congregations, they may also be motivated to covertly agree with their congregation's existing policies so as to put their beliefs and their congregation's choices in conformity with one another. Recall also that the previous chapter showed that religious and political progressives in congregations with male-only policies were just as positive about female ordination as their counterparts in congregations that allow for female clergy. Our list experiment casts some level of skepticism on that finding, however, as it shows that these individuals are likely less approving than they claim in public opinion surveys. Again, this may be because they feel pressure to promote gender-inclusive congregational policies to adhere to the norms of their liberal peer groups.

It is also noteworthy that those in congregations who currently have a female pastor or priest are not only the most supportive but the most consistent in their answers between direct and indirect measures, which were around 90% for each. This finding reflects the recurring theme in our interviews that personal experiences *matter*. It follows that a greater prevalence of female clergy could be associated with greater, and more genuine, support for clergywomen. While this finding offers little to a discussion of how to decrease the gender gap, it does help us better understand the phenomenon. Those who have experience with female clergy are more likely to genuinely and overwhelmingly favor female clergy, while those who do not currently have a clergywoman leading their congregation tend to inflate their stated level of support. It seems that Lehman's (1987) finding about the "social contact" effect is supported by our results: attending a congregation with a female pastor and being exposed to her and her leadership role tends to make people almost unanimously (and genuinely!) supportive of female clergy.

This helps us make sense of some of the findings of our face-to-face interviews and telephone surveys as described in previous chapters. The in-person interviews showed evidence that direct personal experience with a female pastor led to more advocacy for female ordination (in line with Lehman 1987) but did not directly affect stated support independently of a person's congregational policies on gender and leadership. In other words, the public opinion surveys showed that whether a person's congregation *allows* for women to serve as clergy matters more than whether the person's pastor or priest is actually a woman or a man. Here, the evidence shows that direct personal experience with a female pastor or priest boosts levels of *indirect* support for female clergy above and beyond any influence caused by one's congregational policies on gender and leadership. Having a woman pastor might not lead someone to espouse the idea of female clergy to a telephone interviewer, but it does seem to lead someone to be more genuinely supportive of female clergy in ways that can be measured indirectly.

A FINAL WORD OF CAUTION

At this point we wish to re-emphasize the "word of caution" discussed earlier in the chapter. As we described, list experiments have been used by many social scientists to study a wide range of behaviors, but they are relatively new and are not without their critics (e.g. Zigerell 2011). The statistical tools for analyzing list experiment results continue to be developed and tested (Imai 2011). Because of this, we argue that the results presented in this chapter should not be considered definitively more valid or legitimate than the results presented in previous chapters, which relied on explicit self-reporting measures and face-to-face interview responses. In other words, this chapter should not be considered the final word on the subject.

From one perspective, for example, we could argue that our public opinion surveys demonstrate that more than two-thirds of Catholic women favor female ordination in American parishes. This is in line with other polling and evidence on the matter (Cooperman et al. 2014). The social desirability issue, however, makes us cautious about uncritically accepting this as truth. On the other hand, our list experiment results would suggest the distinct possibility that support for female ordination among Catholic women is actually zero. As described previously, though, research on list experiments has shown that they tend to underestimate attitudes and behaviors with widespread support (Jonge and Nickerson 2013; Thomas et al. 2017), which is relevant when assessing attitudes toward female clergy in the United States. Also, many of the findings from our list experiment are based on small subsample sizes and therefore have a large margin of error. This then keeps us from uncritically accepting the list experiment findings as definitive.

Ultimately, each of the perspectives presented thus far in the book tells a different story because they are based on different assumptions and are derived from varying analytical approaches, all of which have strengths and weaknesses. We believe that each approach and perspective has merit and is useful at helping us better understand the phenomenon we are investigating. In our estimation, the "truth" of patterns of support for female clergy in the United States likely lies somewhere in the middle of the various pictures that the evidence has painted in the last three chapters.

While we have cautioned against reading too much into any one statistic presented in this chapter, a birds-eye view of the findings suggests a few broad conclusions that we can be more confident about:

1. Support for female ordination among American churchgoers is probably not as high as suggested in the previous chapter (about 72%), but is likely not as low as suggested in this chapter (about 55%).
2. Levels of support among women are probably lower than among men.
3. Groups with the highest levels of direct support for female ordination tend to be more likely to overstate that support, while those with the lowest explicit levels of support tend generally to give more candid answers.
4. Those in congregations that allow for female ordination have high levels of favoring women's ordination and are likely more sincere about those opinions.
5. There is reason to be skeptical about levels of stated support for female ordination among those in congregations with male-only leadership policies.

Some may interpret these results to mean that the gender gap in opportunities for American religious leadership positions is at least to a moderate extent not a result of gender prejudice or theological beliefs but instead a result of lower levels of advocacy from women themselves. Assuming this is true, it begs the question of why women might be less motivated to view women as their potential congregational leaders in the first place. We examined this question to some degree in previous chapters, but as of yet we have not explored the possibility of childhood socialization. If women see only men in the pulpit during their formative childhood years, will they internalize the message that religious leadership is not for women? It is to this question we turn in our next chapter.

NOTES

1. Although see Rosenfeld et al. (1996) and Malhotra and Krosnick (2007) who show evidence in the opposite direction.

2. Throughout this chapter and beyond the "p" values represent the level of "statistical significance." Recall from the previous chapters that statistical significance is an estimate of the probability that the particular finding in the sample is representative of an actual relationship in the wider population and did not appear simply due to random sampling error. Here, a p-value of 0.54 means that there is a 54% chance that there is no actual difference between the two variables in the wider population and that the difference between the two numbers in our sample is instead due to random sampling error. Thus, we are only 46% confident that the difference in our sample represents a "true" difference. By way of comparison, the standard "cut off" for statistically significant result is p=0.05, or a 95% chance that the difference is real. P-values of less than 0.10 are generally characterized by social scientists as strongly suggestive and less than 0.05 as confident.

3. Unless otherwise noted, we apply the same weighting variables as described in the Data Appendix throughout this chapter so as to increase the generalizability to the wider population. All reported statistics (means, sample sizes, etc.) reflect the weighted values. Note also that the weighting makes the sample sizes appear slightly smaller than they are in reality.

4. "N" refers to the sample size that the mean value was computed from.

5. For comparison: unweighted difference is 1.95 (N=379) and 2.48 (N=412), a statistically significant difference of 53%, virtually identical to the weighted values shown here.

6. The mean of the control group is 2.17 (N=194) while the mean of the treatment group is 2.85 (N=186).

7. The mean values of the control and treatment group are 1.81 (N=152) and 2.54 (N=166), respectively.

8. The mean control and treatment group values are 2.10 (N=183) and 2.50 (N=191).

9. The mean control and treatment group values are 2.05, N=72; 2.97, N=84, p<0.0001.

10. The mean control and treatment group values are 2.24, N=121; 2.75, N=101, p<0.0001.

11. See also Burns et al. (2001, 239) who find that men are generally more supportive of female ordination than are women, both in congregations that ordain women as well as those that do not.

12. As in the previous chapter, we unfortunately cannot display results for Jews, Mormons, or other small groups as there were too few in our sample to make even a "ballpark" meaningful inference for those groups using the list experiment approach.

13. Note that the list experiment gives a level of indirect support of -14% for female clergy among Catholic women. Of course this is impossible as there cannot be negative levels of support. This is an artifact of the statistical weighting procedure and small sample size, as the level of support is a statistically insignificant +26% when not weighted. Despite this difference, the substantive results are the same: no statistically significant difference, meaning that we are not 95% confident that there is any support for female clergy among Catholic women whether using the weighted or unweighted figures.

14. As before, a level of support above 100% is of course impossible. When this happens it is an artifact of the survey weighting procedures and small sample sizes as explained previously. The unweighted level of support is 82% (1.86 vs. 2.68, $p < 0.0001$).

15. There are too few cases in this category to be able to break down into further sub-groups such as gender.

So I'm hoping that the girls following me can look at, not me particularly, but at the larger scheme of female leadership and say "we can do this . . . we can do it because she did it." (Interview 26)

I was ordained to the priesthood in the Episcopal Church [in 2003]. When the service concluded I was greeting people in the shaking hands line and a family of four (mom, dad and two little girls) came up and the mom said, "I know we don't know each other, I hope it's okay that we came. We wanted our girls to see this and know that they can do anything."[1]

I was the first woman priest in my first parish (Episcopal) out of seminary. It was a very Roman Catholic and conservative Lutheran area and many of the children in my Sunday School went to a nearby Missouri Synod Lutheran preschool. One such little girl was asked by her teacher to identify the people from the church from a list of pictures. When she pointed to the man in the collar and stole, the girl shrugged. "Why that's the pastor, dear," [said the teacher], "don't you go to church?" "Yes, I go to church (pointing to the woman on the page) and that's the pastor!" said the girl. "Oh, no dear, that's the Sunday School teacher. Only men can be pastors," said the teacher. "Well," said the girl, "in my church the boss is a GIRL!"[2]

6

CLERGYWOMEN AND YOUNG GIRLS

The Importance of Role Models

ON APRIL 12, 2015, Hillary Clinton formally announced her intention to run for president. This was the second time she had run after narrowly losing the primary contest to Barack Obama eight years earlier. At the time, the oldest daughter of one of us (Knoll) was six years old. Her name is Abigail and she is precocious, having been blessed (or cursed, depending on one's perspective) with having two professional educators as parents. When she saw Hillary Clinton's announcement on the news, she said very innocently and matter-of-factly, "I didn't know that women were allowed to be president."

FIGURE 6.1 Personal photographs by the author

I fully accept the blame for my daughter's misperception on this matter. I suppose I had *assumed* that I did not have to explicitly explain to her that women were permitted to be president in the United States. After some reflection, though, it became obvious that she had likely internalized this message due to the fact that all the presidents she had ever seen or learned about were men and that in her brief six years of life, she had encountered more male than female authority figures in her religious, social, and civic life. Regardless, Abigail was very excited that day to learn that yes, not only could women be president of the United States but also that Hillary Clinton was entering the presidential campaign as a strong contender. For the next year and a half Abigail became Hillary Clinton's most enthusiastic and vocal cheerleader among the six-to-seven-year-old female demographic. To this day she describes a visit to a campaign event at which she got Hillary Clinton's autograph as one of the best days of her young life.

Later that year Abigail was assigned to read a biography of a prominent person as part of a class assignment and then present a monologue to the class as that person. Of course she chose Hillary. In preparation, she read a young adult biography of Secretary Clinton—four times!—and then was extremely proud to

FIGURE 6.2 Personal photographs by the author

represent the candidate to her classmates. She practiced her monologue repeatedly and emphasized all the work that Hillary Clinton had done for women and children.

On Election Day Abigail was indignant that, as a child, she was disenfranchised and would not be able to vote due to her age. She said that she wanted to work for children's rights just like Hillary Clinton had done so that children could someday have the right to vote. She then asked me if she could go to the polling location with me and fill out a sample ballot because even though she knew it would not count, it would be important to her to get to vote for Hillary Clinton. She proudly wore her "I Voted" sticker the rest of the day.

Of course she was disappointed in the outcome of the election, but she went to school the next morning with her Hillary Clinton purple pantsuit jacket on and the "I'm With Her" campaign pin still affixed to her backpack. She said, "I know she lost but I still support her and her example!" After school that day we watched Hillary Clinton's concession speech as well as President Obama's statement on the election results. I asked my daughter what she thought about everything that she had heard and how she was feeling. She said that she was happy about the results. That certainly was not what I had expected to hear. I asked her what she meant and she said: "Well, Hillary Clinton won more votes, even though she lost the Electoral

College. That means that more people wanted a woman to be president! And she was the first woman to get a major party's nomination. That's awesome!"

Surprised at her optimism, I asked if it changed anything that Hillary Clinton still ultimately would not be president. My daughter's response immediately channeled Secretary Clinton's concession speech message to young girls that we had watched just a few minutes earlier[3]: "Nope! When some mean boys at recess tell me that girls should only clean the house and reproduce [like I said, precocious], I will tell them that I am valuable, I am powerful, and I can do whatever I want to do. So *HMPH* to that!"

Politics aside, this provided a clear case study to us on the effect of role models in empowering young people, especially young girls. When Abigail heard Secretary Clinton say in her concession speech, "I know we have still not shattered that highest and hardest glass ceiling, but someday someone will," she turned around and said with a big smile on her face, "I'm pretty sure that someone will be *me*!"

A NEW RESEARCH QUESTION

Up until this point we have focused on the phenomenon of public attitudes toward female clergy as an outcome: why do some people support gender-inclusive leadership policies in their religious congregations while others do not? Now we will change course and examine female clergy as a cause. What effect do women leaders have on those in their congregations? Can female religious leaders affect the attitudes and behaviors of those in the pews? Do female religious leaders serve to empower young girls in the same way that other visible and prominent women do?

This is important because, as we discussed in the introductory chapter, women have made great strides in a number of areas over the last fifty years, yet still remain underrepresented in the political and business worlds as well as the workplace and other areas of society. The rapid increases in female leadership that were spurred on by the 1960s have since plateaued. Whereas many expected that 2016 would be *the* year for women's advancement, "the highest and hardest" glass ceiling remained intact, the number of women in Congress remained unchanged, and the number of female leaders of our nation's places of worship have held steady at about one in ten.

One popular argument among advocates of women's ordination is that gender role models in religion are important because the norms and values of a *religious* community affect one's expectations and interactions with their *political* and wider *social* community. According to one proponent of women's ordination, "what is taught on the Sabbath leaks into our politics, our health policy, violence around the world. It leaks into education, military, fiscal decision-making. These laws get legally and culturally codified" (Shields 2015). In other words, gender equality in religious leadership and decision-making is important because it shapes the patterns of cultural behavior and expectations in a way that increases the likelihood of gender equality and empowerment in the cultural, legal, and political spheres.

Some researchers have argued that religious congregations hold a great deal of potential in helping overcome this disparity between men and women in the acquisition and employment of civic skills. This is because religious congregations provide frequent opportunities for their members to develop organizational and leadership skills that then can carry over into the public sphere. Verba et al (1995) go so far as to say that religious involvement is the "great equalizer" in American society in terms of the building of civic skills and resources. More recent research, however, has shown that men are the primary beneficiaries of these effects in that churchgoing men are still more likely to exercise their skills in the public sphere and also more likely to be recruited for civic leadership. Frieson and Djupe (2017), for instance, suggest that this could be because women are more likely to confine their exercise of civic skills to their religious congregations whereas men are more likely to use these skills in broader society.

Could this be due, in part, to the effect of the underrepresentation of women in American religious congregations? Are women less likely to carry over the skills they learn in religious congregations into the public sphere because of the relative rarity of examples of women in primary leadership positions in their congregations? If so, it suggests that one way to bring about greater parity and representation of women in society would be to start by looking at the role of women in leadership in our places of worship. To examine these questions, this chapter will first review existing research on the effect and importance of role models, with a specific focus on gender dynamics and youth socialization. We will then examine both quantitative and qualitative evidence to determine if there is any relationship between the gender of religious leaders during a woman's childhood or adolescence and levels of her empowerment in adulthood. As we will see, there is good evidence that gender leadership in religious contexts during girls' formative years matters for both personal empowerment and opportunities when they become adults.

THE IMPORTANCE OF ROLE MODELS

There is little question that role models make a difference in the lives of children and young adults. When someone adopts a role model, he or she perceives some similar set of characteristics and then works to become more like that individual, consciously adopting those characteristics (Gibson 2004). For young people, role models are often adults they see in their everyday lives or in media representations. Research has consistently shown that positive role models can contribute to health, education, and well-being in young people (DuBois and Silverthorn 2005; Sánchez, Esparza, and Colón 2008). Role models can impart knowledge about topics of interest and importance (Clark, Martin, and Bush 2001). Studies have also shown that having good role models is important for young adults when it comes to starting businesses and developing entrepreneurship (Bosma et al. 2012; Karimi et al. 2013). Role models are especially important for promoting educational and career achievement among college students (Campbell and Campbell 1997; Clark, Martin, and Bush 2001; Eby et al. 2008; Ghosh and Reio Jr. 2013).

We also know that role models play an integral part in the development of gender identity among young people. It seems that human beings are hard-wired to imitate others, an essential part of the development process (Jones 2009; Meltzoff and Prinz 2011; Oostenbroek et al. 2016; Whiten et al. 2016). Social Learning Theory argues that children learn how to act as adults largely through observation and imitation: they assimilate what they are supposed to do and how to act through what they see in others (Bandura 1976). This process is especially strong for the internalization of gender role identities. Much research has shown that boys learn how to be boys by imitating the adult male role models in their lives while girls take similar cues from adult women role models (Bussey and Bandura 1984, 1999). Some research has suggested that children pick up on gender role cues from adults by how often adult men and women exclusively model a particular type of behavior (Bussey and Perry 1982; Perry and Bussey 1979). In other words, if children see a behavior performed almost entirely by adult men, they will internalize that behavior as masculine and it will be imitated only by boys, whereas if a particular behavior is performed only by adult women, children will understand it to be a feminine behavior to be imitated only by girls.

There is obviously a strong history of distinctive gender roles throughout human history, although there is a good deal of variety depending on culture and context (Wiesner-Hanks 2010). In American culture, women's gender roles have historically revolved around the private/domestic sphere while men's have centered in the public sphere, where there are more opportunities for political and social leadership (Cott 2004). This being the case, boys are likely to internalize that their role is also to exercise leadership and influence in the public sphere while girls perceive their role as confined to the domestic sphere. It is interesting, given these traditional gender roles in American society, that boys tend to be responsive not only to male role models, but also powerful role models, regardless of gender. In other words, they are more likely than girls to emulate whoever has more power in a particular context, whether that person is male or female (Gibson and Cordova 1999). Girls, on the other hand, tend to emulate female role models more exclusively, irrespective of whether those women they seek to imitate are in high- or low-power roles.

It is especially important, then, for young girls to have influential positive female role models in their lives, since they are less likely to seek out role models who are male. This research suggests that young boys are much more likely than young girls to internalize that they are capable of leadership even if they do not have positive male role models in their lives. Young girls, on the other hand, are more responsive to the roles being modeled by the adult women in their lives. If they see women in positions of leadership, influence, and authority, it shows young girls that these things are part of the acceptable female gender role that they then feel empowered to internalize and imitate. This is supported by evidence showing that educational and career aspirations and success among young women are enhanced by a close relationship with a female role model but that young men do about as well in those outcomes with or without a corresponding male role model in their lives (Bettinger and Long 2005; Carrell, Page, and West 2009; Gilbert, Gallessich, and Evans 1983; Hackett, Esposito, and O'Halloran 1989; Lockwood 2006; O'Brien et al. 2017; Quimby and De Santis 2006; Spencer and Liang 2009).

One recent study examined this effect among a group of university students in Switzerland. About 150 students (both male and female) were asked to give a speech related to student fees at their institution. Researchers randomly assigned these students to four different groups. For one group, the researchers displayed a photograph of Bill Clinton on the back wall of the auditorium, large enough so that the students giving the speeches could see it clearly. Another group of students saw a large photograph of Hillary Clinton and another of German Chancellor Angela Merkel, while no photograph was displayed for the last group. Afterward, audience members as well as participants were asked to rate the effectiveness of the speeches, including on aspects such as how well the speakers articulated their messages and the effectiveness of their body language. Female participants were rated higher on their speeches by both themselves and the audience when they had seen prominent images of Hillary Clinton and Angela Merkel at the back of the auditorium, but not Bill Clinton or a blank wall. The researchers concluded that this shows the importance of prominent female role models in boosting confidence and leadership skills for young women (Latu et al. 2013).

This effect is also illustrated anecdotally by New Hampshire Senator (and former Governor) Maggie Hassan in a 2017 interview with *Elle* magazine. After discussing how New Hampshire had a strong tradition of female political leadership in the state legislature and governor's office, she said:

> When I was still governor, I called a colleague of mine who was in the state Senate at the time. He didn't answer, and I left a message. When he called me back later, he said he'd been driving and had his two daughters in the car. They were maybe eight and 11, and they asked him—because they saw it was my name on his cellphone screen—"Are you going to return the Governor's call?" And he said, "Yes." And at some point, one of them asked him, "Dad, did you ever think about running for governor?" And he said, "Well, some people have talked to me about it. What are your thoughts?" And one of his daughters said, "No." And he said, "Why?" And she said, "Well, you can't. You aren't a girl." The fact is role models matter. It really matters to people to see women in leadership, and that's one of the ways that we can break through some of the barriers that still exist—just simply by being there. (Kahn 2017)

RELIGIOUS ROLE MODELS AND GENDER EMPOWERMENT

We argue that leaders in religious congregations routinely act as powerful role models for young people. In the second half of the twentieth century, religious leaders influenced children perhaps more than any other adult authority figure after parents, relatives, and teachers. According to the 2008 General Social Survey, only about 9% of adult Americans said that they never attended religious services growing up (specifically, when they were twelve years old). On the other hand, nearly three-quarters (72.3%) of American adults said that they attended services at least two to three times per month when they were growing up. Regardless of whether they attend religious services now, this means that a large majority of Americans report having attended services regularly in their pre-adolescent years. This would put them in frequent contact with religious authority figures in their congregations. Given that gender roles (whether traditional or progressive) are highly salient and emphasized in many religions (Crandall 2012; Nynäs 2016), it is reasonable to expect that children and young adults would actively internalize gender cues not only from the teachings of their religious traditions, but also from the gender of those who occupy leadership roles in their congregations.

Wave 4 of the Gender and Religious Representation Survey was conducted in October of 2016. It included 815 respondents, 710 of whom came from a nationally representative telephone survey and 105 of whom came from a deliberately targeted internet survey to balance out demographic representativeness for age and race/ethnicity (see details in the Data Appendix). This survey asked respondents two questions that measured their exposure to gender diversity among their congregation's leaders when they were growing up. The first question asked how often women served as the principal leader of their religious congregations. Of the 94.5% of respondents who indicated attending congregations, 60.7% said that they "never" had a woman congregational leader. Another 25.8% said that they had a female leader "some of the time," 8.3% said "most of the time," and 5.2% said that they had a female pastor or priest "all of the time." Clearly, a majority of Americans have only ever had a man serve as their principal congregational leader.

We can break this down further among specific religious traditions. Figure 6.3 shows how frequently those who currently identify with one of the major American religious traditions had a female religious leader when they were growing up. Those who currently identify as Black Protestant had the most female pastors, with nearly a quarter (23.7%) reporting that women served as their congregational leader either most or all of the time. At the other end of the scale, Catholics are most likely to report that they never had a female priest (72.7%), which is surprising only in that it shows once again some degree of decoupling (Chaves 1997) with the other quarter of Catholics reporting that they had a woman serving in the chief leadership position in their congregation at least some of time. (Alternatively, this could at least partially be attributable to fact that some current Catholics may have grown up in

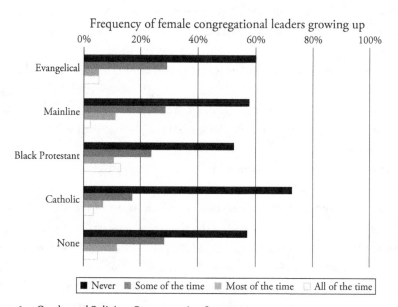

FIGURE 6.3 Gender and Religious Representation Survey

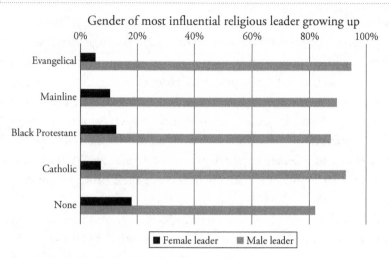

FIGURE 6.4 Gender and Religious Representation Survey

a tradition in which women were permitted to serve as congregational leaders and then converted to Catholicism in adulthood. According to the 2014 Pew Religious Landscape Survey, about 9.5% of those who currently identify as Catholic grew up in a non-Catholic tradition.)

We also asked our survey respondents to think of the "most influential pastor, priest, rabbi or other spiritual leader you had when you were growing up" and then to say whether this person was male or female. Among the vast majority of respondents who said that they attended religious services growing up, 91.3% reported that their most influential spiritual leader was a man, and only 8.7% said that this person was a woman. We can see once again in Figure 6.4 that there are some modest differences between religious traditions. Those who currently report no denominational affiliation had, growing up, the highest level of influential female spiritual leaders, 18%, while Evangelicals reported the lowest, 5.4%. It is also noteworthy that only 11.2% of women report that their most influential spiritual leader when growing up was a woman, compared to 6.1% of men who said the same.

In sum, most Americans interviewed grew up attending religious congregations in which they regularly saw and interacted with men as their primary religious leaders. Only about 14% grew up in congregations in which women were their primary role model of spiritual power most or all of the time. And fewer than one in ten say that their most influential spiritual leader growing up was a woman. Thus, few Americans today were regularly exposed to women in positions of authority as role models in their congregations when they were growing up, precisely at the stage of life when gender-specific behaviors become important to the identity formation process (Hill and Lynch 1983). The remainder of the chapter explores whether this matters in terms of personal and societal empowerment.

PERSONAL EMPOWERMENT: SELF-ESTEEM AND SELF-EFFICACY

We use two different attitudes to measure levels of personal empowerment: self-esteem and self-efficacy. Self-esteem is generally defined as one's sense of his or her own self-worth, or the extent to which individuals view themselves as valuable or important (Donnellan, Trzesniewski, and Robins 2014; Pierce et al. 1989). A host of research has shown that self-esteem has a variety of positive outcomes for people. Those with high levels of self-esteem are less likely to suffer from depression (Silverstone and Salsali 2003; Sowislo and Orth 2013) and anxiety (Pyszczynski et al. 2004). They are also more likely to have successful relationships and higher levels of job satisfaction (Orth, Robins, and Widaman 2012). Adolescents with high self-esteem are also less likely to engage in criminal behavior during adulthood (Trzesniewski et al. 2006). It has also been linked to higher levels of motivation for personal growth and improvement (McLeod 2012).

In contrast, self-efficacy is the extent to which someone believes that he or she has the "ability to influence events that affect their lives" (Bandura 2010). Self-efficacy is a powerful predictor of a variety of positive personal and social outcomes. For example, youth and young adults with higher levels of self-efficacy also have higher levels of academic motivation and performance (Bandura 1993; Multon, Brown, and Lent 1991; Schunk 1991; Zimmerman 2000). Self-efficacy has been shown to reduce anxiety and increase resilience in situations of personal failure (Bandura 1982). It has been linked to higher levels of physical health (Holden 1992), engagement in healthy behaviors such as exercise, maintaining a good diet, and overcoming addiction and eating disorders (Bandura 1997); higher workplace performance (Stajkovic and Luthans 1998)' increased job satisfaction (Judge and Bono 2001); intrinsic motivation to engage in ethical behavior (Welch 2013); and higher levels of persistence, effort, and success in accomplishing difficult tasks (Bandura 1986, 1997; Locke and Latham 2012).

Research has also shown that positive role models play an important part in boosting both self-esteem and self-efficacy (Price-Mitchell 2015). In particular, we see that female role models matter more for women than male role models do for men in boosting self-esteem and self-efficacy (BarNir, Watson, and Hutchins 2011; Ochman 1996; Wilson, Kickul, and Marlino 2007). Bandura (1976) argues that role modeling is especially important in boosting self-efficacy. When people see someone they perceive to be similar to themselves successfully doing a task or overcoming a challenge, they are more likely to believe that they themselves will also be successful at completing that task or overcoming their own personal challenges. Given this knowledge, we can reasonably expect that when young girls or young women observe adult women engaging in religious leadership activities or performing acts of religious authority, they will perceive themselves as being able to competently do those same things and successfully exercise leadership.

In our survey, we measure self-esteem with a straightforward level of agreement with the statement: "I have high self-esteem." Our respondents were generally very positive on this statement, with about 60% saying "strongly agree," 32% saying "somewhat agree," and the remaining 8% saying "somewhat" or "strongly disagree." Self-efficacy is measured with a combination of levels of agreement with three statements: "I will be able to achieve most of the goals that I have set for myself," "When facing difficult tasks, I am certain that I will accomplish them," and "Compared to other people, I can do most tasks very well." Responses to all three are fairly comparable to responses on the self-esteem scale. The good news, it looks like, is that most Americans have fairly high levels of self-esteem and self-efficacy. (See the Data Appendix for more details on these variables as well as others analyzed in this chapter.)

We will examine these relationships using the same multivariate statistical procedures we used earlier in the book. We can examine the effect of our gender role model variables (frequency of women clergy growing up and gender of most influential clergy growing up) on the outcomes of interest (in this case self-esteem and self-efficacy) while controlling for the effect of other factors that could also affect the outcomes. Throughout this chapter, we control for standard demographic and religious variables (religious service attendance and degree of belief orthodoxy) as well as the gender of the respondent's current congregational leader and whether the respondent's congregation allows for women to serve as the primary leader. These last two factors are controlled for because those who experienced influential women clergy growing up may be more inclined to seek out gender-inclusive congregations as adults. Including these factors allows us to statistically control for this possibility. Here, we display the relationships that are statistically significant, meaning that we are confident that the relationships we observed are real and not simply the result of random sampling error. (More comprehensive details about the statistical procedures used in this chapter can be found in the Data Appendix.)

First, Figure 6.5 shows the relationship between frequency of female leaders growing up and levels of self-esteem now. Notice that for women, self-esteem gradually increases with the more female leaders they had in their youth. On a 0-to-1 scale, women's average level of self-esteem increases from 0.74 when they never had a female pastor to 0.92 when they never had a male pastor. This 18% increase is roughly equivalent to the

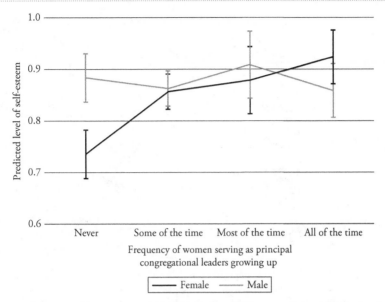

FIGURE 6.5 Gender and Religious Representation Survey; Note: the figure displays the predicted level of self-reported self-esteem depending on frequency of female congregational leaders in one's youth, holding all other variables in the multivariate analysis constant at their means.; Error bars are 95% confidence intervals for each statistical estimate.; The y-axis is modified to show detail.

difference between someone saying that she "somewhat agrees" or "strongly agrees" that she has high self-esteem. In contrast, levels of self-esteem among men are more or less constant regardless of how many women religious leaders they had growing up. It is already known that women tend to have lower levels of self-esteem than men on average (Kling et al. 1999). This finding would suggest that *the self-esteem gap between men and women might be eliminated entirely in a world where women have female clergy at least "some of the time" in their formative years.* It would boost self-esteem for women to levels equivalent with men (if not slightly higher) while not perceptibly changing self-esteem for men one way or the other.

Figure 6.6 also provides some evidence that the gender of a person's most influential clergyperson when growing up matters in terms of one's self-esteem as an adult. The right side of the graph shows that women have lower levels of self-esteem than men when their most influential pastor or priest growing up was a man (specifically, 9% lower), but left-hand side of the graph shows that this self-esteem gap disappears when either respondent's most influential leader was female: women now have levels of self-esteem comparable to those of men.

On the second part of the question, we find no substantive effect of clergy gender, specifically when it comes to self-efficacy, on either men or women when they were growing up. There is, however, an intriguing pattern when it comes to the gender of

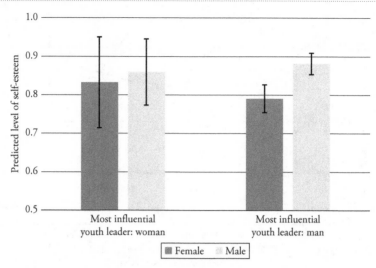

FIGURE 6.6 Gender and Religious Representation Survey; Note: the figure displays the predicted level of self-reported self-efficacy depending on the gender of one's current congregational leader, holding all other variables in the multivariate analysis constant at their means.; Error bars are 95% confidence intervals for each statistical estimate.; The y-axis is modified to show detail.

one's *current* congregational leader. Figure 6.7 shows that in a congregation with a female pastor, priest, or rabbi, women have levels of self-efficacy about 12% higher than men.[4] In congregations with male clergy, however, there is no difference in self-efficacy between men and women. This effect is small, but suggestive that role models continue to matter in adulthood, just as they do in childhood and adolescence. Here, women are slightly more likely than men to feel confident that they can achieve their goals and overcome obstacles when they see a woman as their primary religious leader, while men with female religious leaders are slightly less likely to be confident in their abilities to do the same.

In sum, there is good evidence that female religious leaders acting as role models in a person's youth can help close the self-esteem gap between women and men, boosting self-esteem among women and not affecting self-esteem among men. On the other hand, there is a small degree of mutual exclusivity when it comes to whether someone's current congregational leader is a man or woman: women's self-efficacy is boosted slightly in congregations with a female pastor, while men's self-efficacy is slightly depressed.

SOCIETAL EMPOWERMENT: EDUCATION AND EMPLOYMENT

Now we turn to examining the potential empowering effect of gender clergy role models on two different measures of societal empowerment: educational attainment

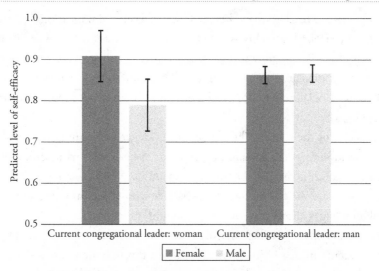

FIGURE 6.7 Gender and Religious Representation Survey; Note: the figure displays the predicted level of self-reported self-efficacy depending on the gender of one's current congregational leader, holding all other variables in the multivariate analysis constant at their means.; Error bars are 95% confidence intervals for each statistical estimate.; The y-axis is modified to show detail.

and employment status. These are other areas in which women have closed the gap with men over the last half-century in American society and indeed, college graduation rates are now higher among young women than young men (Ryan and Bauman 2016). There is strong evidence that education is an empowering resource. Across the board, those with higher levels of education enjoy better health and longer lifespans (Cutler and Lleras-Muney 2006; Furnée et al. 2008; Hummer and Hernandez 2013; Zimmerman, Woolf, and Haley 2015) and earn higher incomes (Julian and Kominski 2011; Tamborini, Kim, and Sakamoto 2015). They also experience better quality of life and general well-being (Lasheras et al. 2001; Witter et al. 1984), in part because more education is strongly associated with reductions in emotional and physical stress as well as increased access to employment, which enables greater control over one's life and choices (Ross and Van Willigen 1997). This is important especially for gender dynamics because better-educated mothers on average produce environments where children have improved educational and health outcomes (Hill and King 1995; Teachman 1987). There is also evidence that a well-educated workforce is a key factor in predicting a country's level of economic strength and prosperity (Berger and Fisher 2013), not to mention overall levels of societal poverty and peacefulness (UNESCO 2011).

As before, same-gender role models are an important driver of educational and employment outcomes, and research has shown that it matters more for young girls and women than for young boys and men. For instance, girls who attend high schools with more female teachers have higher levels of eventual educational attainment than girls who attend high schools with fewer female teachers (Nixon and Robinson 1999). This effect is also shown for young women in college, who have higher career and educational attainment when they have more female professors (Hackett, Esposito, and O'Halloran 1989; Hoffmann and Oreopoulos 2009; Neumark and Gardecki 1996).

Perhaps one of the most striking pieces of evidence of the importance of same-gender role models is the research by Beaman et al (2012), who took advantage of a natural experiment available to them in India. A 1993 law instituted a mandatory gender quota for village councils, requiring that a randomly selected third of all villages allow only women to stand for election as the chief councilor (roughly equivalent to a village mayor). The researchers surveyed over eight thousand adolescents in nearly five hundred villages throughout 2006 and 2007, and compared outcomes between boys and girls depending on whether they were in a village with a man or woman serving as the chief councilor. They found that the gender gap in high school–equivalent levels of education between boys and girls completely disappeared in villages with female chief councilors compared to villages with male chief councilors. Furthermore, female adolescents in these same villages reported higher levels of educational aspirations, as did the their parents for their daughters. Young girls in these villages were even assigned less time on household chores compared to their counterparts in villages with men serving as the chief councilors. The researchers conclude that female role models play a powerful role in shaping educational outcomes for young women and their families.

Given that female political and educational role models make such a pronounced difference for educational attainment and eventual economic security in adulthood, it is possible that female religious role models could exert the same effect. Some clergy in our interviews made the same observation. One female minister, for example, emphasized how she thinks "it's important for girls to see women in . . . every job" (Interview 22). Another female associate pastor stated that seeing women in ministerial positions shows girls that "they can be more than the cooks and the cleaners" (Interview 26).

We can further investigate this relationship using our multivariate tools, as was done previously. Here we estimate the effect of female religious role models during childhood and adolescence on educational and employment outcomes, controlling for a variety of other factors that could also contribute to these outcomes. After all, it could be that some other factor (demographic, religious, or otherwise) is obscuring the relationship between these two things.

We see in Figure 6.8 that even after accounting for a variety of alternative factors such as demographics and mother's level of education, women whose most influential

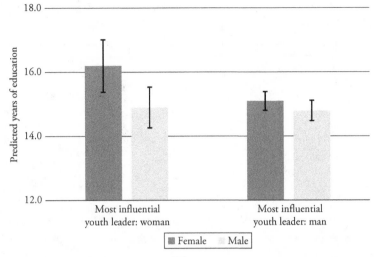

FIGURE 6.8 Gender and Religious Representation Survey; Note: the figure displays the predicted years of education depending on the gender of the most influential congregational leader in one's youth, holding all other variables in the multivariate analysis constant at their means.; Error bars are 95% confidence intervals for each statistical estimate.; The y-axis is modified to show detail.

religious congregational leader growing up was a woman receive, on average, one additional year of schooling than women whose most influential leader was a man. In our survey, the average woman with an influential male leader completes 15.1 years of education, roughly equivalent to high school and three years of college, while the average woman who instead has an influential female religious role model completes 16.2 years of education, enough to make the difference of completing a four-year college degree versus stopping one year short. In other words, the gender of a woman's most influential religious leader growing up can literally be the difference between finishing college or not. Men, for their part, receive the same level of education regardless of the gender of their most influential religious leader.

Figure 6.9 shows that influential female religious role models also matter when it comes to gaining full-time employment. In our survey, 61% of women and 74% of men reported that they were currently employed fulltime outside the home, a gap of 13%. When a woman's most influential religious leader growing up was also a woman, however, that employment gender gap disappears almost entirely: those women are employed at the same rate as men. When a woman's most influential religious leader growing up was a man, the employment gap remains. We see again that men's likelihood of employment is unaffected by the gender of their most influential religious leader growing up.

In sum, the frequency of having women serve as the head pastor, priest, or rabbi as one's chief congregational leader in childhood and adolescence seems to have

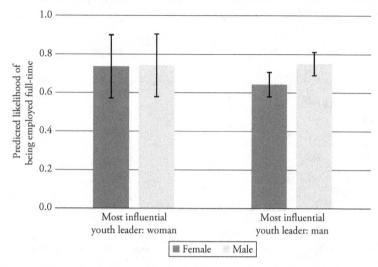

FIGURE 6.9 Gender and Religious Representation Survey; Note: the figure displays the predicted likelihood of currently being employed full-time depending on the gender of the most influential congregational leader in one's youth, holding all other variables in the multivariate analysis constant at their means.; Error bars are 95% confidence intervals for each statistical estimate.

little impact on a young woman's eventual level of societal empowerment as measured by educational attainment and full-time employment. If, however, the young woman's *most influential* congregational leader is also a woman, her future educational attainment is boosted by an average of one year of schooling above and beyond the average level of educational attainment of men. She also becomes just as likely as a man to be employed full time. It seems that influential religious female role models cannot only close the employment gap for women but also give them a boost in terms of education.

These findings complement the host of anecdotal evidence that speaks to the importance of female mentors in the lives of young women as they consider future possibilities and careers. Consider, for example, these three accounts[5]:

I am a recently retired priest. A college student visited my church about three years ago. She had grown up in a wonderful Baptist church and been active in evangelical/fundamentalist youth organizations. She loved church life, many kinds of worship, and discussions about faith, but had not seen the church world as a place for women leaders. Not only had she seen very few women leaders, [but] it had been implied or even sometimes said that women should not be in "upfront" roles. We struck up a friendship, often meeting at a coffee shop for conversation. She has now entered the process towards ordination in the Episcopal church.

Growing up my Godmother took me many times to [a] retreat center in Massachusetts to meet with . . . a woman deacon there, as she was convinced before I was [that] I had a call. [She] spent a lot of time teaching me about her ministry and she taught me about how she navigated being the only female in a male ministry team. Those lessons would be invaluable in the first eight years of my ordained life. She taught me how to be a "bridge" person and to listen to others' concerns and to show them my call. It was a nonconfrontational way of being part of a team and making changes from the inside. Using that method I was able to get the support of the diocese . . . which was opposed to the ordi- nation of women at the time.

Three weeks in a row, I crossed paths with one woman from another church in the lobby of the local hospital: each time she had another gravely ill rela- tive to visit. It felt like no coincidence that we kept meeting. The first time she called to me upon seeing my clerical collar, asked if I was a pastor, asked if she could talk to me about her ministry of feeding homeless people out of her own pantry, and how she, too, might pursue becoming a pastor. The second time she asked me to pray with her for her family member, [and] to pray for her dis- cernment of future ministry. We huddled together in the hospital lobby, and I gave her my card, asking her to call me so that I might offer further support. The third time we saw each other in the same spot, she walked right up to me and hugged me, we prayed together, and she said she would call me. I haven't heard from her, but I keep praying for her, and I am confident that her ministry and discernment continue because the Lord had given her perseverance. When I meet these women in all kinds of places—airports, community gatherings, you name it—they tell me that seeing me, in my clerical collar, gives them hope for their own ministries, gives them the possibility of viewing their calls to service as legitimate and worthy of pursuit.

These examples provide some context to help understand how close female re- ligious mentors can help make a difference for young women and girls in terms of what opportunities they can imagine for themselves as they are growing up. For the women in the first two cases, their female religious mentors made them aware of opportunities that they likely would not have considered without their guidance and example. In the last case, a woman pastor herself sees her example as empowering other women who may wish to pursue similar opportunities and vocations. While these examples focused specifically on pursuing a call to the ministry, our broader survey results show that influential female leaders also make a difference in terms of education and employment in just about any field.

SPIRITUAL EMPOWERMENT: VIEW OF GOD

When we brainstorm ways in which personal or social empowerment occurs, we tend to think in terms of education, employment, and income; we do not always think of how it affects one's personal conception of God. There is, however, much research indicating that individuals' view of God has a strong relationship with how they see themselves, interact with others, and engage with the world in an empowering way.

While there are many ways of thinking about how people view the nature of God, Froese and Bader (2010) put forth a four-part categorization based on whether someone thinks of God as more or less judgmental and more or less engaged in the world. A judgmental God who is engaged in the world is an "Authoritative God" while a judgmental but less engaged God is a "Critical God." A less judgmental but engaged god is a "Benevolent God" and a less judgmental but unengaged God is a "Distant God." All in all, they argue based on survey evidence that roughly half of American believers view God as more judgmental and the other half view God as less judgmental.

In that same vein, Greeley (1993) puts forth what he calls a "Grace Scale" categorization of perceptions of God. Survey respondents were presented with four pairs of words and asked which word of each pair most closely matches how they think about God. These roughly correspond to Froese and Bader (2010)'s differentiation between more/less judgmental as one of the key discriminators in people's views about God. They are: friend versus king, lover versus judge, spouse versus master, and mother versus father. The more often people indicate preferences for the first items in each couplet, the higher they rank on the Grace Scale given that they indicate a preference for a more "gracious" view of God (Froese and Bader 2010, n. 4).

In our survey, we replicated the Greeley (1993) Grace Scale with our respondents. Their responses to each of the four are as follows:

- 43.3% "friend," 35.8% "king," and 20.9% both.
- 41.7% "lover," 40.3% "judge," and 18.0% both.
- 23.6% "spouse," 68.9% "master," and 7.5% both.
- 7.8% "mother," 85% "father," and 7.2% both.

Combining the various responses into a single Grace Scale index, about 58% of respondents were on the "king/judge/master/father" side of the spectrum while the other 42% leaned toward the "friend/lover/spouse/mother" side. For our purposes, we will refer to the former as believing in a more Authoritative God while the latter believe in a more Gracious God (following Froese and Bader 2010 and Greeley 1993).

Using these and similar conceptualization schemes, many have shown that one's view of God is linked to all kinds of important outcomes. According to Froese and Bader (2010), Authoritative God believers are more likely to embrace Biblical literalism, oppose social welfare political policies, see a stronger conflict between science and religion, have stricter preferences on hot-button issues such as gay marriage and abortion, and believe that God causes natural disasters. Research has also shown that Authoritative God believers are less likely to cheat and have more self-control (Shariff and Norenzayan 2011). They are also more likely to hold conservative political beliefs (Froese and Bader 2007).

On the other hand, Gracious God believers have better health outcomes (Ironson et al. 2011) and report higher levels of spiritual and personal well-being, self-adequacy, self-worth, and general life happiness (Francis 2002; Francis, Gibson, and Robbins 2001; Greeley 1989; Wong-McDonald and Gorsuch 2004). They are also more likely to support socially egalitarian social policies, oppose the death penalty, back environmental protection initiatives (Greeley 1989, 1993; Lambert and Robinson Kurpius 2004), help religious minority groups, and volunteer in the community (Johnson et al. 2013). Silton et al. (2014) show that belief in a Gracious God is associated with lower levels of psychiatric disorders such as anxiety, obsession, and paranoia. From a theological perspective, McLemore (2016) argues that a more gracious/feminine view of God is associated with higher levels of spiritual maturity in the Christian mystic tradition. Given that Gracious God believers are more likely to report higher levels of health, well-being, and happiness, one's view of God arguably matters in terms of affecting one's degree of personal empowerment.

In general, research shows a few different sources of one's conceptualization of God, including one's level of self-esteem. Those with higher self-esteem are more likely to believe in a Gracious God (Benson and Spilka 1973; Buri and Mueller 1993; Pritt 1998). The strongest factor, however, is the example set by parents in a young person's life. Those with strict, obedience-focused parents tend to develop a more Authoritative view of God while those with more permissive parents internalize a more Gracious view (De Roos, Iedema, and Miedema 2004; Dickie et al. 1997; Hertel and Donahue 1995).

Given the strong influence of parents in determining one's view of God, it is also possible that other important adults, especially religious leaders, might have a clear impact on whether one believes in an Authoritative or Gracious God. Specifically, Greeley's Grace Scale uses one's gendered image of God as a key component to the scale (whether one thinks of God more as a mother or a father). Piatt (2014) has argued that seeing a woman in the pulpit might also lead girls to understand God as having feminine as well as masculine characteristics, which may help them more easily identify with their conceptualization of God.

Additionally, female clergy may themselves hold religious views that lead congregants to consider a less traditional understanding of God. It is not just the fact of women's presence in the pulpit; it is also about what those female clergy are likely to believe. Smidt (2016, 76) shows that while two-thirds of male Protestant clergy in America are traditionalist in their theological stances, only about a quarter of female Protestant clergy subscribe to literalist, traditional theological faith propositions. He also shows that male clergy are twice as likely as female clergy to hold a belief in absolute moral standards, which is related to their being more likely to hold more literal, orthodox beliefs (98–99). Given that nontraditional theologies are more likely to focus on grace, egalitarianism, and feminism (Briggs and Fulkerson 2014; Smith 1991), it is reasonable to expect that young women in congregations with female religious role models will be more likely to adopt a Gracious view of God than an Authoritative one.

Figure 6.10 shows us that this is indeed the case. Women whose most influential pastor or priest growing up was a woman are much more likely to believe in a Gracious God than women whose most influential leader was a man. On a 0-to-1 scale, with zero being the strongest Authoritative God view and one being the strongest Gracious God view, women with a woman as their most influential religious leader are nearly 20% closer to the Gracious God end of the spectrum. Analyzed another way, roughly one out of every three people, both men and women,

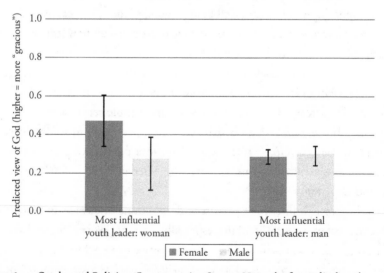

FIGURE 6.10 Gender and Religious Representation Survey; Note: the figure displays the predicted location on the "Authoritative God" to "Gracious God" scale depending on the gender of the most influential congregational leader in one's youth, holding all other variables in the multivariate analysis constant at their means.; Error bars are 95% confidence intervals for each statistical estimate.; The coefficient for the interaction term is significant in the multivariate analysis, despite the overlap in the 95% confidence intervals for the estimates.

lean toward Gracious God belief when their most influential spiritual leader growing up was a man, but when their most influential leader was a woman, that increases to about one out of every two women. Men, for their part, are not significantly affected in their view of God either way. Also, we did not uncover any relationship between adults' views of God and whether they had female clergy in their youth. It seems that the role model effect for young girls on this issue is activated by the presence of a close, influential female congregational leader rather than the overall prevalence of women congregational leaders throughout their childhoods.

"HAVING IT ALL"

Many from more traditional religious backgrounds would likely quibble (if not outright dispute) the conceptualizations of "empowerment" that we have employed throughout this chapter. While we hope that everyone would agree that self-esteem and self-efficacy are important, traditionalists (especially Complementarians in the Protestant tradition, conservative Catholics, or conservative Mormons) may argue that empowerment for women means fulfilling their divinely appointed gender roles as wives and mothers instead of leaving the home to enter the workforce. Do female religious leaders increase the likelihood of a woman either getting married or having children? Our survey results also asked respondents' marital status and number of children. While we did not discover any relationship between the gender of respondents' childhood congregational leader and their likelihood to be married, we did uncover an interesting relationship when it comes to the number of children someone has.

Women whose most influential pastor or priest growing up was a woman have, on average, 2.5 children, whereas women whose most influential leader was a man have 1.7 children.[6] In other words, *women have more children when they experienced influential female religious leaders when they were growing up*, almost equivalent to an entire additional child. Keep in mind that this is after controlling for age, race, education levels, frequency of church attendance, levels of belief orthodoxy, the gender of their current congregation's leader, and other relevant variables. It seems that for women, the gender of their childhood influential congregational leaders *also* matters, leading women with influential women leaders to be more empowered in the way that many traditionalists would define empowerment: having bigger families. (Leaders of traditional religious institutions who are interested in the long-term generational transmission and birthrates in their particular traditions might look to more gender-inclusive leadership policies as one important piece of the puzzle.)

This effect may again be due to role modeling. No small amount of ink has been spilt on the question of whether "women can have it all," or, in other words, a career *and* a family. Smidt (2016, 40) shows that more than 90% of Protestant clergy are currently married. Perhaps when young girls have close female religious mentors who are successful leaders while simultaneously married and raising a family, they internalize the message that they too can do both when they grow up, and perhaps are more likely to have larger families as a result.

SUMMARY AND DISCUSSION

The goal of this chapter was to determine whether gender role models in a religious congregational context matter during congregants' childhood and adolescence in driving levels of personal and societal empowerment for women in adulthood. There is good theoretical reason to expect that this would be the case given the importance of positive role models in young people's lives, and especially in developing and internalizing their own gender role identity. While many people in the United States today may not attend religious services regularly, more than nine out of ten attended services with some degree of regularity as young adolescents. Thus, there was ample opportunity for congregational religious leaders to frequently model gender roles for young people in attendance. When girls and young women see women in positions of religious authority, it shapes their own gender role identity in such a way that they are more likely to feel that they, too, can be leaders and feel empowered to pursue their goals both in their own lives and in broader society.

As predicted, our survey results showed evidence that exposure to female leaders in formative years can boost both self-esteem and self-efficacy for young women, and that this carries on into adulthood. This is important because both self-esteem and self-efficacy are critical factors in a person's physical and emotional well-being as well as one's motivation to pursue education and goals. It is also important because women tend to have, on average, lower levels of self-esteem than men. Our results show that, even after controlling for a host of demographic and religious factors, the more female religious leaders young women have growing up, the higher levels of self-esteem they have as adults. In fact, the presence of female religious leaders in a young woman's life enables her to effectively close the self-esteem gap as an adult. We also discovered evidence that self-esteem among women is boosted by having a particularly influential female religious leader during childhood/adolescence. Combined, this would suggest that the self-esteem gap between men and women today is due at least in part to the absence of any female religious leaders for more than 60% of Americans in their formative years. For their part, men's levels of self-esteem are just as high whether they had more male or female religious leaders growing up. Similar to previous research, gender role models matter for women, but not men, in determining their levels of self-esteem as adults.

In contrast to previous research, however, there is also evidence that levels of self-efficacy among men can be depressed a little when their most influential religious leader was a woman. This has the opposite effect for women, whose self-efficacy increases a little if they had another woman as their most influential religious leader growing up. On this aspect of personal empowerment, it seems that there is some degree of mutual exclusivity: when it comes to feeling that they can make a difference in the world and achieve their goals, men are better served by male spiritual mentors in their youth, and women by female ones. That said, these effects are relatively modest.

When it comes to measures of societal empowerment such as education and employment, we also see evidence that the gender of religious role models matters. This is important because education is linked to all kinds of positive outcomes such as financial security, good health, general happiness, and well-being, not to mention the achievement of potential and self-actualization. When young women have a close influential female religious leader growing up, they acquire, on average, one additional year of education compared to women whose most influential religious leader was a man. Given the average level of educational attainment in the United States, this could often be the difference that leads to completing a four-year college degree. It is also well known that there is a gender gap when it comes to full-time employment (Bureau of Labor Statistics 2014). Among respondents in our nationally representative survey, though, this gap disappears entirely among women who had a close, influential female pastor or priest growing up: they are employed at the same rate as men. (For their part, we see once again that levels of education and employment for men are unaffected by the gender of their childhood religious leaders or mentors.)

We found evidence that people's view of God as either authoritative or gracious is dependent on the gender of their religious leaders when young. This is important because those who tend to view God as more gracious than authoritative also have increased levels of well-being, happiness, and self-esteem, all of which are integrally important for personal empowerment. And it turns out this makes a difference for women. Having had an influential female congregational leader in their youth increases the likelihood that they will believe in a Gracious God rather than an Authoritative God as adults.

Finally, our data show us that women whose most influential congregational leader growing up was a woman tend to have more children, on average, than women whose most influential congregational leader was a man. This suggests to us that influential female religious role models show young women that they do not always have to choose between having a career and raising a family.

CONCLUSION

In conclusion, it matters whether a person's religious leaders growing up are men or women. In general, influential female leaders during one's childhood and/or adolescence have a clear empowering effect on women as adults. It is also important to note that this most often is the case when a female clergyperson is one's most influential leader growing up, and sometimes, but less often, is the result of having had more female clergy throughout one's childhood.[7] It seems that the empowering effect of religious role models in one's youth is dependent on a close relationship with these role models as opposed to the overall frequency of these role models in the pulpit.

This effect is attested to by one of our interviews with a female associate minister who explained that girls in churches with female clergy can look to their female minister as a role model for leadership:

> I think that it gives women the opportunity to say culture is wrong. Like, we can do this. Like, we are capable of being leaders. And to be able to break what they have been taught their entire lives of women are supposed to be, you know, prim and proper and not speak out and not be argumentative and not be, you know, direct. We have been taught from a very early age, myself included—I was always told I was too loud, I talked too much, I was too boisterous. I need to, you know, sit back and behave. On my dad's side of the family I had two cousins. They were male. After dinner, they got to go out to play. I had to be in the kitchen cleaning up. From an early age I was like, "That's not fair." You know, I feel that now especially like young girls can then be like, "Wait." And legit be able to say to their family, "That's not fair." And say why. I feel like—I pray that—we are getting to an age where young girls are able to speak up for themselves and advocate for themselves in ways that I wasn't able to because I didn't have the women leaders to look to. Where now, I can look toward several . . . strong, independent, fiercely, um, protective women leaders who I'm like, "I want to be you when I grow up." [Laughter]. You know what I mean? (Interview 26)

At the outset of the book we described how women's participation in various fields (politics, social, business, etc.) had advanced over the past several decades, but in many ways has recently slowed or stalled. We also described in this chapter how women are less likely than men to use the civic skills they acquire in religious congregations in the wider social world (Friesen and Djupe 2017). Our research indicates that increasing the occurrence and influence of women as congregational religious leaders could go a long way toward helping women to close the gap with men with in terms of personal and societal empowerment. In fact, it could be argued from this evidence that the strong overrepresentation of men in the nation's pulpits is at least partially to blame for the continuing inequality between women and men in society as well as the workplace.

When looking to the results of this chapter, there is reason to believe that the increased presence of female clergy could not only improve the personal lives of women (through the improvements to health and quality of life that are associated with increased self-esteem, self-efficacy, and educational attainment) but also could increase equality in the workplace and political sphere. As described earlier, women whose most influential religious leader was a woman tend to obtain greater levels of education and higher rates of employment. With an increasingly educated and employed female workforce, it is safe to assume that these increases could only help in decreasing the gap in management and other leadership positions in America's businesses.

The connection between religious equality in leadership and political equality is, perhaps, even more direct: levels of self-doubt and self-esteem have been connected to the gender gap in politics. Research indicates that women are less likely than men to feel that they are qualified to run for office and less likely than men to think they would win (Lawless and Fox 2005). Moreover, women have let these misperceptions keep them from running for office (Lawless and Fox 2005). As women are just as likely as men to win when they do decide to run (Anastasopoulos 2016; Lawless 2015), these misperceptions of qualifications have real consequences in terms of gender equality in political leadership. As the evidence in this chapter has shown, clergywomen have a positive socializing effect on women's self-esteem, self-efficacy, education, and employment—all of which are factors that could help women feel they are qualified to run for office and be just as electable as men. As more women believe they can run and win, more will be elected, thus decreasing the gender gap in political leadership. Increasing the presence of clergywomen, then, not only improves the lives of the women in their congregations, but could also serve to improve the state of gender equality throughout the public, private, and political arenas.

NOTES

1. Source: personal correspondence with Rev. Kedron Nicholson of Grace Episcopal Church in Orange Park, Florida, who requested to be identified.

2. Source: personal correspondence with the author.

3. The full passage from the concession speech was: "And to all the little girls who are watching this, never doubt that you are valuable and powerful and deserving of every chance and opportunity in the world to pursue and achieve your own dreams."

4. Unless noted to the contrary, the level of statistical significance in the multivariate model for this relationship and others throughout this chapter attains the traditionally accepted level of $p \leq 0.05$ even if there is a negligible amount of overlap between the error bars depicted in the corresponding graph (see Payton, Greenstone, and Schenker 2003).

5. These accounts also come from personal correspondence with the authors as opposed to the other qualitative interview accounts featured throughout the book.

6. Interaction significant at $p = 0.072$.

7. An alternative explanation for the patterns we describe in this chapter could be due to a self-selection effect. It has been clearly demonstrated that personal/economic empowerment and opportunity are strongly linked to the economic and social context of a person's upbringing (Putnam 2016). Perhaps parents in more affluent and privileged contexts are also more likely to take their children to congregations that have more egalitarian leadership practices and a higher frequency of women leaders (which tend to be Mainline Protestant congregations, which on average draw congregants of a higher socioeconomic status). If this is indeed the case, the relationships we describe here are an example of "correlation but not causation" because the empowerment demonstrated here is due more to the choices of parents than to gender leadership modeling in congregations. To perfectly assess this possibility would require running experiments in which we randomly assign children to parents and randomly assign families to congregations and then observe the levels of personal and economic empowerment that these children attain later as adults. While this is obviously impractical, we do our best to account for these alternative possibilities with the statistical controls described in the Data Appendix, which is a common approach in social science research. For example, we control for standard demographic indicators such as education and income. This is not a perfect measure of a person's childhood socioeconomic context, but the two variables are highly correlated in contemporary American society (Erola, Jalonen, and Lehti 2016). The analyses of personal educational attainment and employment include controls for the level of education and employment status of the respondent's mother during the respondent's childhood, which correlates highly with gender ideology (Davis and Greenstein 2009). We can thus control to some extent for childhood socioeconomic context and parental gender ideology by using these proxy variables. It is also important to note that we further control for the gender of the individual's current religious congregational leader and whether the individual's congregation allows for female congregational leaders. All in all, our various statistical controls significantly increase the likelihood that the relationships we describe here are due to the role model effect that we discuss and not simply a spurious case of correlation but not causation.

It shows them that they can be a leader in the
church. It shows them that they are necessary
in the church. And it shows them that they
can progress in the church. (Interview 30)

7

THE EFFECT OF CLERGYWOMEN

Religious Representation

IN THE PREVIOUS chapter we looked at how gender leadership in American religious congregations can affect wider questions of gender equality and advancement through personal and societal empowerment. In this chapter we turn our attention to how gender and leadership interact to affect the specifically *religious* attitudes and behaviors of those in the pews. This should be of particular interest to the leaders of religious institutions, as they are perennially concerned about issues of congregational growth and retention, as well as general levels of congregational satisfaction among the rank and file in their congregations.

On a more personal level, some have argued that women pastors and priests are important because they are empowering in a specifically *spiritual* or *religious* sense to young women and girls. Seeing women in the pulpit, for example, may increase the likelihood that a woman feels that congregational leaders are responsive to her and her interests: "If you are not reflected in your leadership it is difficult to trust that they are attending to your needs and interests. Yes, I believe that until the leadership is more broadly dispersed, women and people of color aren't able to reach their fullest potential as it pertains to their membership in the church" (Kuruvilla 2015). Professor Susan Shaw has argued that, "the denial of ordination to women maintains patriarchal hierarchies of value, with men in the position of somehow being more like God than women and therefore better able to represent God than women" (Shaw 2015).

These perspectives support the assertion that female clergy is important to both the religious as well as the political empowerment of women in American congregations and society. The acceptance of women pastors and priests at church may lead to a host of indirect effects on general cultural and political norms regarding the role of women in secular life, too. A male-only clergy can both directly and indirectly cause women to internalize narratives of subservience and inferiority, which then affect how they understand their role in the wider political and social world (Jost, Banaji, and Nosek 2004). A male-only clergy can also either directly or indirectly cause men to absorb the idea that women are less suited for positions of leadership and influence in the business or political world, leading to greater disadvantages for women in society as a whole.

But is there any evidence to support these arguments? Advocates of women's ordination are often quick to present theoretical arguments and isolated anecdotes. In the preceding paragraphs we have seen that many have argued that the presence (or even the potential) of women in the pulpit can influence levels of religious enthusiasm, behavior, and empowerment for women in the pews. Systematic empirical evidence in support of these arguments, though, is harder to come by. In the next two chapters we address this deficiency and determine whether there is any systematic empirical evidence to back up these arguments. Are women who attend congregations with female ministers really more engaged in their religious participation? Do they feel more connected to the congregations? Do they display higher levels of religious behaviors or spirituality? Also, does the gender composition of the lay leadership in these congregations matter? What about the congregational policies themselves? Are women in congregations that allow women to serve as the pastor or priest, but who currently have a male leader, different in their religious behavior or attitudes than women in congregations with male-only leadership policies? Are these patterns manifest among other religious or political groups?

Throughout the book we have drawn parallels between the gender gap in the leadership of America's places of worship and trends in women's leadership in other areas of society. Decades of progress and women's advancement in government, business, and religion appear to have plateaued in many ways since the 1990s. In the previous chapter we discussed ways in which progress toward gender equality in religious leadership could be connected to women's advancement in other fields. We saw how female leadership in America's places of worship could help further gender equality in public and private spheres through increases in women's self-esteem, self-efficacy, education, and employment. Although this chapter will focus on the effect of female leadership in a specifically religious context, we also hope to elucidate the connections between leadership in the political and religious realms.

In particular, we will examine the ways in which representation matters in American congregations.

Before examining those questions, though, it is helpful to discuss the theoretical concept of representation, as these arguments implicitly suggest that clergy represent their congregants in some form. To better understand the importance of representation, we turn to the field of political science, which has explored this topic in great detail, both from a theoretical as well as an empirical perspective.

THE IMPORTANCE OF REPRESENTATION

Scholars have identified a variety of forms of representation that are relevant to our topic. First, it is common to discuss representation as "descriptive" or "substantive." Descriptive representation as defined by Hannah Pitkin is "the extent to which representatives 'resemble' or share certain characteristics with the represented" (Dovi 2007, 150). For example, when a Latino voter lives in a congressional district represented by another Latino, we would say that this person is descriptively represented. The same could go for any other relevant demographic characteristic including age, gender, education, or religion. Substantive representation, on the other hand, happens when a person's views or interests are advocated for and pursued by the representative, regardless of whether the representative shares any demographic characteristics with the person. For example, a Catholic woman who cares strongly about pro-life issues can be substantively represented by a pro-life Protestant man so long as the representative is advocating on behalf of the pro-life political interests that the Catholic woman cares about. Similarly, an African American who cares strongly about criminal justice reform for racial minorities can be substantively represented by a white liberal elected official who advocates for reform policies on behalf of minority communities.

Research has found that these different forms of representation have real-world consequences. For instance, Gay (2001) found that African Americans are sometimes more likely to vote in congressional elections if their member of Congress is also an African American. Voter turnout among African Americans reached its highest levels in history during the 2008 and 2012 elections when Barack Obama was on the ballot, only to then drop 7% in the 2016 election, returning to the same level as 2004 (Krogstad and Lopez 2017). Barreto et al. (2004) demonstrated that Latinos in southern California are more likely to vote when they live in a district with a majority Latino population and thus anticipate the election of a fellow Latino to office. Preuhs (2007) found that Latinos in state legislatures are able to preserve state spending on welfare programs that benefit poorer citizens, including many racial/ethnic minority groups (see Dovi 2007 and Mansbridge 1999 for a more comprehensive treatment of descriptive and substantive representation). Representation theorists have sometimes drawn distinctions between "dyadic" and "collective" representation. Dyadic representation happens when one representative directly and exclusively represents a constituent. This happens in single-member districts such as in U.S. Congressional districts of most state legislative seats. Dyadic representation can involve descriptive representation, substantive representation, both, or neither, depending on the characteristics and preferences of the individual and the representative. Collective representation, in contrast, refers to representation that occurs (either descriptively or substantively) by an individual or group in the legislative representative body as a whole rather than direct dyadic representation (Clark 2014; Weissberg 1978). A Democrat living in Kansas, for example, may not have any dyadic substantive partisan representation in his or her congressional district or in the U.S. Senate given that Kansas is usually represented by Republicans, but this Kansas Democrat may be collectively and substantively represented by other Democrats in Congress from California or New York, or the institution as a whole if Democrats have a majority.

GENDER AND POLITICAL REPRESENTATION

When it comes to the political impact of representation, most often scholars of gender and politics have examined the effect of descriptive dyadic representation of female elected officials on the political attitudes and behavior of women in the United States. Are women who are represented by other women either at the local or national levels any more likely to engage in normatively desirable political behaviors than those who are represented by men?

Sapiro and Conover (1997) use the 1992 elections as a case study in analyzing the question of gender difference in electoral behavior. They found higher levels of both interest in politics and political attentiveness among women who live in a districts with female candidates than they did among female constituents without a women running in their districts. In contrast, Dolan (2006), found little empirical analysis to support the connection between descriptive representation and voting behavior. Other research has shown that the presence of a female candidate is even correlated with a decrease in men's interest in the election (Wolak 2015).

There is evidence that helps reconcile these disparate research findings. Reingold and Harrell (2010) argue that the presence of descriptive gender representation does indeed increase political engagement among women in the electorate, but only when that female representative is of the same political party as the constituent. Atkeson

(2003) also shows evidence that the political engagement of women increases when a woman is on the ballot, but only when that candidate is competitive. "Simply having a 'like' candidate on the ballot is not enough to stimulate political engagement," she writes (1053).

Dyadic descriptive representation can also influence other kinds of political outcomes such as trust in one's representative. Jane Mansbridge (1999) argues that descriptive representation can "forge bonds of trust" between a constituent and her representative, thus improving the constituent's "feeling of inclusion" and making "the polity democratically more legitimate in [her] eyes." A study conducted by Ulbig (2007), though, qualifiedly supports Mansbridge's statement. Ulbig examined the degree to which descriptive representation affected trust at the local level. By comparing survey data collected from multiple municipalities, she found that among respondents with a moderate level of political knowledge, the presence of women city council members led to increased trust among women in their local city officials but decreased trust among men.

Descriptive representation has also been linked to increases in political efficacy. In this case, "efficacy" is a political science term referring to the extent to which individuals feel that their government is responsive to their interests and needs (external efficacy) or the extent to which individuals feel they can make a difference and have a meaningful effect on the political system of which they are a part (internal efficacy) (Craig and Maggiotto 1982). Barbara Burrell maintains that women's descriptive representation is able to influence efficacy because "women in public office stand as symbols for other women, both enhancing their identification with the system and their ability to have influence within it" (Carroll and Fox 2013, 11). Burrell's claim has been empirically supported by studies such as Atkeson and Carrillo (2007), which found higher levels of external political efficacy among women who were descriptively represented in the statehouse than those who were not. Lawless (2004), however, found little relationship between descriptive representation and efficacy.

Other researchers have investigated the effect that female elected officials can have as role models for younger women. Campbell and Wolbrecht (2006) find that high-profile candidacies of women for political office in the United States inspire young women to express an increased desire to be politically active. Wolbrecht and Campbell (2007) extend these findings to an international perspective: women and adolescent girls in countries that have more women in national legislatures are more likely to discuss politics with others and express interest in participating in politics.

In sum, descriptive representation can theoretically influence a variety of different behavioral and attitudinal political outcomes including voting, interest, engagement, trust in elected officials, and internal/external political efficacy. Existing research has so far produced mixed results. We can safely say that descriptive gender representation matters in terms of women's political behaviors and attitudes in the United States and around the world, but that the effect is not uniform and is at times contingent upon context.

GENDER AND RELIGIOUS REPRESENTATION

As is evidenced by the above discussion, descriptive representation for female constituents seems to matter for political outcomes, but to varying degrees, depending on context. There is as of yet very little research linking religious descriptive representation to *religious* behavioral outcomes. Why might we expect representation, a political concept, to matter in religious congregations?

Building on the work of Djupe and Gilbert (2008), Djupe and Olson (2013) provide a theoretical framework for the application of representation theory to religious contexts. They investigate the effect of descriptive gender representation in Mainline Protestant congregations on political interest and participation. They argue that religious congregations can, to some extent, be conceptualized and behave like political communities, specifically in terms of the link between representation and behavior. "Having a woman in a leadership role may spark women's interests and participation, in the same way that descriptive representation can increase political discussion, group empowerment, and feelings of self-worth" (Djupe and Gilbert 2008, 226).

There are a variety of organizational similarities, they argue, between congregations and political communities. For example, many congregations choose their clergy through some sort of democratic process. Clergy in many Protestant congregations especially attain their positions through a job search comparable to the system used in some secular occupations. This often consists of a committee selected to represent the congregation as a whole that then uses some kind of democratic process to choose a congregational leader. Because of this, clergy are then incentivized to remain at least somewhat responsive to the opinions and wishes of the majority of their congregants. Just like elected officials in democratic communities, clergy often depend on the approval of their congregation for their job security. Thus they will often pursue activities and priorities that represent the interests and preferences of congregants, similar to how elected officials behave toward their constituents.

Of course, not all congregations select their leadership in this manner. Many American religious traditions, notably the Catholic and Mormon churches, have a primarily hierarchical, top-down process for selecting congregational leaders. Leaders are appointed or selected by a higher governing authority and assigned to the congregation with little direct popular input. That said, it is reasonable to expect that there remains an element of democratic constraint on those congregational leaders even when they are not directly chosen by their congregations. For instance, higher governing authorities have an interest in the smooth operation of their congregations and are sensitive to the attitudes of members and the nature of their relationship with their leaders. The governing authorities thus have an incentive to appoint leaders who, to some extent, will represent the views and interests of those in their congregations. Should influential members of the congregation become dissatisfied with their local leaders, they may be able to apply sufficient pressure to the higher authorities to appoint a new leader more amenable to their preferences.

In their research, Djupe and Olson (2013) found that women who attend religious congregations with women clergy develop more interest in politics but only if those women share the political ideologies and preferences of their clergywoman (similar to the finding of Reingold and Harrell [2010] that descriptive gender political representation influences political engagement among women only if the representative is of the same political party). They also found that these women are more likely to participate in politics but that this effect was limited to those who had lower levels of political participation to begin with. Djupe (2014) extended this research and found that in many Mainline Protestant denominations the presence of women in the pulpit is associated with an increased likelihood of women serving in leadership positions in their congregations as well as participating in politics. This effect, though, is somewhat limited and depended to a large extent on denominational context. He concludes that descriptive gender representation matters "a little bit" in influencing women in religious congregations.

DOES FEMALE LEADERSHIP MATTER?

In Chapter 3 we described what our face-to-face interviewees thought about female clergy in their congregations. Throughout these dozens of interviews we also probed both clergy and laity alike on how they thought that the gender of their congregation's leader might influence the religious behavior or attitudes of those in their congregations. In this chapter we document other major themes and results from these interviews. When discussing their thoughts on whether the gender of their pastor, priest, or rabbi mattered in shaping those in the congregation, people were quick to say that the personality and leadership style of the specific leader was more important than his or her gender. However, they then identified several areas in which they believed that gender may in fact make a difference.

CLERGY PERSONALITY MATTERS MORE THAN GENDER

In our interviews the vast majority of interviewees stated that clergy's individual characteristics, such as personality and experience, matter more than gender in affecting their interactions with the behaviors of the parishioners (similar to Carroll, Hargrove, and Lummis 1983). We found that this theme was mentioned across the board by men and women, clergy and congregants alike. Moreover, this trend does not appear to be bound by denominational policy regarding female ordination or by whether a congregation currently has a woman or man serving as its pastor or priest. Instead, it appears that most people were reluctant to say that they believed that gender "matters."

As one Buddhist man describes, gender does not affect his interactions with religious leaders:

> To me, it comes down to more about their experience and my level of trust in them. And my ability to trust that they're going to take seriously my problem and that they're going to be respectful of whatever it is that I'm going through. So, that to me is really independent of gender because I've had negative experiences with both men and women in terms of leadership positions and how I relate to them. (Interview 58)

A woman who belongs to a Mainline Protestant denomination that ordains women but whose congregation currently has an older male head pastor and a younger female associate pastor describes it like this:

> RESPONDENT: I think it has much more to do with their age and experience than it does their gender.
> INTERVIEWER: Okay, so what does it have more to do with?
> R: Well, it would be really odd, the roles they play—she hasn't been in ministry long enough to have achieved the role of a head pastor. So, I assume she will at some point, but she's just younger right now. You know, she just doesn't have experience to actually be the head pastor of a church.
> I: Right. So does it make a difference to you when you go to church on Sundays whether you're listening to a man or a woman?
> R: No, not really. It has much more to do with maybe what they have to say or their life experience or, you know, something like that. But I can relate to a man just as easily as I can relate to a woman. (Interview 39)

A female Catholic formation minister (a lay member who has undergone training to serve as an unordained ecclesiastical leader) echoed this theme in terms of her interactions with those in her parish:

> I think some of that is more personality than it is whether [it is] a guy or a woman. I'm sure you have guys or women that you would feel more comfortable talking about things than you would your guy friends. . . . So once again, I just don't see it as a male/female issue, I see it as a personality and a ministerial issue. And if during confession—if they're going to confess an abortion, it's anonymous, so it's not like they even know who it is. (Interview 33)

Although many interviewees, especially those from Mainline Protestant denominations that permit women's ordination, went on to discuss the ways in which having female pastors is important (which will be discussed in greater detail shortly), they were hesitant to relate their interactions with their religious leaders and religious behaviors to their clergy's gender. While individuals from both traditions that do ordain women and those that do not emphasized personality as mattering more than gender, their motivations for these statements seemed to differ. Part of the reason that those from denominations that do not ordain women might be hesitant to describe gender as "mattering" is because they exclude women clergy. If gender were proven to make a substantive difference in congregational leadership, the logical conclusion would be to support the inclusion of women in those leadership positions.

The view of individuals from religious traditions that do ordain women, in contrast, seems to be related to their view of gender as a "done issue" in their congregations. Some clergymen and clergywomen who belonged to denominations that do permit female ordination described issues related to gender and ordination as "done deals" and "finished arguments" (Interview 25). This theme of gender as a "done issue" for many congregations may help explain why clergywomen were hesitant to directly state that gender influences their interactions with congregants, even though many went on to describe an effect that they had perceived and attributed to gender. This sentiment of the topic of gender as a "done issue" was not limited to clergypersons. One Buddhist man stated that because "there [has] always been a strong presence of female leadership" since he has been involved in Buddhism, questions of gender are "something that you just don't . . . even think about" (Interview 58).

RELIGIOUS AND SPIRITUAL EMPOWERMENT

Although individuals were hesitant to say that the gender of their religious leader was the primary factor affecting their interactions and religious behaviors, many went on to describe ways in which they believed that clergy gender does, in fact, matter to these outcomes. One of these areas dealt with the possibility of religious and spiritual empowerment for young women and girls. The following is one clergywoman's story of expressing her call at a young age:

> When I was in the first grade . . . the teacher asked everyone in the class to draw a picture of what they wanted to do when they grew up. And so, many others were saying—thirty kids in the class . . . fifteen other girls—and the pictures were for the most part, secretary, teacher . . . airline stewardess . . . they were mommies . . . I drew a picture of myself in a black robe with the Bible in hand. And the teacher literally freaked out because there [was] no . . . point of reference whatsoever to this. And she was so upset that she called my parents . . . and she thought there was something really wrong with me. (Interview 24)

Although this woman succeeded in becoming ordained despite being seen as "an aberration" by authority figures in her youth, many of the clergy and congregants we talked to feared that other young girls that belonged to congregations that do not permit women to be ordained would not overcome this discouragement.

In congregations that do not ordain women, some discussed an overt form of discouragement wherein pastors defined gender roles from the pulpit. As one male parishioner describes it, "from the pulpit they told us that . . . there are a couple things that women just wouldn't be considered for: a pastor, preacher, and then the elders" (Interview 53). It follows that a woman in such a congregation, in which the gender limitations were so distinctly defined and readily discussed, would hesitate to follow, or even acknowledge, a call to ordination.

Some described a more subtle form of discouragement. Even in congregations that were not as vocally opposed to ordaining women—or in traditions that permitted female ordination but did not currently have a female pastor—women could see a "glass ceiling" to their options for leadership. One young African American man described how the absence of women in key church leadership positions affects how young girls might think about the options that are available to them:

> I believe that whenever you grow up and you don't see people like you doing something, you steer away from it. For example, when I was growing up a young African American male in the city, I grew up watching a lot of basketball.

Everybody who was African American where I was played sports: basketball, football, what have you. I didn't see a lot of black astronauts. I didn't see a lot of black police officers. I didn't see a lot of black lawyers. So in my mind those jobs weren't cool to me. The cool jobs were the athletes so I tend to go towards that. Now, a female in the church . . . and especially an African American female where you don't see too many African American black pastors, they're not going to go towards that job. They'll see choir director, youth leader is a female or maybe working in the staff kitchen, they could see that as a leading role, they can see the nursery which are all jobs that are real genderized. But those are the jobs that you'll see most African American women having in the church, you'll see them in the choir or in the nursery or in the kitchen. They don't see a lot of African American women being pastors and since you don't see that it's uncommon and it's not right. So . . . I believe that if there were more African American female pastors it would encourage young ladies to pursue that and go into it but it's so rare and so uncommon that you really don't see it that much.

This interviewee believed that the presence of female church leaders in the African American community would certainly prompt young girls to pursue the clergy as a career possibility. The presence of women in these leadership positions could be empowering in the same way that Jackie Robinson was to a prior generation of African Americans:

Oh, yeah without a doubt. Without a doubt . . . people want to see people like them. . . . Once Robinson goes into the professional baseball league other African Americans want to follow, we don't want to play in the Negro league anymore, we want to play in the MLB. It's like in the church, little girls right now see growing up that Mom wants to be in the kitchen or in the choir, they don't see Mom wanting to be a pastor. But once that first person comes—that first African American female in the pulpit they see will make them think about pursuing that. (Interview 47)

This theme of female empowerment can be seen in multiple accounts of clergywomen who describe their role in inspiring and motivating younger women in the church to pursue a call to ministry. One Disciples of Christ minister in her fifties detailed how she "never really had [a female pastor] to look up to when she was little" (Interview 24). Because there were so few female pastors around, she was viewed as an "aberration," and grew up being told that "there was something wrong with [her]" (Interview 24). Female clergy can thus serve the role of providing proof that a young girl's call is legitimate. One female minister sees her role as helping "to break . . . barriers that once were there" (Interview 27). Through her example, a young girl in her congregation who pretends to be a pastor when she goes home can "say 'yes, it is a possibility,' and allow her to have hopes and dreams and not be told 'no, those—that can't happen.' I think that's incredible" (Interview 27). In sum, through their own leadership example, female clergy can inspire women in their congregations to lead.

While clergy and congregants from traditions that *do* ordain women consistently discussed female clergy's empowering effect, the individuals we talked to from traditions that do *not* ordain women tended to explain how other women within their churches could fill a similarly inspiring role. One Catholic woman, for example, explained that her daughter had felt a call to ministry from a young age. She believed that seeing women such as nuns in leadership positions could inspire her daughter: "So, for her to see women in those positions, of course, it helps . . . tend the soil a little bit more so that they can say 'yes. This is a possibility. This is . . . something that I could be called to.' Just even open it up, you know, so they can hear about it." (Interview 29). This same woman grew up in a Mainline Protestant denomination in which her pastor gave her "opportunities to be in ministry":

> I had some really beautiful experiences with my pastor growing up who gave me opportunities to teach. He gave me opportunities to be in ministry. We would go to the juvenile detention center once or twice a year. We would do services there. So, I never felt any imposition of just this "women can't do this." But I also never felt like "do this because you're a woman." I felt like "follow the Lord. Trust him. Do what he is calling you to do." And I was very blessed to have a pastor who gave me opportunities to do that. (Interview 29)

It is interesting that while she "never felt any imposition of . . . 'women can't do this,'" she did not discuss the potential that her daughter might one day feel that same "imposition" within her current tradition that ordains only men to be priests.

Other individuals from traditions that do not ordain women, or that do ordain women but who currently have a man serving as the primary religious leader, mentioned the "first lady" (the pastor's wife) or other women who teach Sunday school or lead studies of religious texts as serving as role models for women within the church. One woman who attends a congregation that permits women to be ordained but does not currently have a woman as the main pastor stated that "there are other ways of serving within the church that would inspire young people" (Interview 39). Several individuals discussed the notion that those role models could be found in other positions—even though women could not, or currently did not, serve as the primary religious leader, there were women serving in leadership roles throughout the church.

In congregations in which women cannot be ordained, in some instances it appeared as though individuals emphasized the ways in which women could lead within the religious community in an attempt to compensate for the one position that was reserved only for men. "Women can do a host of things. It's just that the office of the pastor is reserved for men," explained one African American man from a congregation that does not ordain women. He further emphasized the ways in which women could be involved: "there are ninety-nine ministries that women can do in the church, except that one God has reserved for men" (Interview 41).

Some women connected these opportunities for involvement to their sense of efficacy within their religious community. Because "women are serving all over the church . . . you don't feel like you're in any way being suppressed or anything like that. There are plenty of opportunities to serve" (Interview 52). Because women see that they have "plenty of opportunities to serve," even in religious traditions in which they cannot be the primary religious leader, they may not think that their congregation's policy on female ordination "hinders [them] from teaching or being effective in the ministry or having a voice." By looking to the ways in which they can be involved, women within congregations that do not ordain women can still feel that "[they're] all important people" (Interview 17) and not underprivileged.

GENDERED ISSUES

Our interviews further revealed that many people perceive gender to matter between clergy and congregants when it comes to the discussion of specific gendered issues. Topics such as miscarriage, abortion, sex, and parenting were often mentioned as benefitting from female counsel. It is worth noting that Deckman et al. (2003) found that the largest gap of opinion between male and female clergy was on the topic of abortion. They found a tendency on the part of clergywomen to be more leftleaning than clergymen on a host of issues, including gendered issues such as abortion and women's rights.

From our conversations with clergy and congregants, the phenomenon of gendered issues being difficult to discuss with individuals of the opposite gender appears to be present across religious traditions—although congregational stance on female ordination affects how the question is regarded. Traditions that ordain women tend to emphasize the necessity of a clergywoman in discussing these topics, while some individuals from congregations that do not have female religious leaders point to other nonclergy women in the church as being available to talk with congregants about these issues. This fits with what we observed in the previous two chapters: congregational context tends to mediate the impact of most other factors when it comes to gender and religious leadership.

A female pastor of youth and families discussed how young men in her youth group do not come to her about certain issues (for example, sex or romantic feelings), while younger girls are more likely to bring up sensitive topics with her:

> RESPONDENT: I try to surround myself with volunteers who cover a range of socio-political kind of formats so that at any one point in time those youth feel comfortable going to somebody in the group. Whether it's me or whether it's one of my volunteers, I want them to know they can come to any one of us and we can be a listening ear for them.
>
> INTERVIEWER: So do you see youth gravitate toward people who are more like them, whether it's by gender or by some other marker?
>
> R: Yeah. because they want to know that you're going to understand them.
>
> I: And I guess gender's a clear way that they would.
>
> R: Very clear. . . . I mean, I remember being a teenager. So much of it is around sexuality. The boys are not going to come and talk to me about sex. It's just not going to happen. That is like [short laughter], you know, hands off. I, she won't understand me. But another young man they might feel more comfortable going to. It's all about who they feel comfortable seeking guidance from. So I try to put people in places where there will be an option for any youth who might have questions or concerns or whatever to be able to go to somebody there. . . . The girls can then come to me and say, "this happened to me. Somebody said that I was a bitch because I was being assertive." And I can be like, "yeah. That blows. And that's not fair. That's not right. And here is what I've done in my past when that has happened." And I can relate to them on that level. . . . So, like I said before, teens need that role model of their own who looks like them in a sense because they think they understand it. (Interview 26)

Another female Episcopal priest described how she frequently talks with women from other churches "who need to talk to a woman" and are referred to her by their male pastors or Catholic priests:

> A woman who's been raped really does not want to talk to a man. We just know that psychologically it retraumatizes her. Women who are dealing with issues of fertility . . . there is a comfort level that women often have with other women that they're just not going to have with a man. . . . And what happens in denominations where there are no women [to talk to about issues of] the grief of miscarriage. Or the very exhausting and emotional choice of whether or not

to terminate a pregnancy. Or what happens when a woman finally speaks the truth about sexual abuse. You know, those are things, what happens, where does that go? Well, maybe it goes to a therapist, but maybe it doesn't. (Interview 25)

Other clergy and congregants, however, differed on the necessity of having an ordained woman to discuss these issues. While most everyone we talked with agreed that there are some issues that could be better understood by another woman, they also believed that this woman did not necessarily have to be a pastor or priest. One Catholic priest put it this way:

> There have been many times when I have said to women, "you need to talk with one of your lady friends." Or, "why don't you have a talk with"—when I was at the Newman Center—"with Sister [So and So]." And then sometimes I'll tease, and say, "because you know, the women stick together." And I think that's true. I think women understand women and men understand men, and women need time to be with women and men need time to be with other guys. (Interview 19)

An older Catholic female parishioner said that she goes not only to her priest for guidance but also to the women in her Bible group. "I see these women as my peers and as my best friends. Yes, we go to each other for guidance. The way only a woman could get guidance from a woman, if you understand what I'm saying, [would be] as peers and as best friends" (Interview 30).

WOMEN BETTER UNDERSTAND WOMEN

Another theme that emerged from our interviews is the idea that women can better understand women. Many discussed how women were more comfortable going to other women when seeking guidance on topics religious or otherwise. As we saw with gendered issues, some individuals qualified their statements by saying that it was not necessary for women to have a female pastor to go to but could talk with, and relate to, other women within the church.

Many interviewees saw women as better able relate to other women because of shared and similar experiences. These experiences could include gendered issues such as childbirth but could also be related to societal expectations about how women should live and act. The ability for women to better relate to women was often used to explain how having women clergy was advantageous for women in the congregations. An African American woman in her late twenties explained her belief in the importance of a diverse clergy by noting that having clergy from "different walks of life," including different genders and ethnicities, made clergy more able to connect with people in various situations (Interview 46). A female pastor told a story of how a female congregant had come up to her and said, "it's so nice to have somebody here who finally gets us," someone who "finally gets the . . . stresses of life" (Interview 24). In other words, one strength of permitting women to become pastors, priests, or imams is their ability to relate to the 50% of the population (or more in churches, as women tend to attend at higher rates than men) that is not typically represented.

A male Southern Baptist minister agreed that women could better relate to women but did not see this as necessitating female ordination. Rather, he referred women in his congregation to more "spiritually mature" women for help with the specific issue:

> When it comes to men and women, obviously I'm a guy so I'm going to gravitate more towards men in terms of the things that we have in common and the things that we're interested in and so that makes my relationships with the men in the church much easier than relationships with women in the church. But there's also kind of an aspect of intentionality in that, whereas I seek to invest more of my ministry in the men of the church. And that's not to say that there's anything against the women in the church, but I feel like I can't relate to the women as well. So in some ways we rely on other women in the church who are spiritually mature. . . . They can reach out to other women in the church [and] can minister to them more effectively than I can in certain situations. (Interview 5)

As we saw earlier, most of the people we spoke with found other factors, such as personality and personal experience, as mattering more than gender in shaping their interactions and involvement with their clergy. At the same time, statements such as those from the congregant mentioned above ("it's so nice to have somebody here who finally gets us") demonstrate the ways in which gender still matters in the life of the congregation.

CONGREGATIONAL ATTENDANCE AND INVOLVEMENT

Our interviews also revealed that in some cases, the gender of the pastor or priest can affect levels of attendance and involvement from those in the congregation. Several individuals reported more families attending their church since having a female pastor. One Lutheran (ELCA) man in his sixties sees this phenomenon as being related to women's prominent role in deciding which church their family attends. "I think mothers play a big role in deciding what church you go to. And if the mother can relate better with the female pastor, that may encourage them to choose a church that has a female pastor" (Interview 34).

Despite this man's perception that the "connection between having a female pastor" and the surge in the number of young families within the church, the extent to which gender plays a role remained ambiguous to the interviewee. When his pastor was asked about the same phenomenon, she perceived it to be related more to her own personal gift with children rather than her gender specifically:

> For me personally, I think I have a—God has blessed me with an ability to really love kids and younger people. And so I authentically love them, and I like being with them. And they like being with me. I have a lot of joy when I'm with them, and our children's sermons are fun. I was talking to my president about our confirmation—how fun that is—and the kids wanting to sit with me at confirmation [laughter]. It's just like "they want to sit by me!" . . . I think that women, some women, when you have good relationships and can relate really well with people then, then it just becomes, well, "that's my pastor. And this is the relationship that I have with my pastor." And I have kids that I've known since they were little, and now are bigger, and I've been their pastor. And it's just been this relationship of love and understanding and watching them grow and encouraging them in the faith and . . . them always knowing that a woman can be a pastor. (Interview 27)

Clergy gender was also discussed as having a potential influence on youth attendance. A female associate pastor of youth and families described a change in the makeup of the church's youth group after she became the primary youth minister. Since becoming associate pastor, "I actually have more females coming to youth group than I do males. Where before it was the other way around with the male youth directors that this church has had in the past" (Interview 26).

CONGREGATIONAL CHOICE AND "SELF-SORTING"

Our interviews revealed another way in which clergy gender could shape the religious behavior of those in their congregations: individual congregational choice. Some individuals discussed clergy gender and/or a church's stance on female ordination as being factors that they consider when selecting a church to attend. One

woman who recently joined the Seventh-day Adventist church discussed her difficulty in attending a congregation that does not permit women to serve in certain
leadership roles. Although she joined the church despite this issue, she worries that
her church's stance may prevent others from even considering visiting its services.

> It might be okay with those that are going, but what about if we want to attract
> other people that think more like me? You know, maybe we're keeping women
> away that would be a part of your church if they could see women in leadership
> or be allowed to do something if they wanted to. (Interview 56)

Another woman in her mid-thirties who attends a nondenominational Evangelical
church introduced this theme of self-sorting as an explanation for why conversations
about women's leadership didn't take place in her church: people know initially
what the church believes in regard to ordaining women, and they do not attend that
church if its stance on female ordination bothers them. "I don't know that we see
that a lot because like when they start coming [here], they obviously know up front
so it's not like they come and then they complain about it. You know what I mean.
So I'm sure that does deter a lot of people" (Interview 49). Instead, they select a
church to attend that more closely aligns with their beliefs.

Although only a few individuals introduced this theme of self-selecting a congregation based on its stance on female ordination, it does fit within a larger, national
trend of religious and political self-sorting over the last several decades. Scholars have
shown that in contemporary American society people are more likely to modify their
religious beliefs to match their politics than they are to modify their politics to match
their religious beliefs (Bishop 2009; Margolis 2018; Putnam and Campbell 2012,
chap. 5). Here we see some evidence that a congregation's policy on female ordination
can serve as a convenient shortcut to help potential members know whether the congregation and its policies are generally more progressive or more traditional.

SUMMARY AND CONCLUSION

This chapter has begun to investigate the impact of gender and leadership on the religious attitudes and behaviors of American congregants. This question was motivated
and informed by political science research on the concept of representation. It has
previously been shown that descriptive representation affects political behavior and
attitudes among a host of demographic and political groups including women, ra-
cial/ethnic minorities, and other political groups. People sometimes respond differently when someone who looks like them is on the ballot or represents them in

a political office. This is also important because it speaks to wider questions on the extent to which the gender gap matters. Political science research has shown many of the ways that representation matters in a political context, and in this chapter we set out to see how it might affect religious attitudes and behaviors in religious communities. To inform this discussion, we talked with clergy and congregants in various religious traditions. Through these conversations, we wanted to see whether gender representation in a religious context affects those in the pews; and if it does matter, in what ways does it make a difference?

Based on the research of Djupe and Gilbert (2008), Djupe and Olson (2013), and Djupe (2014), we theorized that religious congregations can in many ways behave similarly to political communities and that religious leaders can function similarly to elected representatives in terms of the effect that descriptive representation exerts on the attitudes and behavior of those in their congregations. In essence, the theory is that churchgoers implicitly internalize the characteristics of the person in the pulpit and respond accordingly. Building on this research we began to investigate the responses from our dozens of face-to-face interviews with both clergy and congregants. We tried to learn whether these interviews revealed any indication that the gender of a person's pastor or priest has a discernible impact on those in the pews. Our interviews revealed a few common themes.

First, many people believe that the presence of female clergy ("religious gender representation") can have an empowering effect on young women and girls, similar in many ways to the empowering effect of minority representation on minority groups in the political sphere. Several of our interviewees described how seeing women in a position of religious leadership can help girls and young women feel that they also have the freedom to pursue a call to the ministry. Our interviews also revealed that this empowering effect is not limited only to the religious sphere. Similar to the results of our wider survey discussed in the previous chapter, several of our interviewees noted that the presence of a woman in the chief leadership role at church can signal to girls and young women that they can be leaders in the secular and professional worlds as well.

Second, several people noted how female priests are often better at relating to women in their congregation, especially when it comes to ministry and counseling on gender-related topics such as pregnancy, childbirth, rape, and miscarriage. Third, some clergy and congregants have observed the presence of a female pastor to be associated with an increase in the level of attendance from families and young people—in other words, it seems to exert a "mobilizing" effect. Fourth, some of those we spoke with face to face observed that the presence or absence of gender-inclusive leadership can be a reason that people decide whether to begin or continue attending a particular congregation. Few went so far as to say that individuals select a church based on their personal preference of having a male or female clergyperson, but instead pointed out that clergy gender is an easily identifiable indicator of whether their own political and ideological views will align with those of the congregation.

Finally, our interviews revealed that despite these areas for which clergy and congregants believed female religious representation in leadership to matter, most were simultaneously of the opinion that it matters less than the particular personality and leadership style of the individual leader. Those in congregations with female clergy seemed motivated to brush off gender and leadership as a "done issue," while those in congregations with male-only clergy were motivated to argue that it was not a major problem because unordained volunteer or informal female mentors could be found in most congregations. Looking at interviews conducted in the 1970s, Carroll et al. (1983) found a similar pattern. "[Clergy] do not, however, perceive their gender to be as important as other differences between themselves and their role-partners among laity and clergy, such as value, style, theological, and personality differences." Several decades later, this still seems to be the case.

There are many insights that we have gained through our examination of these interviews. We have seen ways in which gender representation matters in a religious context. Similar to the effect of gender representation in politics, it can have a mobilizing effect for certain demographics and also motivate more women to pursue positions of leadership. We also found female clergy to matter when discussing specific gendered issues. Even though individuals tend to state that personality matters more, these conversations revealed a number of ways in which gender representation does, in fact, matter. Although the parallels are not exact, it seems as though gender representation in America's places of worship makes a difference in much the same way as it does in secular contexts. We turn now in our next chapter to the results from our nationally representative public opinion surveys. As we will see, a statistics-based analysis of these same questions reveals many results that both support and diverge from those presented in this chapter.

THE EFFECT OF CLERGYWOMEN

Religious Empowerment and Mobilization

IN THE PREVIOUS two chapters we set out to examine the question of how female clergy influences those in their congregations, both from a personal and societal empowerment perspective as well as a religious and spiritual perspective. This was motivated by a desire to examine the ways in which gender representation matters in a religious context. Given the pervasiveness of the gender gap in leadership in both religious and secular contexts, combined with research that shows ways in which political gender representation affects constituents, we set out to see if similar effects could be found in America's places of worship. In the previous chapter we examined our face-to-face interviews and found that many people perceive gender to matter when it comes to religious leadership, and perceive that female clergy is important to empowering young women and girls. They also noted that the gender of a religious leader makes a substantive difference in how these leaders interact with their congregations. That said, most were of the opinion that whether one's pastor or priest is a woman or man matters *less* than the personality and leadership style of that particular congregational leader. In this chapter we now turn to our nationally representative public opinion surveys to examine the same questions. Is there any large-scale statistical evidence that the gender of clergy affects the religious attitudes and behaviors of those in their congregations? A quantitative perspective is important as it can add a dimension of evidence that our qualitative interviews are not able to capture. For example, our qualitative interviews, while very insightful, also focused on individuals from a single geographical region in central Kentucky. Our public opinion survey, in contrast, sampled congregants from around the country. Also, qualitative interviews capture people's *perceptions*, which can often draw conclusions from just a few personal experiences or anecdotes. These certainly add richness and depth to our understanding of the topic, but the random-sample public opinion surveys are able to determine whether those anecdotes are generalizable to the wider population. We can better discern, for instance, if there is systematic evidence that women in congregations with female clergy have higher rates of attendance or other religious behaviors, even controlling for the impact of other important demographic, religious, and political factors.

In this chapter we approach our question as other scholars have approached their quantitative studies of the effect of political representation. As described in earlier chapters, the basic procedure is to collect information about attitudes and behaviors from a random sample of individuals. Contextual information is then added to this sample, including some important characteristics of each individual's elected representative, such as a member of Congress or state legislator. For example, if a researcher has a random sample of people across the United States and knows the gender of each individual and whether he or she voted in the previous election, the researcher can then add to the data an indicator of whether the individual's state governor is a man or woman. This data can then be used to perform a statistical analysis to determine whether women in states with female governors are more likely to vote than women in states with male governors. If this turns out to be the case, it is evidence of the mobilizing effect of descriptive gender political representation.

The approach we take in this chapter is similar. Our Gender and Religious Representation Survey includes a random sample of American churchgoers from all major American denominations, including those that ordain women and those that do not. This is an advancement over previous research that primarily focuses on Mainline Protestant denominations that ordain women (Lehman 1987). We also have several measures of each person's demographic characteristics as well as their social, political, and religious attitudes and behaviors. Our survey also records whether each person currently has a clergywoman or clergyman in his or her congregation as well as other indicators of gender representation. This chapter will analyze the results of a variety of statistical tests to see, for example, whether women in congregations with female pastors or priests also report higher levels of spirituality than women in congregations with male pastors or priests. This will allow us to directly test whether there is any systematic and generalizable evidence that female descriptive representation in religious congregations matters in shaping people's religious behaviors and attitudes.

DEFINING AND MEASURING GENDER REPRESENTATION AND RELIGIOUS
ATTITUDES/BEHAVIORS

We rely on Waves 1 through 3 of our Gender and Religious Representation Survey for the analysis presented in this chapter. In this survey we measure gender representation in three key ways: 1) the presence of a woman as the principal religious leader in a congregation; 2) congregational policies regarding whether women are permitted to serve as the principal religious leader, regardless of whether the person currently occupying the position is male or female; and 3) the proportion of women currently serving as small group leaders and lay ministers in the congregation. (Details on how each of these variables is operationalized and coded can be found in the Data Appendix.)

Why do we use these three distinct measures of gender representation? Recall from the previous chapter that dyadic representation (either descriptive or substantive) is the one-to-one direct relationship between a constituent and his or her representative, while collective representation occurs when a person is represented (either descriptively or substantively) by one or more people in the representative body as a whole, even if none of these representatives is directly assigned to this person. Adapting these theories to the context of religious congregations, dyadic descriptive representation would be characterized by a woman having a female pastor (or a man having a male pastor), while collective descriptive representation would occur when a woman belongs to a congregation in which women hold various leadership positions—in small groups, ministries, service organizations—or a man belongs to a congregation in which men hold these leadership positions. We therefore measure religious gender representation in both ways: 1) presence of a woman serving as the principal religious leader and 2) the proportion of women serving in the lay congregational leadership.[1]

We also measure religious gender representation in a third way: whether the congregation's policies permit women to serve as the principal religious leader, regardless of whether the leader at the time is a man or woman. In Chapter 2 we saw that about 45% of those in our Religion and Gender Representation Survey attend congregations in which women are not permitted to serve as the principal religious leader. It is possible that even the *potential* of realizing gender representation by having policies in place that permit both men and women to be ordained as clergy might be sufficient to signal to the congregation that the views of both men and women are represented in the leadership and decision-making process.

Our goal is to assess the influence of religious gender representation on religious attitudes and behaviors of those in the pews. Social scientists often draw a distinction between religiosity and spirituality. Religiosity generally refers to a person's religious behaviors while spirituality reflects inner experience and feelings (King and Crowther 2004). The survey measured aspects of both of these, including religious behaviors (frequency of religious service attendance, personal prayer, volunteering in one's congregation, devotional scripture reading, talking about religion with others) and spirituality (frequency of feeling a deep sense of spiritual peace and well-being, a deep sense of wonder and connection with the universe, God's presence and love, and that one is guided by God in the midst of daily activities).

We also measure respondents' trust in their congregations. In a political context, trust in one's political system has been shown to make a difference in explaining support for government action to solve societal problems (Chanley, Rudolph, and Rahn 2000) as well as approval of incumbent political leaders. This has important consequences for the general effectiveness of the political system (Hetherington 1998, 2006; Hetherington and Rudolph 2015). It is reasonable to suspect that something similar may happen in religious congregations. Trust in one's congregation could affect support for its leaders and confidence in its ability to address concerns of relevance to the individual. Here, we measure religious congregational trust by agreement with this statement: "Generally speaking, I can trust my church or congregation to do what is right." Congregational trust may be especially responsive to the gender of leadership because prior research has shown that the frequency and quality of people's interaction with their congregational leaders is a strong predictor of the amount of trust they have in their congregation (Seymour et al. 2014). It is likely that certain people may be more inclined to develop a strong relationship with their congregational leader if they perceive that leader to be similar to them, and gender is a clear and salient heuristic of potential similarity.

In Chapter 6 we examined how gender role models can affect levels of personal self-efficacy, the feeling of confidence that individuals can meet their goals and overcome challenges. In Chapter 7 we discussed previous research as it relates specifically to a political context, discussing how gender representation in politics can influence political efficacy. Recall that "external efficacy" in a political context is the extent to which individuals believe that a government or other organization is responsive to their needs and interests, while "internal efficacy" is the degree to which they feel they can make a difference and bring about change in that community or government. Applied to a religious congregational context, we measure external religious efficacy by the extent to which a respondent agrees that "I feel that my church or congregation leaders care a lot about what people like me think." Internal religious efficacy is measured by respondents' agreement that "People like me have a lot of influence over the decisions made by my local church or congregation."

Finally, we measured personal identification with the congregation by this statement: "I identify as a member of my church or congregation and I am proud of that identity." Identification with a community is a significant component of in-group association, which is an important source of one's loyalty and commitment to the community as well as measure of the extent to which someone would defend the community against threats from out-groups (Tajfel and Turner 1986).

Our survey includes three key causal (independent) variables and thirteen outcome (dependent) variables. One approach would be to analyze the relationship between each of the causal variables and each of the outcome variables, making for thirty-nine separate combinations of variables to analyze and present. We assume that few readers have the interest or patience for such an adventure. We therefore have opted to simplify and combine the various outcome variables into three index variables that measure religious behavior, spirituality, and congregational efficacy/identity, making for three causal variables and three outcome variables: a total of nine relationships to examine.[2] As we did before, we can investigate this question further by performing a multivariate regression analysis of our data. Recall that this tool identifies the *unique* effect of a particular factor on the outcomes of interest while statistically controlling for the effect of other demographic, social, religious, and political factors that might also influence the outcome.[3] This allows us to determine whether the association between gender leadership and religiosity, spirituality, and efficacy/identity still hold true once we have accounted for these other possible explanations.

We performed this multivariate regression analysis on all nine relationships that we discussed previously as well as on a variety of possible "interactive relationships" associated with each of these nine analyses. For example, we examined if the relationship between having a female pastor and the level of one's religious behaviors is different for men than for women, or for younger versus older individuals, or religious traditionalists versus modernists, or political liberals versus conservatives. In this chapter we give an overview of the substantively relevant results.[4] (For a detailed discussion of how we created these three combined index outcome variables or the nuts and bolts on this chapter's methodological approach, we refer readers to the Data Appendix.)

THE EFFECT OF GENDER LEADERSHIP ON RELIGIOUS ATTITUDES AND BEHAVIOR

Figure 8.1 shows how congregational policies regarding female leadership affect men's and women's levels of congregational efficacy/identity. To help with substantive

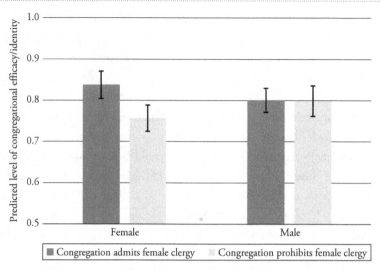

FIGURE 8.1 Gender and Religious Representation Survey; Note: the figure displays the predicted level of congregational efficacy/identity depending on whether the individual's religious congregation admits or prohibits female clergy, holding all other variables in the multivariate analysis constant at their means.; Error bars are 95% confidence intervals for each statistical estimate.; The y-axis is modified to show detail.

interpretation of the results shown in Figure 8.1 and others in this chapter: imagine a number line on a 0-to-1 scale, with the lowest possible values of congregants' efficacy/identity (the feeling that they have no say in what their congregation does, that their leaders are not responsive to them, and they have very little personal identification with and pride in their congregation) represented as 0 and the highest possible levels of their efficacy/identity (strong agreement that they have voice in their congregation and that leaders are responsive to them and are proud of their strong sense of identity with their congregation) as 1. Then imagine four hypothetical people who are identical in every way except that two are men and two are women, and within each gendered pair, one attends a congregation that permits female clergy and the other attends a congregation that does not. Figure 8.1 shows us that the woman attending the congregation that permits female clergy is 8% higher on the 0-to-1 efficacy/identity spectrum (0.76 versus 0.84) than the woman attending the congregation with male-only policies. The two bars representing men in Figure 8.1 show us that congregational policy on gender leadership does not change levels of efficacy/identity for men regardless of the congregation's gender leadership policies.

We see a similar relationship in Figure 8.2 between collective gender representation and congregational efficacy/identity. Women who attend congregations in which at least half of the ministry and small group leaders are also women have levels of efficacy/identity about 7% higher than women who attend congregations

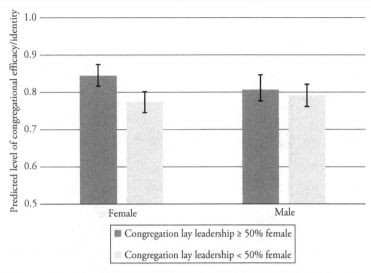

FIGURE 8.2 Gender and Religious Representation Survey; Note: the figure displays the predicted level of congregational efficacy/identity depending on whether women constitute at least half of the lay leadership of the congregation, holding all other variables in the multivariate analysis constant at their means.; Error bars are 95% confidence intervals for each statistical estimate.; The y-axis is modified to show detail.

in which men make up the majority of the congregational leadership. Again, we see that this factor does not affect men's levels of efficacy/identity one way or the other.

Much of the discussion about descriptive gender representation focuses on the Millennial generation. Some have argued that younger churchgoers are especially sensitive to gender dynamics in both civic as well as religious institutions. According to Twenge et al. (2015), the "never attend" rate among high school girls has grown 125% since the 1970s compared to 83% for high school boys. They speculate that "given shifts away from traditional female roles, females may have been affected more than males." In a discussion of this study, *Washington Post* reporter Danielle Paquette quotes a twenty-four-year-old young woman whose resolve to attend church "fizzled" during her first semester at college: "at church, the woman would be the person in the background. As long as I can remember, I would think: This is ridiculous. I'm not that person" (Paquette 2015).

Our survey results show *some* degree of support for this explanation. As can be seen in Figure 8.3, women under forty who attend congregations with a male pastor or priest have levels of religious behavior about 10% lower than other young women who attend congregations with a female clergyperson.[5] Conversely, it could be interpreted that levels of religiosity are 10% higher for women Millennials when they attend congregations with female pastors or priests.

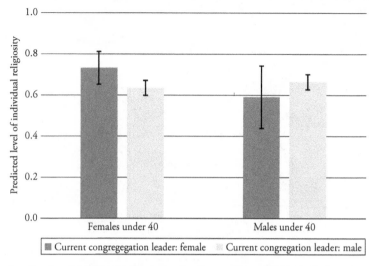

FIGURE 8.3 Gender and Religious Representation Survey; Note: the figure displays the predicted level of individual religiosity among those under 40 years old depending on the gender of the current congregation leader, holding all other variables in the multivariate analysis constant at their means.; Error bars are 95% confidence intervals for each statistical estimate.

Could collective female representation compensate for male-only congregational leadership policies? This possibility was brought up several times in our qualitative interviews from both clergy and congregants who said that it did not matter if the pastor or priest was a woman because other positions of lay leadership in the congregation were filled by women. In other words, they argued that women in congregations that do not allow women to serve as the principal leaders can still be empowered by having more women in lay leadership positions. Consider these quotes from two women from the Evangelical Protestant tradition:

There are so many other avenues in our church to lead. Whether it's in women's ministry or whether it's in a Bible study. . . . It's not like some churches where the women are silent and they don't do anything. I mean we have so many opportunities within our congregation for women to step up and lead that I just don't think, . . . to my knowledge, no one has had an issue with not being able to preach or lead an adult ministry . . . I don't know of any circumstances where that's the case. (Interview 48)

Women are serving all over the church so it's not—you don't feel like you're in any way being suppressed or anything like that. There are plenty of opportunities to serve. (Interview 52)

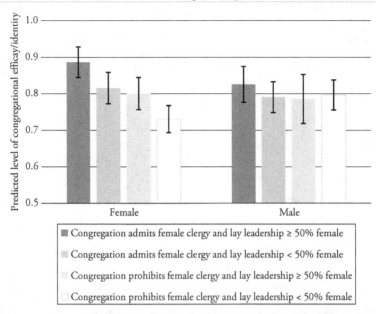

FIGURE 8.4 Gender and Religious Representation Survey; Note: the figure displays the predicted level of congregational efficacy/identity depending on whether the respondent's congregation admits or prohibits women to serve as the principal leader and whether the lay leadership in the congregation is at least half female, holding all other variables in the multivariate analysis constant at their means.; Error bars are 95% confidence intervals for each statistical estimate.; The y-axis is modified to show detail.

Our survey results suggest that a higher occurrence of women in the lay ministry can *somewhat* compensate for a male-only leadership policy, but not completely. As can be seen on the left-hand side of Figure 8.4, both the congregational gender policy *and* the proportion of women in the lay ministry matter in driving levels of efficacy/identity for women.[6] Efficacy/identity goes up for women when they are in congregations that ordain women (the two highest bars) regardless of whether their congregation has a majority female or majority male lay ministry. At the same time, Figure 8.4 shows that efficacy/identity is higher for women when they are in congregations that have majority female lay ministry leaders, regardless of whether their congregation ordains women. The figure also shows that the strongest effect for women occurs when they have both inclusive gender policies *and* majority female lay leadership, but each serves to empower women to a lesser degree in the absence of the other. We can also see on the right-hand side in Figure 8.4 that there is little (and statistically insignificant) variation in efficacy/identity for men in these same circumstances.

Our public opinion survey analysis also shows that collective gender representation can influence the extent to which the gender of the congregational pastor

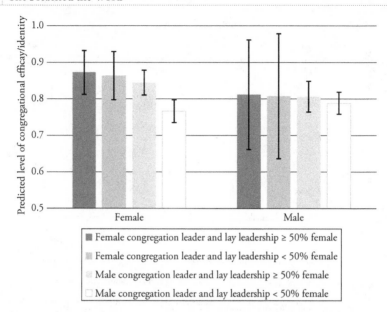

FIGURE 8.5 Gender and Religious Representation Survey; Note: the figure displays the predicted level of congregational efficacy/identity depending on the gender of the current congregational leader and whether the lay leadership in the congregation is at least half female, holding all other variables in the multivariate analysis constant at their means.; Error bars are 95% confidence intervals for each statistical estimate.; The y-axis is modified to show detail.

or priest affects levels of efficacy/identity for women. The left-hand side of Figure 8.5 shows that levels of efficacy/identity for women in congregations in which men comprise the majority of the lay ministry are 10% lower when they are in congregations in which men serve as the head pastor or priest.[7] On the other hand, we also see that when women make up more than half of the congregational lay leadership, levels of efficacy/identity for women are the same regardless of whether the head pastor or priest is a man or woman. Also, the right-hand side of Figure 8.5 again shows that these contextual factors do not matter one way or the other for men.

In terms of personal spirituality, Figure 8.6 shows that the impact of collective gender representation on levels of spirituality is also contingent on gender, although the effect is very small and only weakly statistically significant.[8] Women who attend congregations in which women make up more than half of the congregational leadership have levels of spirituality about 3% higher than those who attend congregations in which the congregational leadership is dominated by men.

Finally, we can use our survey results to statistically estimate levels of religiosity, spirituality, and efficacy/identity for a series of hypothetical individuals in congregations that have varying degrees of gender leadership balance. Specifically,

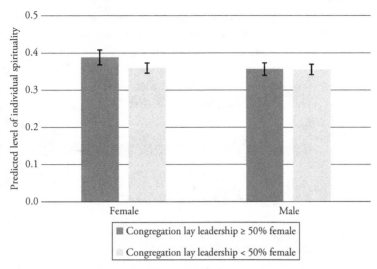

FIGURE 8.6 Gender and Religious Representation Survey; Note: the figure displays the predicted level of individual spirituality depending on whether the lay leadership in the congregation is at least half female, holding all other variables in the multivariate analysis constant at their means.; Error bars are 95% confidence intervals for each statistical estimate.; The y-axis is modified to show detail.

we can compare men and women in three different types of congregations: 1) a congregation with "male-dominant leadership," in which women are excluded from the clergy and the lay leadership is majority male; 2) a congregation with "female-dominant leadership," in which women are admitted to the clergy, a woman is currently serving as the principal congregational leader, and women make up half or more of the congregation's lay leadership; and 3) a congregation with "gender-egalitarian leadership," in which women are admitted to the clergy, men and women are equally likely to serve as the congregation's principal religious leader, and the lay leadership is equally balanced between men and women. In our survey, congregations with male-dominant leadership make up about 29% of all congregations while those with female-dominant leadership make up about 5%. How do men and women in these different congregations compare on the religious attitude and behavioral variables we have been investigating so far?

The bars in Figure 8.7 show the estimated levels of religiosity, spirituality, and efficacy/identity for both men and women in our three hypothetical congregations along with the maximum potential levels of male and female leadership as well as egalitarian gender leadership. Recall that each of these outcomes is represented on a scale of 0 to 1, with 0 representing the lowest frequency of religious behaviors, spiritual experiences, and levels of efficacy/identity and 1 representing the highest.

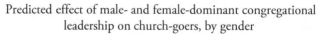

Predicted effect of male- and female-dominant congregational
leadership on church-goers, by gender

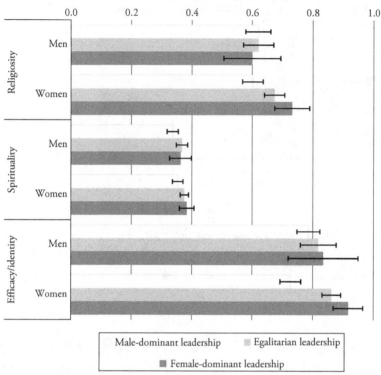

FIGURE 8.7 Gender and Religious Representation Survey; Note: the figure displays the predicted
level of each outcome for men and women in three hypothetical congregations: one that maximizes female leadership, one that maximizes male leadership, and one that shares leadership equally between
men and women, holding all other variables in the multivariate analysis constant at their means.; Error
bars are 95% confidence intervals for each statistical estimate.

(A full table with numerical figures corresponding to Figure 8.7 as well as other
similar tables in this chapter can be found in the Data Appendix.)

The estimates show that women in congregations with the strongest degree of
female leadership have levels of religiosity about 13% higher than those of women
in congregations with the maximum amount of male leadership. Women in
congregations that maximize female leadership engage in religious behaviors more
frequently than women in congregations that maximize male leadership. More intu-
itively, this is roughly equivalent to a difference of attending religious services once
or twice a month instead of a few times a year, or engaging in religious behaviors like
prayer and scripture reading at least once a week compared to daily. For their part,
men have virtually identical levels of religiosity regardless of whether they are in a
congregation that maximizes male or female leadership.

Figure 8.7 also shows that levels of congregational efficacy/identity for women increase by about 19% when they move from a congregation with male-dominant leadership to one with female-dominant leadership. This is roughly equivalent to the difference between a woman saying that she "somewhat agrees" versus "strongly agrees" with statements such as, "my congregation's leaders care about what people like me think," "I identify as a member of my congregation and am proud of that identity," and "I trust my congregation or church to do what is right." It is also noteworthy that levels of congregational efficacy/identity are slightly lower on average for women in male-dominant congregations than men in these same congregations.

As before, men have similar levels of efficacy/identity regardless of whether they are in a male-dominant, female-dominant, or gender-egalitarian congregation. This means that a man who attends a congregation that has a female leader and a majority-female lay leadership body is just as likely to say "people like me have a lot of influence over the decisions made in my local church or congregation" or "I trust my church or congregation to do what is right" as another man in a congregation with a male pastor or priest, male-only clergy, and a majority-male lay leadership team. As we can see, this is *not* true for women.

Figure 8.7 also shows that men have *slightly* higher (3%) levels of spirituality when they are in gender-egalitarian congregations compared to male-dominant congregations. In general, the frequency with which both men and women report that they "feel a deep sense of spiritual peace and well-being" or "feel God's presence and love" or "feel a deep sense of wonder and connection with the universe" appears to be the roughly same regardless of the gender balance of the leadership in the congregation they attend.

Perhaps the most interesting finding in Figure 8.7, however, is that levels of religiosity and congregational efficacy/identity for women in gender-egalitarian congregations are closer to the levels of women in female-dominant congregations than they are to those of women in male-dominant congregations. In fact, there is no statistically significant difference between levels of religiosity and efficacy/identity for women in gender-egalitarian congregations and those in female-dominant congregations, both of which are higher than for women in male-dominant congregations.

What this means is that purely female-dominant leadership is not necessary to maximize the frequency of religious behaviors and congregational identity and trust among women in these congregations. Rather, women benefit just as much from an equal balance of men and women in their congregation's formal and lay leadership as they do from exclusively female leadership. Further analysis shows that this effect is due more to a congregation's policy on gender and leadership and the proportion of lay leadership who are female than the frequency of women serving as the principal congregational leader (results presented in the Data Appendix). A congregation in which the pulpit is open to women and in which the lay leadership is evenly balanced between women and men produces women with levels of congregational efficacy/identity equal to those of men. It is only in congregations in which women are barred from the pulpit or the altar and make up a minority of lay leadership and ministers do we find women who have less trust in their leadership and less pride in and emotional commitment to their congregation.

FEMALE LEADERSHIP AND BELIEF ORTHODOXY

In previous chapters we found that support for female ordination is driven by a variety of factors, including religious behaviors and attitudes as well as political orientations. Might it be that these factors also influence whether someone is empowered or disempowered by the presence or absence of female clergy in a congregation? There are compelling reasons to predict that this might be the case. American political parties differ in their approaches to gender egalitarianism in society and the extent to which the government influences the role of women in the workplace and societal leadership positions. Also, belief orthodoxy often influences attitudes toward societal gender roles, with people who are more orthodox tending to support traditional gender roles and those who are more theologically progressive favoring egalitarian gender roles. It is also possible that those with different levels of support for inclusive gender roles in secular society would be differently affected in their religious beliefs by the presence or absence of gender-inclusive practices in their religious congregations. We can therefore begin by performing the same analysis as before, but this time focusing on the impact of religious belief orthodoxy instead of gender.[9]

Figure 8.8 shows that when controlling for various demographic, social, religious, and political factors, theological progressives (those who say they their churches or congregations should either adopt modern beliefs and practices or adjust them in light of modern circumstances) have levels of congregational efficacy/identity that are about 10% lower than those of theological traditionalists when they attend congregations headed by a man, but there is no statistically significant difference between the two when they attend congregations headed by a woman. Similarly, Figure 8.9 shows that theological progressives in congregations with a male pastor or priest have levels of spirituality that are about 5% lower than those of theological traditionalists in the same congregations. It also shows that levels of spirituality are the same for theological progressives and traditionalists in congregations led by women.

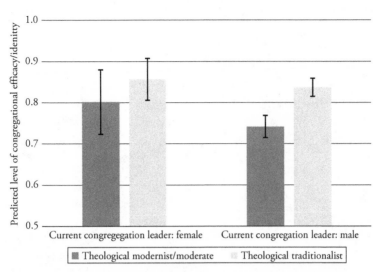

FIGURE 8.8 Gender and Religious Representation Survey; Note: the figure displays the predicted level of congregational efficacy/identity depending on whether the current congregational leader is male or female, holding all other variables in the multivariate analysis constant at their means.; Error bars are 95% confidence intervals for each statistical estimate.; The y-axis is modified to show detail.

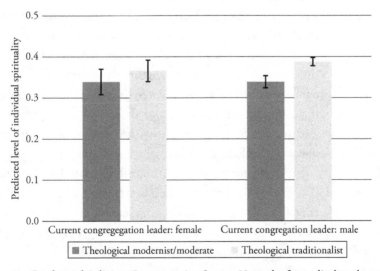

FIGURE 8.9 Gender and Religious Representation Survey; Note: the figure displays the predicted level of individual spirituality depending on whether the current congregational leader is male or female, holding all other variables in the multivariate analysis constant at their means.; Error bars are 95% confidence intervals for each statistical estimate.; The y-axis is modified to show detail.

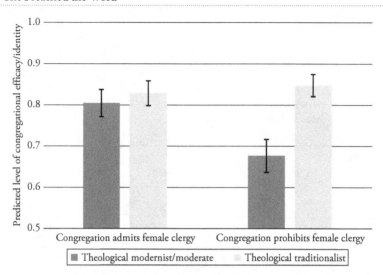

FIGURE 8.10 Gender and Religious Representation Survey; Note: the figure displays the predicted level of congregational efficacy/identity depending on whether the congregation admits or prohibits female clergy, holding all other variables in the multivariate analysis constant at their means.; Error bars are 95% confidence intervals for each statistical estimate.; The y-axis is modified to show detail.

Another important finding can be observed in Figure 8.10. Theological traditionalists appear to have relatively high levels of congregational efficacy/identity regardless of whether they attend a congregation that admits or prohibits female ordination. For theological progressives, however, the gender policies of their congregation make a difference: levels of efficacy/identity are approximately 13% lower for theological progressives when they attend congregations with male-only clerical policies compared to congregations that allow women to serve as clergy.

As before, we can predict levels of religiosity, spirituality, and efficacy/identity among hypothetical theological traditionalists and progressives depending on whether they attend congregations with male-dominant, female-dominant, or gender-egalitarian leadership practices. Recall that this statistical estimation combines the effect of all three types of gender representation: whether the congregation allows for female clergy, the gender of the current clergyperson of the congregation, and the proportion of men and women in lay leadership.

The results shown in Figure 8.11 indicate that theological progressives who attend congregations with gender-egalitarian or female-dominant leadership have levels of congregational efficacy/identity about 18% and 23% higher, respectively, than do progressives who attend congregations with male-dominant leadership. This effect is similar to that shown in Figure 8.7 for women. Theological progressives respond equally well to congregations that evenly split the leadership between men

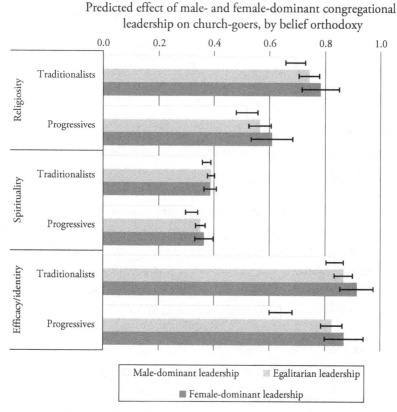

Predicted effect of male- and female-dominant congregational leadership on church-goers, by belief orthodoxy

FIGURE 8.11 Gender and Religious Representation Survey; Note: the figure displays the predicted level of each outcome for theological progressives and traditionalists in three hypothetical congregations: one that maximizes female leadership, one that maximizes male leadership, and one that shares leadership equally between men and women, holding all other variables in the multivariate analysis constant at their means.; Error bars are 95% confidence intervals for each statistical estimate.

and women and to congregations that magnify the presence of females in the congregational leadership. As was the case for women, gender equality is sufficient to prevent the decline in congregational efficacy and identity for theological progressives. In the presence of gender-egalitarian leadership, theological progressives are just as likely to say that they trust their congregation's leaders to do what is right or that they are proud of their identity as a member of that congregation. It is only in congregations with male-dominant leadership that theological progressives are diminished in their emotional attachment to the congregation.

We also see in Figure 8.11 some faint evidence that boosting the presence of women in leadership positions seems generally to result in slightly higher levels of religiosity, spirituality, and congregational efficacy/identity for theological progressives and traditionalists alike when compared to congregations that focus solely on male leadership. The key pattern seems to be that more female leadership leads to a little more religiosity, spirituality, and efficacy/identity for theological progressives as well as for traditionalists.

FEMALE LEADERSHIP, POLITICAL IDEOLOGY, AND POLITICAL PARTISANSHIP

We turn now to our examination of how political ideology and partisanship interact with female congregational leadership to influence religiosity, spirituality, and efficacy/identity. Figure 8.12 shows that the gender leadership policies of a congregation make a difference for political liberals: their levels of congregational efficacy are 13% higher when they are in congregations that admit women clergy compared to those that have only male clergy. Their levels of efficacy/identity are also about 10% lower than conservatives' levels when they are in congregations with male-only gender leadership policies. Their levels of religiosity are boosted by about 10% when they attend congregations with a female leader (result not depicted). As seen in Figure 8.13, levels of religious efficacy/identity among Democrats are also about 8% lower in congregations that prohibit female clergy compared to levels for Democrats in congregations that ordain women.

It is important to see in Figures 8.12 and 8.13 that political conservatives and Republicans have generally high levels of trust, identification, and efficacy

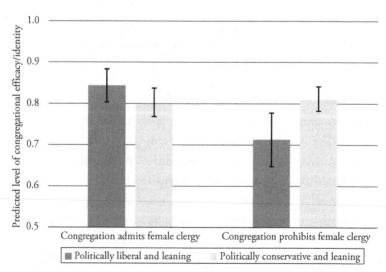

FIGURE 8.12 Gender and Religious Representation Survey; Note: the figure displays the predicted level of congregational efficacy/identity depending on whether the congregation admits or prohibits female clergy, holding all other variables in the multivariate analysis constant at their means.; Error bars are 95% confidence intervals for each statistical estimate.; The y-axis is modified to show detail.

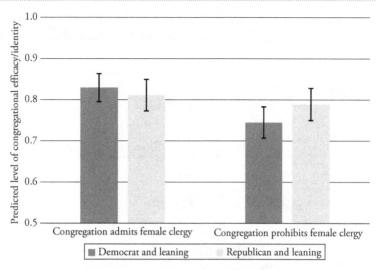

FIGURE 8.13 Gender and Religious Representation Survey; Note: the figure displays the predicted level of congregational efficacy/identity depending on whether the congregation admits or prohibits female clergy, holding all other variables in the multivariate analysis constant at their means.; Error bars are 95% confidence intervals for each statistical estimate.; The y-axis is modified to show detail.

associated with their congregations regardless of whether their congregation ordains women. Political liberals and Democrats, however, have lower levels of trust, identification, and efficacy when they attend a congregation that does not ordain women compared to one that does, and the effect is stronger for liberals than for Democrats.

Our final piece of evidence is found in Figures 8.14 and 8.15. Here we once again examine statistically estimated comparisons between hypothetical conservatives and liberals, Republicans and Democrats in three different types congregations: those with male-dominant leadership, female-dominant leadership, and gender-egalitarian leadership. Again, these combine the effect of all three types of religious representation in leadership while statistically controlling for a variety of other demographic, religious, and contextual factors that could also contribute to levels of religiosity, spirituality, and congregational efficacy/identity.

Figures 8.14 and 8.15 show that both liberals and Democrats are demobilized in their levels of religiosity and congregational efficacy/identity when they find themselves in congregations with male-dominant leadership. Specifically, liberals and Democrats have levels of religiosity that are 15% and 11% lower when they attend congregations with male-dominant leadership as compared to female-dominant leadership. Their rates of congregational efficacy/identity are reduced even more by male-dominated leadership, with dips of 24% and 17%, respectively. Similar to what we have observed before with women and theological

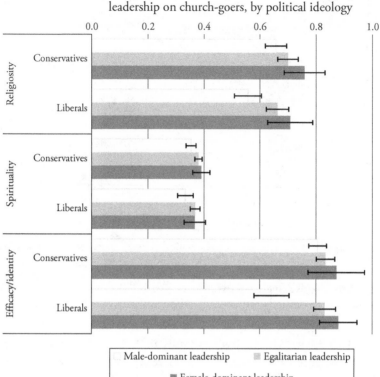

Predicted effect of male- and female-dominant congregational
leadership on church-goers, by political ideology

FIGURE 8.14 Gender and Religious Representation Survey; Note: the figure displays the predicted
level of each outcome for political liberals and conservatives in three hypothetical congregations: one
that maximizes female leadership, one that maximizes male leadership, and one that shares leadership
equally between men and women, holding all other variables in the multivariate analysis constant at
their means.; Error bars are 95% confidence intervals for each statistical estimate.

progressives, levels of religiosity and efficacy/identity are just about as high for
liberals and Democrats in congregations that ordain women and attain gender
parity in the lay leadership as they are in congregations that amplify female leadership. Comparable to earlier patterns, liberals and Democrats do not need ex-
clusive female leadership to stay strong in their religiosity and congregational
efficacy/identity; they respond just as well to congregations that share the leadership evenly between men and women.

Figure 8.14 also shows that political conservatives actually have levels of religiosity about 10% higher in congregations that maximize female leadership
compared to those that maximize male leadership. They also have a very small
(3%) increase in their levels of spirituality in gender-egalitarian congregations
than those in male-dominant congregations. (A similar increase is found among

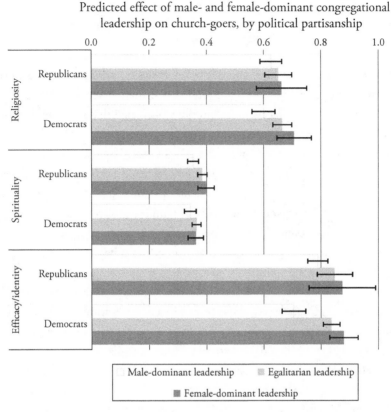

Predicted effect of male- and female-dominant congregational leadership on church-goers, by political partisanship

FIGURE 8.15 Gender and Religious Representation Survey; Note: the figure displays the predicted level of each outcome for Democrats and Republicans in three hypothetical congregations: one that maximizes female leadership, one that maximizes male leadership, and one that shares leadership equally between men and women, holding all other variables in the multivariate analysis constant at their means.; Error bars are 95% confidence intervals for each statistical estimate.

Republicans, as shown in Figure 8.15) On the other hand, there are no statistically significant differences in congregational efficacy/identity for conservatives and Republicans when comparing male-dominant, gender-egalitarian, and female-dominant congregations.

From these results it seems that seeing more women in congregational leadership inspires political conservatives to attend religious services, pray, and read scriptures a little more often, and they are just as happy and trusting in their congregations as they are when men are at the helm. Political liberals and Democrats, in contrast, are less trusting of their leaders and less emotionally connected to their congregations in the presence of male-dominant leadership, and a little less likely to attend services, pray, and talk to others about their faith than they are when their congregations share the leadership evenly between men and women.

COMPARING OUR FACE-TO-FACE INTERVIEWS WITH PUBLIC OPINION
SURVEY RESULTS

This chapter and the last have approached our key questions from two different perspectives and yet we nonetheless found that in many cases they tended to tell the same basic story. Our face-to-face interviews revealed that many who attend religious services perceive the presence of a woman at the pulpit to have a religiously empowering effect on young women and girls in that they may feel more inspired to pursue a call to the ministry or to be more engaged in their religious lives and congregations. Some also believed that a female pastor may have a positive influence on attendance and involvement, especially by families and teenagers.

Our quantitative results found evidence of a complementary type of empowerment: the presence of female leaders or gender-inclusive policies can produce a modest boost in levels of religiosity, spirituality, and congregational efficacy/identity among women in those congregations. More specifically, we uncovered evidence that the presence of female pastors or priests in a congregation is associated with a small increase in levels of religiosity (church attendance, volunteering, prayer, etc.) among women of the millennial generation. The face-to-face interviews suggest that this is likely because they feel that they are better able to relate to their congregational leader if that leader is a woman. This is especially noteworthy as the research described earlier in the chapter indicated that young women are particularly likely to have dropped out of religious lifestyles over the last several years. We also found that expanding all three types of female leadership in a congregation, or even equalizing clergy and lay leadership between men and women, can produce a moderate increase in attendance and other religious behaviors among women and also among political liberals and Democrats.

As we described earlier, one of our interviewees pointed out that gender and leadership is a nonissue in her congregation because everyone already knows what their congregation believes on the topic and they would not attend if they disagreed with their congregation's position (Interview 49). While this may be a bit of an overstatement, one of the most consistent findings from our public opinion surveys is that those on the left side of the religious and political spectrums (theological modernists, political liberals, and Democrats) are disempowered in their levels of congregational efficacy/identity and demobilized in their religious behaviors in the absence of any female clergy. We saw in Chapter 4 that these same individuals are more supportive of female ordination regardless of their congregations' policies on the topic. It makes sense that they would also then feel disempowered in these congregations when they feel that their congregations do not represent their beliefs and values.

While this evidence suggests that gender leadership in American congregations certainly matters in terms of its impact on those in the pews, we also note that its effect is perhaps not as universal or strong as advocates often assume. Many of the quantitative results shown here are modest in size and manifest most often in their effect on congregational efficacy and identity. There were also many contexts in which efficacy/identity, behavior, and spirituality were *not* substantially affected (or not affected at all) by the presence or absence of women in a congregation's leadership. These quantitative findings align well with statements from several of our interviewees who maintained that while the gender of a congregational leader is important, the individual personality and leadership style of the pastor or priest matter more.

SUMMARY AND CONCLUSION

We introduced the previous chapter by asking whether women who are in congregations with more inclusive gender policies or practices would respond with higher levels of religious empowerment as expressed through their religious behaviors, levels of spirituality, and feelings of efficacy, trust, and identity toward the congregation. This was motivated by many arguments that advocates of female ordination have made in previous years as well as political science research on the concept of representation and the effect it can have on the political behavior of minority groups in society. Given the pervasive gender gap in female leadership in both religious and secular contexts, we wanted to gain a better understanding of the extent to which this gender gap influences the religious behavior of American congregants. To what extent and in what ways does gender representation affect individuals in America's places of worship?

A summary of this chapter's quantitative public opinion results is found in Table 8.1. On the whole, the results we uncovered are moderate but positive for women in congregations with more gender-inclusive leadership, whether in policy or practice. In contrast, those on the left side of the theological/political spectrum (both men as well as women) are in some ways impaired by the presence of male-only policies or practices in their congregations and bolstered by female-oriented congregational leadership.

It is important to again note that the effect of gender-inclusive leadership on religious attitudes and behavior of parishioners, where manifest, seems to create only upsides and no downsides, with very few exceptions. Where the effects are present, they serve only to *increase* religiosity, spirituality, and especially congregational efficacy/identity among women and sometimes even among men. (This is similar to

TABLE 8.1

Summary of results: gender congregational leadership on religiosity, spirituality, and efficacy/identity

	Effect on religiosity	Effect on spirituality	Effect on efficacy/identity
Currently have a woman as congregational leader compared to a man (9% of congregations)	Women under age 40 are 10% higher. Liberals are 10% higher.	Theological liberals are 5% lower on spirituality compared to traditionalists in congregations led by men; *no difference in spirituality led by women.*	Liberals are 9% higher. Democrats are 5% higher. Theological progressives are 10% lower than traditionalists when they have male clergy; *no difference between the two when they have female clergy.*
Current congregation permits women to serve as congregational leader compared to those that do not.(55% of congregations)	Liberals are about 7% higher, matching levels among conservatives.	Everyone is 2% higher.	Women are 8% higher. Theological progressives are 13% lower in congregations with male-only policies; *traditionalists are high regardless of gender policies.* Liberals are 13% higher. Democrats 8% higher.
Women make up more than half of congregational lay leaders compared to those where they do not. (37% of congregations)	Everyone is 5% higher.	Women are 3% higher.	Women are 10% higher. This can also help compensate for male-only congregational policies among women.
All three types of female leadership present (5% of congregations) compared to all three absent (29% of congregations)	Women are 13% higher. Liberals are 15% higher. Democrats are 11% higher.		This can also help compensate for male clergy among women. Women are 19% higher. Theological progressives are 23% higher. Liberals are 24% higher. Democrats are 17% higher.

Karp and Banducci 2008, who show that the presence of more women in national legislatures produces more positive attitudes about the political process for both women *and* men in those countries.) If anything, we see that the absence of female leadership can actually decrease levels of efficacy/identity among women, theological progressives, and political conservatives.

In this sense, this chapter's findings are similar to those reported by Djupe and Olson (2013) and Djupe (2014) who found contingent and somewhat limited effects of gender representation on the political attitudes and behaviors of women in Mainline Protestant congregations. Ultimately, Djupe (2014) concluded that female leadership matters "a little" in shaping the political attitudes and participation of women in their congregations. Our analysis can be described similarly: descriptive gender representation much of the time matters a little in shaping the religious attitudes and behaviors of American churchgoers, although sometimes it can matter a lot, especially for women and liberals.

More specifically, our results also show that, hypothetically, if female leadership were equalized in religious congregations by implementing gender-inclusive leadership policies and making sure that lay leadership positions were equally distributed between men and women, Democrats and political/theological liberals would avoid being disempowered and demobilized in their levels of religiosity and feelings of efficacy/identity toward their congregation. We also see that equalizing the presence of women in the nation's pulpits would not substantively affect levels of religiosity or congregational efficacy/identity for men, Republicans, or political/theological conservatives. To look at it another way, male-only clergy is often disempowering and demobilizing to women and those on the left, but equalizing gender leadership empowers women and those on the left without affecting men and conservatives either way. In levels of religiosity and congregational efficacy/identity, especially, there are only upsides to maximizing female clergy and religious leadership and a few significant downsides for maintaining male-only leadership policies and practices.

These results have some important theoretical implications. First, they show that the empowering potential of descriptive representation is not limited only to political contexts. Similar to what we saw in Chapter 6 regarding the effect of gender and role models in a person's youth, we have shown here that women can be affected by the *current* presence, absence, or even the *potential* presence of other women leaders in their religious congregations. This theoretically advances the research started by Djupe and Olson (2013) and Djupe (2014), who showed that female representation can motivate women in religious congregations to engage in civic and political activities. It also corresponds with research by Seymour et al. (2014), who showed that the strength of people's relationships with their clergy are a key factor that enhances trust in their congregations. In this case, our results suggest a potential linking mechanism: women in congregations with female leaders may be more likely to develop stronger ties with their congregational leaders, as they perceive their leaders to be similar to them. It seems that human social behavior can respond similarly to gender leadership cues whether in political or religious contexts.

Second, these results suggest that descriptive representation in religious contexts can have a spillover effect into other social domains. Representation theory predicts descriptive representation to have the most salient effect on the groups being descriptively represented. Specifically, we should expect that the presence or absence of women in congregational leadership should primarily influence the women in the pews. While we uncovered evidence of this, we also found evidence that descriptive representation can exert an effect on groups *not* defined primarily by gender, specifically groups defined by theological orthodoxy or political orientation. It seems, then, that the influence of descriptive representation is not always limited to the groups being represented. In this case specifically, it may be possible that theological and political liberals are more likely to develop close ties to their religious leaders when those leaders are women, perhaps on the assumption that women are generally more likely to agree with them on their theological and political orientations (see Deckman et al. 2003 and Smidt 2016, for example). This potentially has important and wide-reaching implications for our understanding of representation in both religious as well as political contexts.

Third, the finding that descriptive gender representation can manifest itself along theological and political lines in addition to gender lines is perhaps not surprising once we consider that the last few decades have witnessed a tectonic shift in the political, religious, and ideological coalitions of the American public. In the middle of the twentieth century, religion defined politics by group membership status: Protestants were Republicans and Catholics and Jews were Democrats. Fast-forward to the early twenty-first century, when religious group affiliation is now only weakly associated with partisanship. The new fault lines are religious behaviors and belief orthodoxy: devout traditionalists are Republicans while less-active progressives are Democrats, regardless of whether they are Catholics, Protestants, or subscribe to a different doctrine. There is now a strong alignment between religious orientation and political partisanship that was not the case several decades ago (Putnam and Campbell 2012, chap. 11).

Pair that with research by Mark Chaves (1997), which argues that women's ordination serves as a "signaling" device that religious communities use to communicate their ideologies to one another and to form denominational alliances. Religious traditions that want to signal their embrace of post-Enlightenment modernity and classical liberal individualism have done so by embracing women's ordination over the last half-century. Those who wish to signal both to society and to other traditions that they are resisting modernism and holding fast to "traditional values" do so by maintaining male-only leadership policies.

Given these realities, it is not surprising that political liberals and Democrats, who are more likely to espouse Enlightenment egalitarian and individualistic views when it comes to gender and society, are more negatively affected in their feelings of congregational efficacy and identity by the absence of female leadership in religious congregations: they feel that their interests and values are not being represented in the structure and organization of their congregations.

The results from this chapter can also serve to reassure defenders of male-only clergy who worry that having a woman in the pulpit will demotivate men or drive them away from their congregations (see Lehman 1981, 1985, chap. 5; Pivec 2006). The results show that these concerns are unfounded. There is no evidence from either our qualitative or quantitative evidence that more female leadership (whether in the pulpit or lay leadership) or more inclusive gender leadership policies depress religious behaviors or attitudes among men *or* women, theological traditionalists *or* progressives, Republicans *or* Democrats. Quite the opposite, in fact: these findings suggest that female leaders are a little better in some ways at motivating their congregations to higher levels of religiosity and personal empowerment in their congregations.

If anything, our results indicate that the lack of female leadership often serves to religiously *disempower* women, theological progressives, and political liberals. Some of our strongest findings are that congregations with male-dominant leadership arrangements significantly drive down feelings of congregational efficacy, trust, and identification among these groups. It also depresses levels of church attendance, prayer, scripture reading, volunteering, and other religious behaviors among women, political liberals, and Democrats. This is important because these are some of the groups most likely to have left organized religion in recent years. If congregations were to implement more gender-inclusive policies and practices in their leadership positions, this might help slow or even stop this exodus, and contribute to the diversity, growth, and long-term vitality of these congregations.

NOTES

1. Collective representation theoretically could also be manifest by the gender makeup of the denomination's regional, national, and global governing boards, conferences, or other authoritative bodies. We unfortunately do not have the data available to determine this level of contextual information for each survey respondent, but is a compelling topic for future research.

2. More details about the three combined index variables can be found in the Data Appendix; all statistical analyses in this chapter apply the same data weights as described in previous empirical chapters and in the Data Appendix.

3. The control variables we use in each of the multivariate models in this chapter are: gender of congregational leader, whether the congregation permits female clergy, whether at least half of the congregation's lay leadership is composed of women, belief orthodoxy, political ideology, political partisanship, age, black, Latino, education, income, Jewish, and non-Christian. As was the case in Chapter 4, we include Jewish and non-Christian as control variables due to the difference of cultural, congregational, and theological structures that may influence support for female religious leaders in those traditions.

4. In other words, we present and discuss the findings for those relationships in which the independent variables were statistically significant in the multivariate models. In some cases, the error bars overlap slightly in the figures despite a statistically significant ($p \leq 0.05$ unless otherwise noted) relationship in the regression estimate. For more on statistically significant relationships having overlapping error bars, see Payton, Greenstone, and Schenker (2003).

5. This relationship is statistically significant at $p = 0.06$.

6. In more technical terms, the interactive effect of the two variables in the regression model is insignificant but the two constituent terms are.

7. This relationship is statistically significant at $p = 0.08$.

8. This relationship is statistically significant at $p = 0.09$.

9. To keep things concise, we collapse the political orthodoxy variable into a binary variable with two categories: religious traditionalist (my religion or church should "preserve traditional beliefs and practices") and religious moderate/modernist (my religion or church should "adjust beliefs and practices in light of new circumstances" or "adopt modern beliefs and practices").

CONCLUSION

Clergywomen Matter

IN MAY OF 2016 the United Methodist Church (UMC) gathered in Portland, Oregon, for its quadrennial general conference to discuss issues facing the church and to consider revising church law and policies. A few days before the gathering a satirical news article reported the following:

> A new proposal to ban "self-avowed, practicing women" from ordination is gaining momentum.
>
> A sizable number of delegates to the denomination's General Conference are also seeking to defrock en masse the women ordained since the UMC first gave in to the culture of radical feminism 60 years ago.
>
> One #Defrock4Jesus movement leader is Institute on Religion & Democracy's Twitter-troll-in-chief Mark Tooley, who claimed proponents had secured enough votes to win. "Methodist membership has been in free fall since women's ordination was condoned. Simple logic tells who's to blame. We must repent and revert to the biblical understanding of women being silent in church." (Graves-Fitzsimmons 2016)

The purpose of the article was to satirize the decision that the UMC faced regarding the proposed ordination of "self-avowed, practicing homosexuals," which (at the time of this writing) is prohibited by church law. Ultimately, the conference decided to delay discussion on the issue and appointed a special commission to further research and consider the proposal (Miller 2016). The fact that the ordination of women was used to satirize the proposed ordination of LGBT individuals speaks to how much the conversation on women's ordination has changed over the last century in many American religious denominations.[1]

We described in the introductory chapter that women's ordination continues to be a highly salient and controversial issue in many religious communities. Those that ordain women currently engage in conversations about the balance of men and women in clerical positions as well as issues like the pay gap and work-life balance. Those that do not ordain women are often *forced* to have conversations about the issue, whether driven by external pressures or internal advocacy. When Pope Francis appointed a committee to study the possibility of ordaining women as deacons in the world's largest Christian denomination, the action demonstrated that discussion and conversation on this issue will continue for some time to come (Povoledo and Goodstein 2016).

Questions about women's ordination in America's congregations do not exist in a vacuum. These conversations take place within wider discussions of societal gender roles and the advancement of women in the economic, social, and political spheres. While much progress was made in the 1970s, 1980s, and early 1990s toward closing the gender gap in various aspects of society, it was followed by a stalling effect that has been evident since about the mid-1990s. Given that gender equality in the economic, social, and political spheres is linked to gender equality in the religious sphere, we set out to answer two key questions in this book: 1) who supports women's ordination in their congregations and why?, and 2) what effect do female pastors, priests, rabbis, and other leaders have on those in their congregations? As political scientists, we used the tools of our discipline to analyze both face-to-face interviews as well as a nationally representative telephone/internet public opinion survey that measured the opinions and behaviors of hundreds of people. In addition to shedding light on the role of women and leadership in religious congregations specifically, we hoped to determine whether the role of women in religious leadership can help us understand other patterns in women's advancement and gender roles in American society over the last several decades. This book documents what we learned.

SUMMARY AND REVIEW OF KEY RESEARCH FINDINGS

Similar to other research (Chaves and Eagle 2015), our Gender and Religious Representation Survey found that slightly over half of our respondents attend congregations that allow women to serve as the principal religious leader, though only about 10% of congregations currently have a woman serving in that capacity. About 16% of congregations that ordain women currently have a woman serving as the head pastor, priest, or rabbi. Also, about 40% of our respondents attend congregations in which women make up at least half of the lay ministry and small group leaders. Women make up at least half of the lay ministry almost 60% of the time in congregations with a clergywoman and about a third of the time congregations with a clergyman. About 72% of American congregants report that they support women being permitted to serve as the chief leader in their congregations. This stated level of support is moderately consistent across a variety of demographic, religious, and political subgroups. Support is higher than 50% virtually across the board, including stated support of about 85% for Mainline and Black Protestants and about 70% for Catholics and Evangelical Protestants.

When asked to explain their views on female clergy being permitted to serve in their congregations (either for or against), our face-to-face interviewees cited scriptural authority, personal experiences with a female pastor or priest, and gender stereotypes as influencing their opinions. Scriptural authority and gender stereotypes were selectively used to justify *both* support for and opposition to the idea of female clergy. Several female pastors also noticed that most of the resistance that they encounter tends to come from middle-aged and older women.

When asked if they would *personally* prefer a man or woman as their congregation's chief leader, about half of American churchgoers said that it did not matter one way or another. Of those who do have a preference, the vast majority prefer men and a few prefer women. In all, less than 10% of our survey respondents explicitly stated that they would prefer a woman as their personal congregational leader compared to a little over 40% who said they would prefer a man. This is the case even among those who would personally prefer that their congregation allow women to serve as clergy. Those who would specifically prefer a woman to be their personal congregational leader tend to come from congregations that currently have a female leader, while those who would prefer a man tend to be men who are religiously active and orthodox and who are in congregations with male-only policies.

Our public opinion surveys also revealed that those who support female clergy in their congregations tend to have a few key characteristics in common. They tend to be more progressive in their belief orthodoxy (more likely to believe that their religion or church "should adopt modern beliefs and practices"), less active in their religious attendance and behaviors, more likely to identify politically as Democrats, and also more likely to attend congregations that currently allow for women to serve as pastors or priests. We also found some evidence that those with a lower sensitivity to the "purity/sanctity" moral foundation (Haidt 2012) are more likely to be supportive.

Analysis revealed congregational context to be a key mediating factor in explaining this support for female ordination. The vast majority of churchgoers in congregations that allow for female clergy support women's ordination, regardless of their level of belief orthodoxy, religious behaviors, or political attitudes. Opinions diverge, though, in congregations with male-only leadership policies. In these congregations, religiously active and theological/political traditionalists are more likely to endorse their congregation's position of male-only ordination while religiously less-active and theological/political progressives are more likely to buck their congregation's position and claim support for female ordination. All in all, there is little evidence that gender matters a great deal in explaining support for or opposition to female clergy. Whether a person is a man or a woman makes little difference in explaining preferences on this topic once other religious and political factors are accounted for.

We suspected that there is some degree of social desirability that affects how our respondents answered questions on this topic in our surveys; it is possible that some people who in reality oppose women's ordination might have felt pressure to say the opposite so as to not appear sexist to the interviewers. We tested this possibility with a list experiment survey approach and found evidence that this is indeed the case. The results from this survey tool suggest that support for female clergy is likely closer to around 55% rather than the 72% indicated by direct responses to the question, meaning that around one in six American churchgoers may feel pressure to say "yes" on the issue of female ordination when they privately think "no." This social desirability effect helps explain the disparity between the high percentage of stated support for gender equality in leadership (approximately 72%) and the low percentages of congregations that are actually led by a woman (approximately 9%).

Our list experiment results also showed evidence that actual support for female ordination is much lower among women than among men, including the provocative finding that the list experiment was not able to confidently uncover any degree of support among Catholic women despite the fact that about two-thirds of Catholic women express support when asked directly. Further, the list experiment showed that there is actually less support among the groups that were most likely to *say* that they support female ordination. These include theological and political progressives as well as those who attend congregations with male-only leadership policies. That said, the list experiment approach is not without its critics, and we urge caution in the interpretation of the findings from this particular survey tool.

Given our initial questions about the role of women in wider society as well as their personal and economic empowerment, we examined whether having women exercise leadership in religious congregations in people's youth could affect their levels of self-esteem, self-efficacy, educational attainment, employment, and view of God as adults. We found that female role models do indeed make a difference in each of these aspects of individual empowerment. Most often, it works through the gender of someone's most influential pastor or priest growing up, although the overall frequency of women clergy growing up also makes a difference.

Our results showed that having had influential female religious congregational leaders when growing up is associated with higher levels of both personal and economic empowerment for women as adults, to the extent that the gender gap on these two outcomes disappears entirely. Further, influential religious leaders in a girl's youth are associated with increased levels of educational attainment, self-efficacy, self-esteem, and even more gracious views of God as adults. This is important because it strongly suggests that part of the gap in personal, economic, and societal empowerment between men and women today is at least partially attributable to the lack of female role models and representation in religious congregations when people are young. It also suggests that an increase in women's leadership in America's places of worship could help women's advancement in secular fields. Improvements in women's self-esteem, self-efficacy, employment, and educational attainment could help close the gender gap in both business and political arenas.

We also examined the role of gender and clergy when it comes to how people relate to their congregations. In our face-to-face interviews, most were quick to say that gender "doesn't matter" but then went on to describe several ways they believed it *does* matter. For example, many respondents talked about how women at the pulpit can be inspiring and empowering for young women and girls in terms of how they view their potential in both the secular and religious worlds, although others pointed out that female lay leaders could produce the same effect in the absence of a head clergywoman. Other interviewees observed that clergy gender can affect what issues parishioners can talk about with their leader in a pastoral setting and that it can influence which groups of people are more likely to attend the congregation.

Our public opinion surveys revealed that theological and political progressives are somewhat *disempowered* in a religious sense when they are in congregations with male leaders and male-only leadership policies. There is also evidence that inclusive gender policies have a moderate *empowering* effect for women in terms of their levels of religious behavior, spirituality, and efficacy/identity in their congregations. Many of these effects are often modest, however. Female clergy (or its absence) appears to matter "a little" in terms of either boosting or dampening religious attitudes and behaviors but it appears to matter a bit more for theological and political liberals than for women. There is also no evidence that female pastors or priests are associated with any decreases in desirable religious outcomes among men, theological traditionalists, or political conservatives.

While the effects of female clergy are in many cases modest, we also found that if a congregation were to *equalize* female inclusivity and leadership by allowing women to serve as congregational leaders and ensuring that half of the lay leadership was made up of women, levels of religious behavior and efficacy/identity would improve substantially among women in the congregation as well as among theological progressives and political liberals. Conversely, the same statistical analysis estimates that male-only congregations that have a majority-male lay leadership body are associated with *lower* levels of religious behavior and efficacy/identity among women and theological/political progressives. Currently, about 30% of American congregations maximize male leadership while only about 5% maximize female leadership.

THE PERSISTENT GENDER GAP IN RELIGIOUS LEADERSHIP

At the outset of this book we situated the gender gap in religious leadership within a broader framework of gender inequality in leadership throughout American society. In both secular and religious contexts, in business and in political arenas, women's advancement appears to have stalled since about the mid-1990s after a spurt of activity in the 1970s and 1980s. Despite widespread stated support for gender equality in politics, employment, and business, the numbers of women in leadership positions remains far from representative of their numbers in the American public. This is the case in religious congregations as well. In Chapter 2 we saw that about two out of every three American worshipers state support for female clergy, but only about one in ten American congregations is led by a woman. While we do not have simple or clear-cut explanations for these trends, our findings from Chapters 2 through 5 revealed a number of helpful insights that provide pieces of the overall puzzle. For example, Chapter 3 showed that among the clergy and congregants we interviewed, scripture and sacred texts emerged as two of the most frequently cited motivations that influenced whether people were in favor of female clergy. These findings were echoed in our quantitative analysis in Chapter 4, which showed that belief orthodoxy is one of the primary predictors of support or opposition. The importance of scriptural authority and belief orthodoxy to an individual's stance on female ordination suggests that sincere theological belief is a primary factor in explaining the gender gap in clergy leadership.

While sincere theological belief is undoubtedly a contributing factor for many, further analysis pointed to the importance of congregational context. This appeared first in Chapter 3: we found that the vast majority of our interviewees hold the same opinions on the topic of female ordination as their congregations. Analysis in Chapter 4 confirmed the importance of congregational context: while belief orthodoxy mattered in predicting support for female clergy among those in congregations with male-only leadership policies, congregations that currently have a woman in charge can claim that the vast majority of *both* theological traditionalists and theological modernists are supportive of female clergy. This remained consistent even after testing for a social desirability effect. This suggests that sincere theological belief is certainly one factor in explaining why people oppose female clergy, but congregational context is just as, if not more, important in explaining the phenomenon. One explanation as to why so few congregations are led by women is simply that individuals tend to support what they are familiar with and to follow the cues of their congregational leaders, and nearly half of American worshipers report that they attend congregations in which those leaders defend male-only clerical policies.

Political partisanship can further explain the gender gap in religious leadership. Based on the research of Chaves (1997) that a congregation's stance on clergywomen signals its political or ideological stance combined with studies by Deckman et al. (2003) and Olson et al. (2005) that show clergywomen to be more politically and theologically liberal than clergymen, we predicted that political conservatives and Republicans might hesitate to support female clergy. Chapter 4 provided qualified support for this prediction. Republicans/conservatives were more likely than Democrats/liberals to oppose female ordination, but only in congregations led by men. In congregations led by women, however, Republicans and Democrats alike supported female ordination. Partisanship, then, can help explain opposition to female clergy, but its effectiveness is contingent on congregational context.

While theological belief, congregational context, and political partisanship all reinforce opposition to female clergy and/or the gender gap, they alone are not sufficient to explain the discrepancy between the 72% who state support for gender equality in the abstract and the 9% of congregations that are led by women. Our findings from the list experiment described in Chapter 5 provide some additional insights. Using a survey method that allowed us to indirectly gauge more candid preferences from survey respondents, we found that genuine support for female clergy is likely somewhere around 15% lower than answers to survey questions indicated. This discrepancy is driven primarily by about a third of those who state a preference for allowing female clergy in their congregations to public opinion surveyors but then indicate opposite feelings when given the opportunity to do so candidly and indirectly.

Our list experiment findings also strongly suggest that support for female clergy is in reality much lower among women than it is among men. We found that while about three-quarters of women say they would support their congregations if they were to allow a woman to serve as the principal leader, this figure drops to 40% when women have the opportunity to indirectly express their candid opinions. Also, about 45% of our sample mentioned in Chapter 5 attend congregations that do not currently allow women to serve as the principal religious leader. When asked directly, nearly half of those individuals say they support women being able to serve as their congregation's leader. But in the list experiment, which is designed to allow people to express their unguarded views, support for women clergy drops to about 10%. In all, this suggests that genuine support for gender-inclusive congregational leadership policies is lower than we might expect, based on survey results.

Perhaps the most telling finding from our research that speaks to this issue, as we saw in Chapter 2, is that when asked directly, only about 9% of American worshipers say they would prefer that a woman be the leader of their congregation. This figure is only 11% among women. Even among those who report wanting their congregation to permit female clergy *in principle,* about 14% express a preference for *their* clergyperson to be a woman compared to 30% who prefer a man (with the remaining 56% indicating no preference). When personal preferences for male clergy are twice as high as preferences for female clergy—even among those who support female clergy in the abstract—it is not likely that the remaining half of those in the ambivalent middle will put up a strong fight to hire a female pastor or priest in their congregation (see also Witham 2005, chap. 3). It is also notable that the proportion of American congregants who express an explicit preference for female clergy in their congregations is essentially identical to the number who attend a congregation currently led by a woman: about 9%. Suddenly the vast chasm between stated support for female clergy and actual frequency of female clergy in America's congregations is easier to fathom.

FEMALE CLERGY AND WOMEN'S EMPOWERMENT

In Chapter 7 we described the arguments of some advocates of women's ordination as they relate to female empowerment. Some have argued that seeing a woman in a position of religious and spiritual authority is important for other women because it influences their level of activity, engagement, and identification with their congregation and with religion in general, similar to how women and other minority groups can be mobilized politically when represented by someone of their same group identity. In our conversations with clergy relayed in that chapter, many maintained that their presence has served as an inspiration for girls in their congregations. Because those girls grew up seeing a woman lead, they knew that they, too, could pursue a call to ministry. In this way, clergywomen seem to empower girls within their congregations to believe in themselves and in their potential to lead.

Our quantitative results found supporting evidence in that women have higher levels of efficacy/identity in congregations with more female leadership and sometimes have higher levels of religious behaviors as well. However, we emphasize that this effect is moderate. It remains the case that more women regularly attend religious services in the United States than men and that women outnumber men in denominations with male-only leadership policies (Grant 2015).

Throughout this book we have also discussed how our research might speak to wider questions of the persistent gender gap in the workplace, in paychecks, and in politics. Some have argued that women's leadership in the religious sphere is important because it can have a spillover effect in the secular and professional worlds (Shields 2015). For example, Lawless and Fox (2005) found that one of the major reasons that women are underrepresented in elected office is because they are less likely than men to perceive themselves as qualified for the job. Wiseman and Dutta (2016) also found that states with higher levels of religiosity have higher pay gaps between men and women even after controlling for a host of other demographic and political factors. They argue that religious norms can influence how both employers and employees perceive the relative value of work by men and by women, which accounts for why religious culture influences the size of the pay gap. Might the prevalence of women's ordination in American congregations influence the extent to which women view themselves as qualified to run for office and employers assess the value of work done by women?

Our qualitative face-to-face interviews revealed that many people certainly *perceive* women's ordination to make a difference for young girls, specifically in terms of societal empowerment. Clergy and congregants alike were often of the opinion that seeing a woman in a chief position of leadership at church would help girls and young women internalize that they can occupy positions of power and influence in other areas. We already discussed how clergywomen saw their presence as inspiring girls to believe they could lead in a religious sphere, but many clergy and congregants extended this belief to clergywomen inspiring a sense of empowerment in general.

Our surveys found that fewer than 10% of congregations currently have a female pastor or priest. This means that the vast majority of churchgoing girls and young women see men occupying the principal position of power in their congregations. It is possible that this could affect the degree to which these girls feel they are qualified to be leaders in other areas. For example, this might influence their perceived level of qualification to run for elected office later in life, which may help explain why women are underrepresented in elected office. It also means that the vast majority of churchgoers regularly see a man in the chief position of congregational leadership, which may unconsciously influence how they perceive the value of men's professional work versus women's professional work. This, in turn, may help explain the connection between state-level religiosity and the persistent gender gap in the workplace and in earnings.

The findings outlined in Chapter 6 further support this connection. Our survey results showed that having influential female religious leaders in one's youth has important effects on levels of self-esteem, self-efficacy, and educational attainment among women. For example, women who report that their most influential religious leader in their youth are today as adults employed at rates equal to men. Given the strong connection between self-esteem, self-efficacy, education, employment, and income, we cannot help but conclude that the relatively low rate of female leadership in America's congregations is at least partly responsible for the persistent gender gap in other areas of American society. Our results do not permit us to calculate directly the influence of clergy gender on exact numbers of female CEOs, governors, or college presidents, but our research strongly supports the overall argument that gender equality in our places of worship is an essential piece of the puzzle when it comes to gender equality in society at large. To the extent that America's congregations ordain and hire women as their leaders, we believe that the gender gap in other areas of society will shrink and perhaps in some cases disappear entirely. In sum, the evidence produced by our research powerfully suggests that gender equality in religious congregational leadership is a necessary precondition for gender equality in American society at large.

THE EFFECT OF POLITICS ON RELIGIOUS BEHAVIOR

Religion has influenced politics throughout the history of the United States. Scholars have documented a variety of ways in which religion has shaped social movements (Johnston 2014; Marsh 2006; Smith 1991, 1996; Wiktorowicz 2003), informed presidential rhetoric (Roof 2009; Shogan 2007; G. A. Smith 2008), and infused itself in campaigns and elections (Green, Rozell, and Wilcox 2006; Stecker 2011). They have also documented the various ways in which individual-level religious behaviors and attitudes can influence political opinions and voting patterns (Abramson et al. 2015; Putnam and Campbell 2012; Smidt, Kellstedt, and Guth 2009). Less well documented, though, is how people's *political attitudes* can influence their *religious behavior.*

Chapter 4 demonstrated one way in which political attitudes can shape religious opinions. We saw that individuals' political ideology is a key predictor of whether they support women's ordination in their congregations. The results discussed in Chapter 4 showed that in some cases political attitudes overpower religious doctrine when it comes to women's ordination: liberals and Democrats are more likely to break with the policy of their church when they attend congregations that allow only male clergy, and indicate support for women's ordination. Conservatives and

Republicans, though, tend to defer to whatever policies their congregations have in place: they are in favor of women's ordination when their congregations allow it but are averse when their congregations prohibit it.

We also saw in Chapter 2 another way in which politics can drive religious behavior: people's political ideology is associated with their choice of religious congregation. Liberals and Democrats gravitate toward congregations that allow women to serve in top leadership positions while conservatives and Republicans tend to select congregations that have more male-oriented leadership policies and practices. This, in turn, can influence the general theological orientations and social priorities that the congregations espouse in their efforts to retain and increase their membership. In the marketplace of American religion, there are strong incentives for congregations to pursue goals that are approved by a majority of both their current and potential members. This can serve to perpetuate the status quo when it comes to congregational gender leadership policies.

Our findings also confirm and extend the influential work of Chaves (1997), who argued that women's ordination is a key signaling device that religious institutions use to communicate with each other in their effort to seek and maintain denominational coalitions. "Rules about women's ordination have become one of the key primary markers of a denomination's cultural location" (40). Embracing or resisting women's ordination is thus a key indicator of whether the institution wishes to culturally identify as more liberal/progressive or more conservative/traditionalist. Beyond that, however, Chaves (1997) also argues that women's ordination reflects the denomination's overall orientation toward "modernity" as defined by the Enlightenment prioritization of individual over group rights:

If these connections remain as culturally salient as I believe them still to be, then to resist gender equality is to resist a modernizing, liberal agenda within which individuals have distinctive moral standing qua individuals, and not as members of "natural" groups—families, races, genders—possessing certain "natural" rights and functions. To support gender equality was, and remains, to support the larger project of modernity; to resist gender equality was, and remains, to resist that project.

From this perspective, rules about women's ordination largely serve as symbolic display to the outside world, and they point to (or away from) a broader liberal agenda associated with modernity and religious accommodation to the spirit of the age. From this perspective, a denomination's formal policy about women's ordination is less an indicator of women's literal status within the denomination and more an enactment of its position vis-a-vis the liberal and modern agenda of institutionalizing individual rights.

Women's ordination, then, is about something more than females in religious leadership. (192)

Chaves primarily focused on how these signals are communicated and received between denominations themselves. The research of this book has broadened this finding to the individual level of those in the pews. Chapter 4 showed that some of the strongest advocates for women's ordination are political liberals and Democrats and Chapter 8 demonstrated that liberals and Democrats are also the groups most strongly affected by the presence or absence of female congregational leadership. If women's ordination advertises a denomination's orientation toward modernity, then it seems that those in the pews are picking up on that signal loud and clear. Political liberals and Democrats, who are generally much more supportive of the modern prioritization of individual rights, are also most likely to be demobilized in their levels of congregational efficacy and identity when their congregations maintain male-only leadership policies. They perceive that their congregational leaders do not generally share their fundamental social and ethical values.

This is another way in which politics drives religion in contemporary American society. Chapters 7 and 8 show that gender representation exerts an influence on behavior in religious contexts just as it does for behavior in political contexts. While the selection method for congregational clergy varies by religious tradition and denomination, we argued in Chapter 7 that there is at least some element of democratic choice when it comes to congregational leaders. There is good reason to think that clergy are incentivized to be responsive to the wishes and interests of those in their congregations, just as political representatives have an incentive to pay attention to the views of their constituents. Our research has shown that "religious representation" in congregations matters for the attitudes and behaviors of those in the congregation, which is an important theoretical contribution to our understanding of the nature of leadership, authority, and human behavior. The effects of representation are not limited to political contexts.

Chapter 8 also demonstrated that descriptive gender representation can activate the same effects as substantive representation. By this we mean that the individuals most responsive to female leadership in their congregations were not necessarily other women. Indeed, Chapter 4 discussed that women are just as likely to indicate support for female ordination as men while Chapter 5 revealed that support for women's ordination is likely *lower* among women than it is among men. Chapter 8 indicated that the effects of female religious leadership are sometimes present for women but are much stronger for political liberals and partisan Democrats. Descriptive gender representation can thus have a spillover effect into other domains, in this case political identity groups. This is another theoretical contribution to our understanding of the nature of representation and another example of how politics can drive religious behavior in American congregations.

Attendance and membership rates in Mainline Protestant denominations have been declining for the past several decades (Cooperman and Smith 2015). The satirical article we cited at the beginning of this chapter linked this recent decline to the choice to begin ordaining women in the 1950s, 1960s, and 1970s. It is obvious that the author is skeptical of this causal relationship, but it reveals that this is an argument that nonetheless strikes a chord with many religious leaders.

The logic is that compromise on traditional doctrines and practices (such as allowing women to serve as the congregation's primary religious leader) detracts from the vitality of tradition in the eyes of devout members who desire structure, certainty, and a strong resistance to the shifting winds of social change. This is supported by scholars who have identified the trend that "strict" churches, which are almost always theologically conservative and traditionalist in their outlooks, tend to grow and attract members at faster rates than churches with fewer behavioral expectations of their adherents (Finke and Stark 2005; Iannaccone 1994). A surefire way to lose members, according to this school of thought, is to give in to pressure on social and political issues, including women's ordination.

While our findings do not address this question at the aggregate level, we do not find much support for this perspective at the individual level. Theoretically, if this argument is correct we should expect to see individuals in congregations that ordain women and especially those with female pastors to have lower levels of attendance and congregational identification than those who attend congregations with male-only leadership policies. Our research has uncovered no support for this hypothesis, however. In fact, we observe just the opposite: levels of attendance and other religious behaviors are slightly *higher* in congregations that ordain women and moderately higher for younger women in congregations with a female pastor or priest. We also found that trust and identification with one's congregation is higher for both women and liberals when they attend congregations with higher levels of female leadership. At the individual level, at least, there seems to be no evidence to support the concern that women's ordination will weaken people's commitment to a congregation. This was the case even for theological traditionalists and political conservatives, whose levels of religious behaviors and congregational efficacy/identity were just as high in congregations that ordain women as in those that do not.

Of course, this analysis examines only those who report attending a religious congregation at least occasionally, so we are not able to see whether women's ordination affected those who no longer attend a congregation at all. We can further address this question by examining responses to Waves 2 and 3 of our Gender and Religious Representation Survey. After asking respondents to report about how often they attend religious services, we asked a follow-up question to those who said that they attend never, seldom, or a few times a year: "Which of the following factors, if any, would affect your decision to attend religious services either more or less often?" Options included "having friends or family in the congregation" and "having meaningful opportunities to volunteer and give service." They also included "if the principal leader of the congregation were the same gender as you" and "if the congregation permitted women to serve as the principal leader, regardless of whether the current leader was male or female." We wanted to see if there were any evidence that a congregation's policies on gender and leadership would influence people to attend religious services more often, specifically those who rarely or never attend.

Table 9.1 reports the results of these survey questions. Similar to the results of our face-to-face interviews described in Chapter 7, it seems that infrequent church attenders do not care much whether a congregation has a male or female leader, or at least they don't care enough that it would motivate them to attend more regularly. About two-thirds of women and almost three-quarters of men said it would not matter. About 15% of both men and women said that they would attend more often if their congregational leader were the same gender as them, but about an equal number said this would make them *less* likely to attend more often.

On the other hand, Table 9.1 also shows that less-frequent attenders may be a little more responsive to the gender policies of potential congregations. About 32% said that they would be more likely to attend a congregation if it permitted women to serve as the principal leader whereas about 16% said they would be *less* likely, with the other half ambivalent. This is more or less the same for women as for men. Among infrequently attending Millennials, however, 43% said that they would be more likely to attend if their congregation were to permit women to serve as the congregational leader, similar to the 45% of Democrats and 40% of political liberals. This is noteworthy especially because Millennials and liberals are less likely to attend religious services than their older and conservative counterparts. It suggests that male-only leadership policies may be at least part of the story that explains why younger people attend religious services at lower rates than older people.

TABLE 9.1

Reported likelihood of attending religious services more frequently among infrequent and never-attenders[a]

	Much/somewhat more likely	Much/somewhat less likely	Would not matter either way (volunteered response)
"If the principal leader of the congregation were the same gender as you."			
Overall	15.6%	16.0%	68.4%
Women	15.7%	20.6%	63.7%
Men	15.4%	12.0%	72.6%
"If the congregation permitted women to serve as the principal leader, regardless of whether the current leader was male or female."			
Overall	31.7%	15.8%	52.5%
Women	32.3%	17.1%	50.6%
Men	31.3%	14.6%	51.6%
Millennials (under 40)	43.3%	11.2%	45.5%
Non-Millennials (over 40)	25.1%	18.4%	56.5%
Liberals	39.7%	9.5%	50.8%
Conservatives	18.7%	25.2%	56.1%
Democrats	44.7%	11.2%	44.1%
Republicans	18.1%	25.6%	56.3%

[a] *Source:* Gender and Religious Representation Survey; Question wording: "Which of the following factors, if any, would affect your decision to attend religious services either more or less often? Please indicate whether each factor would make you much more likely, somewhat more likely, somewhat less likely or much less likely to attend religious services at a particular congregation." (Asked only of those who indicated that they attend religious services infrequently or never.)

Nevertheless, we do not claim that our data are able to provide a direct test of the strict church hypothesis (Finke and Stark 2005; Iannaccone 1994). The survey findings in Table 9.1 are a snapshot of Americans at a single point in time and do not tell us whether these individuals were in a religious congregation in the past or why they attend at lower rates than others. Our wider survey findings in this book also do not measure whether the respondents have at any point moved from a conservative to a liberal church (or vice versa) in response to the congregation's gender leadership policies. Moreover, the results say nothing about the relative growth rate of the respondents' congregations over time. What our evidence does demonstrate, though, is that most individuals who currently attend congregations whose pastor is a woman are just as religiously active and invested in their church communities as those whose priest is a man, which should give pause to the conventional wisdom that modernization by a religious tradition inevitably leads to decline and apathy among adherents.

A FURTHER EFFECT OF POLITICS ON RELIGIOUS BEHAVIOR

While our findings challenge the argument that women's ordination is to blame for the decline in Mainline Protestant denominations over the past half-century, they do support another hypothesized relationship for this decline. Putnam and Campbell (2012) analyzed decades of public opinion data on American religious and political attitudes and concluded that the drop in attendance among younger Americans is more likely due to the strong link between the "religious right" and conservative politics in the 1970s and 1980s.

Their argument, in brief, goes like this: younger people are generally more politically liberal than older generations. Those who came of age in the 1990s and early 2000s observed an environment in which religion and politics had become polarized along with the rest of society: highly religious people tended to identify as conservative and vote Republican, and more secular individuals tended to identify as liberal and vote Democratic. Many of these younger people, having a liberal political identification, thought to themselves: "If being religious means being conservative, then being religious isn't for me!" They perceived organized Christianity at large (progressive as well as traditional denominations) as part and parcel of the religious right's political-religious coalition, so the liberal-leaning Mainline denominations suffered in attendance as a result (Miller 2016). This is because those who would have attended Mainline congregations due to their ideological affinity were so turned off by the religious right that they decided to opt out of organized religion entirely. Traditional denominations, for their part, did not initially experience the same decline because conservative young adults did not see a conflict between their religious and political identities.

This, according to Putnam and Campbell (2012, chaps. 3–4), is at least part of the reason why Mainline denominations (many of which ordained women in the twentieth century) have seen a decline in affiliation while conservative-leaning denominations (which have mostly maintained their male-only leadership policies) have stayed level (Cooperman and Smith 2015). One could even argue from this perspective that the political activities of theologically traditional denominations in the second half of the twentieth century indirectly contributed to the decline of membership in theologically progressive denominations during that same time. The link between Mainline denominations' ordaining women and losing membership is thus a classic case of "correlation but not causation."

Our findings add complementary support for this alternative explanation. We have extended the argument of Chaves (1997) that congregations use gender policies to communicate their basic cultural and theological orientations. We have also found that political liberals and Democrats can be negatively affected by male-only leadership policies in religious congregations, particularly in their levels of congregational efficacy, trust, and identity (see Chapter 7). It seems that political constituencies do pick up on cues religious leaders provide (whether intentionally or unintentionally) and respond accordingly in adapting their religious attitudes and behaviors. Those who feel cognitive dissonance caused by a conflict between their political identities and religious communities will try to eliminate the dissonance one way or another, often including a separation from the religious community. When liberals in these traditional congregations decrease their attendance or stop altogether, many of them may simply decide to stay home instead of seeking out a congregation more in line with their political and theological ideals. (For more information on this effect and other potential mechanisms linking partisan identity to changing religious identity, see Djupe, Neiheisel, and Sokhey 2017 and Margolis 2018.)

WHAT SHOULD CONGREGATIONS DO?

We explained in our introductory chapter that our goal is not to provide prescriptive recommendations to religious institutions or leaders about what they should do in their congregations regarding gender and leadership. Nor do we feel it our place to engage in theological conversations on the topic. As we said, we believe that these decisions are best left to the congregations and institutions themselves. We also believe, though, that our research has provided vital information that can inform these discussions and provide additional hard data to the conversations. We acknowledge that religious organizations base their decisions on factors *other* than those we have analyzed in our work. A congregation may decide that maintaining purity of doctrine or observing tradition is ultimately more important than creating conditions that encourage the types of personal or religious empowerment that we discuss here. Still, we will offer a few observations that religious leaders and congregations may wish to consider as dialogue continues on issues of gender and religious leadership.

First, we emphasize that the empirical effects of gender and leadership that we have documented in this book are sometimes substantial, but just as often are modest. As Djupe (2014) found in his analysis of gender leadership and voting, our results show that women's ordination matters "a little" in affecting the behavior of those in the congregations, especially when it comes to religious outcomes specifically. Our findings suggest that whether a congregation chooses to ordain women will likely not "make or break" that organization's viability, at least in its short-term future. We have shown that gender policies will likely make a difference in terms of who decides to join a congregation as well as regarding who is affected and in which ways. The results from Chapters 3, 4, and 5 also consistently showed that most people generally support whatever policy their current congregation has on the issue of gender and leadership. There is no compelling evidence that the decision to maintain a male-only leadership structure *or* to allow women to serve as the principal religious leader will result in either a massive increase in attendance or a fatal blow to a church or other religious congregation in the short-term future.

Second, our results from Chapters 6, 7, and 8 demonstrate that there is almost zero discernible downside to ordaining women in terms of the religious attitudes or behaviors of those in the congregations. No one is negatively affected by attending congregations that have gender-inclusive leadership policies and women pastors or priests. In fact, levels of religious behavior and spirituality are sometimes *higher* in congregations with more egalitarian leadership. Chapter 6 also showed that for the most part, women are positively empowered in their levels of self-esteem, self-efficacy, education, and employment if they have influential female clergy in their youth, while men's attainment of these personal and societal resources are just as high regardless of the gender of their clergy when they were growing up. Moreover, Chapter 8 showed that male-dominant leadership policies *depress* religious behaviors and attitudes among theological and political progressives.

In other words, everyone has positive religious outcomes in congregations that ordain women and hire women priests, pastors, and rabbis: men and women, traditionalists and progressives—all benefit. But some people have lower religious outcomes in congregations that do not ordain women, specifically women, religious progressives, and political liberals. Looking at it another way, men, traditionalists, and conservatives are just as active in congregations that ordain women, but progressives and liberals are not quite as active and "plugged in" in congregations that do not. It seems that choosing to ordain women, practicing gender-inclusive pastoral hiring practices, and having equal women's representation in the lay leadership, then, are associated with positive religious outcomes for the widest spectrum of congregants whereas declining to do these things is associated with negative outcomes for a narrower spectrum of congregants.

Our Gender and Religious Representation Survey reveals that approximately one-third of politically and theologically liberal worshipers in the United States currently attend a congregation that does not allow female clergy (31.8% and 35.5%, respectively). That is about seventy million people who are potentially disempowered and demobilized to some extent in their levels of congregational efficacy/identity due to a mismatch: they attend congregations in which their social values are not reflected in the gender leadership policies. These individuals still attend, though, even though they are lower in their levels of efficacy and trust compared to their liberal counterparts who attend congregations with gender-inclusive leadership. Time will tell if they will continue to make the effort in the short- and long-term future, and who knows how many other political or theological liberals had *already* left their congregations with male-only leadership by the time our survey took place?

Third, it is important to remind religious leaders that male-only gender leadership policies and practices also have been shown to have a disempowering effect on women when it comes to psychological resources such as self-esteem and self-efficacy. Of course this is not the only factor that contributes to lower levels of self-esteem in American society, but our surveys have shown evidence that after controlling for a host of other social and religious factors, *these gaps in self-esteem only exist between men and women who never had a female congregational leader growing up*, that is to say, about three-fifths of the entire U.S. population. Among those in our nationally representative sample, this self-esteem gender gap disappears entirely even among those who said they had female clergy only "some of the time" growing up. This is important because, as explained in Chapter 6, low self-esteem is a predictor of depression, anxiety, criminal activity, lower levels of motivation, and poorer overall quality of life. *The extent to which male-only leadership policies are maintained, then, can detrimentally affect the emotional and psychological health and well-being of women later in life.* We believe that religious leaders have an obligation to consider this type of evidence as they review policies on gender and leadership in their congregations and how those policies affect their members.

We also point out that congregations and denominations that currently extend the priesthood to women still struggle to achieve gender parity in the leadership of their congregations. Chapter 2 showed us that women currently make up only about 16% of the principal congregational leaders where women are admitted and invited to do so. It remains difficult for young women and girls to find female clergy even in congregations in which they are, in principle, available. These congregations may consider ways to increase the balance between women and men in their local leadership positions. At the very least, we recommend that congregational leaders from traditions that currently ordain women, and especially from those that do not, design and implement more intentional and aggressive mentoring programs for girls and female adult religious leaders. Chapter 6 showed us that positive and important emotional and psychological effects were just as often linked to the gender of their *most influential* congregational leader when growing up as they were to the frequency of female leaders in their childhood congregations.

Further, the evidence shown in Chapter 6 indicates that the gender gap in full-time employment does not exist among the 9% of American men and women who had a woman as their most influential religious leader growing up, though it persists among the 91% of Americans whose most influential religious leader was a man. This is important because employment contributes to economic independence and increases control over one's life, choices, and opportunities. In order for young women to benefit from the positive and empowering effect of female religious role models, their congregations must allow and encourage women to serve as congregational leaders in the first place. It is difficult to overstate the extent to which strong women religious leaders and mentors are important in the lives of young women in religious congregations. We also emphasize once again that men are not disempowered by the presence of female clergy, but women *are* disempowered by the *absence* of female clergy in their youth. Again, there are only advantages in personal and societal empowerment when it comes to the presence of influential female congregational leaders in a person's childhood and adolescence.

Fourth, some have argued that ordaining women would result in a fundamental change to a religious institution's doctrine, language, policies, priorities, culture, and identity (see Nesbitt 1997, 161, for example). Some would view this as a welcome change and others an undesirable outcome, especially given that religious institutions tend to value stability and tradition over uncertainty and change. Either way, we are somewhat skeptical of this prediction. As we discussed in Chapter 2, research has shown that male and female clergy, while possibly different in many ways, are not *drastically* different in their leadership styles and approach to the ministry (Lehman 1993). The general consensus, both from previous research as well as our own, is that clergy personality matters more than gender when it comes to many aspects of the interaction between pastors and their congregations. Thus, we predict that if a denomination were to begin to ordain women it would likely produce some changes in policies, doctrinal emphases, and institutional priorities. Some have shown evidence, for instance, that when it comes to moral reasoning, women tend to prioritize care over justice whereas men tend to prioritize justice over care (Gilligan 1982). This might result in some changes of emphasis or applications of doctrine, but we think it unlikely to fundamentally alter the core identity and mission of a congregation or institution, especially given the large amount of self-selection in contemporary American religious congregations (Putnam and Campbell 2012).

Fifth, we offer a prediction as to how issues of gender and leadership might affect the choices facing religious institutions in the not-too-distant future. We described previously that congregations use their policy on gender and ordination to signal their position on the social and theological spectrum as well as their orientation toward modernity and group orientation versus individual rights. As political and cultural polarization continues to intensify in American society, both political and theological progressives who attend male-only leadership congregations will likely continue to experience cognitive dissonance between their personal values and the policies of their congregations. Many may ultimately decide that they must choose between their political identities and their religious communities. Given that Americans are more likely today to alter their religious beliefs to conform to their political values as opposed to the other way around (Putnam and Campbell 2012, chap. 5; Djupe, Neiheisel, and Sokhey 2017; Margolis 2018), they may seek out a different congregation with more gender-inclusive policies—or opt out of organized religion altogether.

This presents institutions that uphold male-only leadership policies with a difficult choice. As we said previously, staying the course on male-only leadership will likely not "break" the institution, at least in the short term. It may, however, contribute (whether directly or indirectly) to attrition from liberals and limit potential converts to only conservatives, many of whom are already heavily invested in their own congregations and religious communities and unlikely to want to change. On the other hand, changing policy and opening the leadership to women would likely result in less (if any) attrition from theological and political liberals and would likely not affect conservatives either way, as our research has shown that traditionalists and conservatives are in general not disempowered or demotivated by gender-inclusive leadership policies.

Making the effort to keep liberals, though, would undoubtedly result in more theologically and politically diverse congregations, which would also produce a community more heterogeneous in its orthodoxy and levels of commitment. Chapter 8 showed us that it is not necessary to switch from male-dominant to female-dominant leadership, though. Congregational leaders should not interpret our research as implying that they must only ever select women as congregational leaders and lay ministers. The results demonstrated that merely *equalizing* gender leadership is sufficient to prevent religious disempowerment and demobilization among women, progressives, and liberals. This can be accomplished simply by inviting women to serve as a congregation's principal leader as often as men and by making sure that the lay ministry positions are shared evenly between men and women. In other words, matriarchy is not the only answer to the disempowering effects of patriarchy in America's congregations—simple equality would work just as well.

We also cite other research that has shown that theological traditionalists in congregations that subscribe to male-only leadership are supportive of expanding the clergy to women *if* they perceive the change as coming from authoritative ecclesiastical leaders (Cragun et al. 2016). This implies that ordaining women would not be opposed by theological traditionalists if the decision to do so came from the top rather than the bottom. Indeed, our findings discussed in Chapters 3 and 4 strongly indicate that people's preferences on female clergy are strongly associated with the existing policies of whatever congregation they attend. Denominational leaders thus have a good deal of influence over how their communities respond to female ordination, as we demonstrated in Chapters 3, 4, and 5; congregational context is a key variable in the prediction of support. We agree with Nesbitt (1997, 167), who argues that congregational and denominational leaders are the most influential voices on the question of women's ordination.

In sum, we believe that organizational leaders who stay the course on policies supporting male-only clergy will likely produce a leaner, more niche-specific religious community: one that perhaps is not as large in membership but also one that is more internally homogenous and cohesive in its perspectives and commitment to the organization's values and goals. Presumably, traditionalists would regard such internal harmony as desirable, but not the erosion of membership that would be required to achieve it. Those who adopt more inclusive policies when it comes to gender and leadership, on the other hand, will likely produce communities in which more people feel welcome (desirable) but which are also more ideologically diverse with potentially a greater degree of variety in member commitment to the organization's teachings, priorities, and mission (potentially undesirable). At the same time, our findings have shown that this variety in belief does not come at the expense of attendance, religious behaviors, spirituality, or identification with the congregation.

Again, there are other factors for religious leaders to consider when it comes to gender and leadership aside from those we have outlined above. We are not in a position to speak to the various theological or scriptural arguments on this question. Maintaining orthodox practice and belief may ultimately be deemed more important than issues of congregant behavior, retention, diversity, empowerment, efficacy, and psychological/emotional health. We leave it to religious leaders and communities to decide which set of outcomes they regard as more important in the long run for their organizations.

CONCLUSION

Lehman (1985) concludes his landmark and pioneering book on women's ordination with a plea for religious institutions to consider the perspective of history:

> Will the churches' reactions to the current feminist movement become something of which they will eventually be proud or ashamed? The way in which

they respond to women wishing to participate in the full range of ministries of the Church will be a major determinant in how future ethical historians evaluate the churches' coming to grips with the human movements of the twentieth century. The inconsistencies between claiming to be the defenders of the highest moral values on one hand and barring any group of people from full participation in the church's ministries on the other are too apparent to gloss over. . . . If the churches boldly endorse women's broadening sense of call to ministry, history is likely to give them high marks. If they refuse to recognize the legitimacy of women's call to serve in places heretofore reserved for men, they will surely find the judgment of history against them. (296)

More than twenty years later, one can infer that Sentilles (2009) senses that the ground continues to shift as she concludes her ethnographic study of women clergy:

Girls and boys, men and women, people all across the country, are seeing ministers like Eli and Michelle and Gari, Tristy and Callie and Sharon and Connie, Laurie and Monica and Liza and Eve, . . . and they know that something else is possible, that they can have a church where they belong, that they can believe in a God who welcomes all. There is no going back. We have already won. (310)

Time will ultimately tell if these predictions bear out. In the meantime, there is still much work to do in understanding how gender and leadership interact in religious congregations and communities. In our book we have endeavored to provide a new perspective on these questions because we believe it to be an important and far-reaching topic worthy of study. Our research confirmed in some ways what we had assumed and yet surprised us in many others. Gender and leadership clearly matter, but not entirely in the ways that we suspected.

We believe that arguments, either for or against an issue, are strengthened when informed by empirical evidence. Our goal has been to contribute such evidence to the conversations on women's ordination. In general, our research has persuaded us that gender representation matters in the leadership of religious congregations. It is clear that more women in religious leadership is empowering to those in the congregations and that they would help make these congregations more attractive to a broader swath of Americans. The evidence has also convinced us that more gender equity in congregational leadership would foster a generally healthier psychological, spiritual, and social environment for American worshipers, especially for women and theological/political progressives, and with very little downside to men and conservatives.

Most important, we were also persuaded that the *lack* of gender equality in congregational leadership is, at least to a moderate degree, one source of the persistent gender gap in social and economic equality in America. We believe the evidence we have presented is persuasive that increasing women's leadership in America's places of worship would do much to ameliorate the gender gaps in broader secular and political contexts. Our research has also shown that the paucity of female leadership in religious congregations is associated with lower levels of self-esteem and self-efficacy in women, which in turn affects overall levels of emotional and physical health, which in turn can affect everything from pursuing education, running for public elected office, and general levels of happiness. Implementing gender equality in religious congregations could thus improve levels of physical and emotional health for American women, improve their overall quality of life, and make much progress toward closing the gender gap in society. Conversely, *failing* to do so will likely serve to perpetuate existing inequalities in the personal, social, economic, and political spheres.

Finally, our survey evidence indicated that American worshipers are fairly responsive to the policies of whatever congregation they happen to attend, which to us indicates that institutional and congregational leaders have the primary opportunity and responsibility to consider this evidence and to respond accordingly on these issues in a way that produces the most positive spiritual, religious, psychological, emotional, and societal outcomes for their congregants. As we have seen throughout, most worshipers "follow the leader" on this issue.

Of course, we do not intend this to be the final word on the topic. We encourage researchers, activists, theologians, and clergy alike to continue gathering data, testing arguments, thinking critically, and seeking inspiration about the role of women in religious organizations while discussing the matter with due civility and respect for differing opinions and perspectives. Neither do we know what the future ultimately holds for the nexus of gender, ordination, and religious leadership. We do know, though, that religious institutions, cultures, doctrines, policies, and communities are always in a state of flux as they respond to external and internal factors that pull them in different directions. Gender roles in churches, synagogues, mosques, and temples have evolved and changed throughout history in response to these forces and they will continue to be debated, revised, reinterpreted, and re-envisioned going forward. We hope that our book will make a valuable contribution to this process.

NOTE

1. As of the time of publication, the blog post had been removed but the Twitter link is still available at: https://twitter.com/RNS/status/728638104463024128.

Data Appendix

As explained in the text, a research team of seven advanced undergraduate students conducted seventy-one semistructured interviews with clergy and parishioners located primarily in central Kentucky, where we at Centre College are located. One of us (Bolin) was an interviewer, while the other (Knoll) was the research seminar instructor that semester. The research team received intensive training on qualitative interviewing methods based on Rubin and Rubin (2011), Saldaña (2012), and Seidman (2012). The interviews took place between September and December of 2015.

To keep consistency with the quantitative survey data, all of our interviewees attended services at least occasionally. Most of the congregants we talked with tended to be actively involved in their congregations because of the way in which we found our interviewees and arranged the interviews. Each of our researchers was assigned a particular religious tradition (e.g., Catholic, Evangelical Protestant, non-Christian, etc.) and then contacted various places of worship in those traditions in the surrounding central Kentucky region. They then asked the clergypersons themselves for interviews as well as to refer members of the congregations who might be interested in talking to us. This is a commonly practiced interviewing technique called snowball sampling "in which one participant leads to another" (Seidman 2012, 58).

Of those we talked with, 12% were a part of an Evangelical Protestant denomination, 16% belonged to the Mainline Protestant tradition, 14% were Historically Black Protestant, 14% were Catholic, 10% were Jewish, 5% were Mormon, 14% were "other Christian," and 14% were "other non-Christian" (figures do not add to 100% due to rounding). We note that our sample is of course not representative of the wider American religious population. This is because our goal was to capture a variety of American religious traditions and denominations, including those representing only a minority of the population. As is often the case with "mixed-methods" research approaches, we rely on our national quantitative survey data for representativeness and statistical significance and turn to our in-depth qualitative interviews for additional depth, detail, and nuance (Jick 1979).

All of the people we talked with were over the age of eighteen. Our interviewers estimated and recorded the age of each interviewee, the oldest of whom was in his eighties. About half were above the age of fifty and the other half below age fifty. Of the clergypersons, about two-fifths were below the age of fifty and the other three-fifths were ages fifty or older. We talked with twenty-seven clergypersons (nine clergywomen and eighteen clergymen) and forty-six congregants (thirty-two women and fourteen men). Fifty-five percent of the individuals we interviewed were women and 45% were men. Racially, 68% of individuals were white, 22% were black, and 10% were "other" or unknown.

These interviews followed a semistructured format whereby the researcher "has a specific topic to learn about, prepares a limited number of questions in advance, and plans to ask follow-up questions" (Rubin and Rubin 2011, 31). After conducting and transcribing the interviews, we used a combination of descriptive and in vivo coding methods. As described by Saldaña (2012, 88), descriptive coding "summarizes in a word or short phrase . . . the basic topic of a passage." In vivo coding, in contrast, "refers to a word or short phrase from the actual language found in the qualitative data record" (91). In other words, codes in the in vivo method are "the terms used by [participants] themselves" (Strauss 1987, 91).

Following these coding methods, we read through each of the transcripts and analyzed the data by utilizing "codes"—that is, either descriptive words or phrases that summarized a passage or the actual words that participants used. After reading several interviews, certain themes such as "personal experiences/support" emerged, and we would use these phrases to code related sections in the following interviews. Once we had a clear list of common themes, we also found it helpful to refer to our coded transcripts and find quotes related to those themes. Unless otherwise stated, the analysis we present in our chapters is based on a combination of clergy and congregant interviews, as they tended to reveal similar trends.

We present quotes from our interviews throughout this book, at times preferring to present longer block quotes instead of short excerpts so as to give fuller context to the themes that the quotes reveal. We also did some very minor editing for presentation's sake, removing words like "um" and "ah" but never altering the substance of a quote.

Table A.1 presents the full list of interviews and some basic characteristics of each individual. The interviews are cited throughout using the interview number as found in this table. We also present in Table A.2 the question outline that we used to begin and structure the interview conversations.

QUANTITATIVE DATA

The primary source of quantitative data we use in this book comes from a series of four "waves" of the Gender and Religious Representation Survey, which included telephone- and internet-based public opinion surveys conducted throughout 2015 and 2016. Waves 1 and 2 were collected in March and September (respectively) of 2015 via a random-digit dialed telephone survey of all adult Americans over age eighteen except for those in Alaska and Hawaii (which were impractical given time zone considerations). Wave 3 was an internet survey that sampled adult Americans over age eighteen and was conducted by the Qualtrics organization in October 2015. Waves 1 and

TABLE A.1

Face-to-face interview respondents and characteristics

Interview	Clergy or congregant	Gender	Race	Approximate age	Tradition	Denomination/family
1	Clergy	Male	Black	50s	Historically Black Protestant	Baptist
2	Clergy	Male	Black	60s	Historically Black Protestant	AME
3	Clergy	Male	White	50s	Evangelical Protestant	Non-denominational
4	Clergy	Male	White	50s	Evangelical Protestant	Assemblies of God
5	Clergy	Male	White	30s	Evangelical Protestant	Southern Baptist
6	Clergy	Male	Black	50s	Non-Christian	Islam
7	Clergy	Male	White	50s	"Other Christian"	Unitarian Universalist
8	Clergy	Female	White	30s	Non-Christian	Reform Judaism
9	Clergy	Male	White	40s	Non-Christian	Conservative Judaism
10	Clergy	Female	White	50s	"Other Christian"	Unitarian Universalist
11	Clergy	Male	White	40s	Non-Christian	Chabad Judaism
12	Clergy	Male	White	80s	"Other Christian"	LDS
13	Clergy	Male	White	70s	"Other Christian"	Jehovah's Witness
14	Clergy	Male	White	30s	"Other Christian"	Jehovah's Witness
15	Clergy	Male	Indian	50s	"Other Christian"	Seventh Day Adventist
16	Clergy	Male	White	50s	"Other Christian"	LDS
17	Clergy	Male	White	50s	"Other Christian"	LDS
18	Clergy	Male	White	50s	Catholic	Catholic
19	Clergy	Male	White	60s	Catholic	Catholic
20	Clergy	Male	White	40s	Catholic	Catholic

(continued)

TABLE A.1

Continued

Interview	Clergy or congregant	Gender	Race	Approximate age	Tradition	Denomination/family
21	Clergy	Male	Black	40s	Catholic	Catholic
22	Clergy	Female	White	60s	Mainline Protestant	Presbyterian Church (U.S.A.)
23	Clergy	Female	White	30s	Mainline Protestant	Episcopal
24	Clergy	Female	White	50s	Mainline Protestant	Christian Church (Disciples of Christ)
25	Clergy	Female	White	40s	Mainline Protestant	Episcopal
26	Clergy	Female	White	30s	Mainline Protestant	Presbyterian Church (U.S.A.)
27	Clergy	Female	White	50s	Mainline Protestant	Evangelical Lutheran Church in America
28	Congregant	Female	White	70s	Catholic	Catholic
29	Congregant	Female	White	30s	Catholic	Catholic
30	Congregant	Female	Black	60s	Catholic	Catholic
31	Congregant	Female	White	60s	Mainline Protestant	Episcopal
32	Congregant	Female	White	60s	Catholic	Catholic
33	Congregant	Female	White	50s	Catholic	Catholic
34	Congregant	Male	White	60s	Mainline Protestant	Evangelical Lutheran Church in America
35	Congregant	Male	White	50s	Mainline Protestant	Presbyterian Church (U.S.A.)
36	Congregant	Male	White	70s	Mainline Protestant	Episcopal
37	Congregant	Female	White	50s	Mainline Protestant	Episcopal
38	Congregant	Male	White	30s	Catholic	Catholic
39	Congregant	Female	White	40s	Mainline Protestant	Episcopal
40	Congregant	Female	Black	40s	Historically Black Protestant	Baptist

41	Congregant	Male	Black	40s	Historically Black Protestant	Baptist
42	Congregant	Female	Black	20s	Historically Black Protestant	Baptist
43	Congregant	Female	Black	20s	Historically Black Protestant	Baptist
44	Congregant	Female	Black	30s	Historically Black Protestant	Baptist
45	Congregant	Female	Black	50s	Historically Black Protestant	Baptist
46	Congregant	Female	Black	20s	Historically Black Protestant	Baptist
47	Congregant	Male	Black	20s	Historically Black Protestant	NA
48	Congregant	Female	White	40s	Evangelical Protestant	Non-denominational
49	Congregant	Female	White	30s	Evangelical Protestant	Non-denominational
50	Congregant	Female	White	20s	Evangelical Protestant	Assemblies of God
51	Congregant	Female	White	60s	Evangelical Protestant	Assemblies of God
52	Congregant	Female	White	40s	Evangelical Protestant	Non-denominational
53	Congregant	Male	White	50s	Evangelical Protestant	Non-denominational
54	Congregant	Male	Indian	80s	Non-Christian	Hindu
55	Congregant	Female	Bosnian	20s	Non-Christian	Islam
56	Congregant	Female	NA	NA	"Other Christian"	Seventh-day Adventist
57	Congregant	Female	NA	20s	Non-Christian	Islam
58	Congregant	Male	NA	40s	Non-Christian	Buddhist
59	Congregant	Female	White	NA	Non-Christian	Buddhist
60	Congregant	Male	NA	60s	Non-Christian	Islam-Sufi
61	Congregant	Female	Indian	20s	Non-Christian	Hindu
62	Congregant	Female	Black	50s	Non-Christian	Islam
63	Congregant	Male	Black	30s	Non-Christian	Islam
64	Congregant	Male	White	20s	Non-Christian	Reform Judaism
65	Congregant	Male	White	NA	"Other Christian"	Unitarian Universalist

(continued)

TABLE A.1

Continued

Interview	Clergy or congregant	Gender	Race	Approximate age	Tradition	Denomination/family
66	Congregant	Female	White	30s	Non-Christian	Orthodox Judaism
67	Congregant	Male	White	60s	Non-Christian	Conservative Judaism
68	Congregant	Female	White	50s	Non-Christian	Reform Judaism
69	Congregant	Female	White	50s	"Other Christian"	Christian Science
70	Congregant	Female	White	60s	"Other Christian"	LDS
71	Congregant	Female	Black	30s	"Other Christian"	Jehovah's Witness
72	Congregant	Female	White	30s	"Other Christian"	Jehovah's Witness
73	Congregant	Female	White	50s	"Other Christian"	Jehovah's Witness

2 were directed by the authors and fielded by student researchers at Centre College, who generously provided funding for the survey.

Waves 1 and 2 attained a total sample of 1,354 telephone responses (including incompletes), which were combined with 349 responses (also including incompletes) collected from the internet sample in Wave 3 for a total of 1,703 cases. In total, 56.5% of our telephone sample was collected via landline and 43.5% was collected via cell phone.

At the completion of Waves 1 and 2, demographic analysis of the data revealed that our survey responses were biased toward older and white Americans, as is often the case in telephone-based surveying (Kohut et al. 2012). Thus, the sample for the Wave 3 internet survey was structured in such a way as to compensate for those demographic biases, oversampling younger and non-white respondents. Specifically, Wave 3 sampled adult Americans between the ages of eighteen and sixty-four, 40% between the ages of eighteen and thirty-four, 40% between the ages of thirty-five and forty-nine, and 20% between the ages of fifty and sixty-four. It also sampled quotas by race/ethnicity: 20% white, 25% black, 40% Hispanic/Latino, 10% Asian, and 5% "mixed/other." While this helped generate a sample that was much closer to national averages of the adult population, some unrepresentativeness remained in our combined sample. Thus, we constructed a weighting variable to adjust for any remaining demographic biases for gender, age, and race, based on figures from the 2014 ACS survey (one-year estimates) administered by the U.S. Census Bureau. After accounting for responses with nonmissing data in each of those three categories, our final sample size of the combined surveys is 1,334. (We should note, though, that missing data in some other categories often results in a somewhat lower sample size included in the various multivariate models that we estimate.)

The following year we fielded Wave 4 of our survey, which was a combination of telephone and internet responses with identically worded questions. The telephone survey for Wave 4 was fielded in October 2016 via the same random-digit dialed telephone survey of adult (age eighteen or older) Americans, except for those in Alaska and Hawaii. After eliminating incompletes and those that lacked the appropriate demographic statistics to receive a weighting variable, 710 usable cases remained (38.1% landline and 61.9% cellphone). These responses were supplemented with 105 internet-based surveys again collected by the Qualtrics organization in November 2016. The internet surveys were specifically targeted to oversample racial minorities and younger individuals so as to account for demographic biases in the telephone sample (thirty black responses, fifty-five Hispanic/Latino, ten Asian, and ten "other"; thirty ages eighteen to thirty-four, sixty-five ages thirty-five to forty-nine, ten ages fifty to sixty-four). Because Wave 4 focused on separate questions from Waves 1 through 3, these responses were for the most part kept separate and all calculations presented are weighted to match representativeness on gender, age, and race/ethnicity from the 2014 ACS survey as described above. This resulted in 815 usable cases for Wave 4 (although due to nonresponses on some other questions there are sometimes fewer cases included in the multivariate models presented here).

There is one final aspect to consider regarding our data sample. Our sample of interest is those who attend religious congregations in America and are exposed at least to some extent to the leadership in those congregations. We therefore limited our data collection sample specifically to those who report attending religious services at least "seldom." In effect, this means that we exclude the roughly 13% of the American population who report that they "never" attend religious services "aside from weddings and funerals" (as per the 2014 Pew Religious Landscape Study). Our sample thus consists of adult Americans who attend religious services infrequently (less than

Face-to-face interview outline

Where possible, interviewers noted the gender, race, and approximate age of each respondent.

Questions for clergy:
- Tell me about your experiences, positions, backgrounds, etc. here?
  - What inspired you to do what you do?
  - Tell me briefly about your spiritual journey.
- What is your relationship with the sacred texts of your religion?
  - How does that relationship affect your views on popular social issues?
- How are your interactions with members in your congregation? What are they like?
  - How are they different for men vs. women?
  - How are they different for older vs. younger members?
- What conversations currently are going on regarding gender and leadership in your congregation/religion?
  - Do you think it's important for women to be in a position like yours? Why or why not?
- Generally speaking, do you tend to identify as more of a theological progressive/liberal, more of a theological traditionalist/conservative, or somewhere in between?
- What question have I not asked that I should ask?

Questions for congregants:
- Tell me about your experiences, positions, backgrounds, etc. here in this congregation.
  - What do you do here? What's your role? Do you enjoy that?
  - How long have you been here? Do you participate in small groups or other opportunities? What does that mean for you?
  - Do you like your participation and involvement in this congregation? Why or why not? How much does this have to do with your pastor/priest?
  - Tell me about your leader/pastor/priest. What's your relationship with him/her? What's that like?
- There are lots of conversations today about gender and leadership in American churches. What do you think about those conversations?
  - What do you think of these issues specifically applied to your congregation/religion?
  - Does it matter to you whether your pastor/priest is a man or woman? Does it make a difference? Why?
  - If you were struggling with a spiritual problem and you sought out guidance, would the gender of the person matter to you? Why? How?
  - Would you prefer that your congregation permit women to serve as pastors/priests? Why?
- Regardless of your congregation's policy on the topic, would you personally prefer a man or woman to serve as your personal pastor/priest? Why?
  - Do you think it matters that woman can/cannot serve in these positions? Why?
- What question have I not asked that I should ask?

"a few times a year") across the spectrum to those who report that they attend "more than once a week."

Ideally our demographic weighting variable would weight according to the age, race, and gender of those who attend religious services at least "seldom" as well. The Census Bureau, however, does not track religious behavior information. Thus, there is no known objective measurement of the demographic composition of the American churchgoing population separate from that obtained by other public opinion surveys. To investigate this further we compared the weighted and unweighted frequencies of the age, race, and gender groups both including and excluding the "never" attenders in the 2007 Pew Religious Landscape Study as well as the 2012

American National Elections Study. In the vast majority of cases, the frequency changes in the demographic subgroups were less than 1%. We argue, then, that using demographic information from the Census Bureau to construct our demographic sampling weights has only a very small impact on our final results even though the two samples are not 100% identical.

Ultimately, we make no claims in our analysis that our findings are generalizable to the *entire* American population at large, but rather that they are representative of the adult population who attend religious services with some degree of frequency, including a very low degree of frequency. That said, this population consists of approximately 87% of the American adult population according to the 2014 Pew Religious Landscape Study (again, we exclude *only* those who report "never" attending religious services outside of weddings and funerals). We do not claim to speak to the other 13% who never attend religious services and thus (presumably) are largely, if not completely, unaffected by the dynamics of gender leadership in religious congregations.

It is also important to note that while our survey sampled the comprehensive swath of American religious traditions, some are too small a proportion of the American population to have produced a sufficient number of cases to be able to produce generalizable results focusing solely on those groups. These include Jews, Mormons, Muslims, Buddhists, and other minority religions. They are included in our statistical analyses as they are Americans who attend religious services, but we are unable to provide any reliable information as to how gender leadership *specifically* affects their religious behavior and attitudes. We leave it to future researchers to zoom in more closely on those religious subgroups.

Chapter 2 Additional Information

The multivariate model predicting preferences for the gender of one's personal congregational leader was performed with a multinomial logistic regression procedure. The dependent variable was a three-point measure of preference: -1 if the respondent indicated a preference for a male pastor or priest, 0 if the respondent volunteered a response of "doesn't matter" or "no preference," and +1 if the respondent indicated a preference for a female congregational leader. In the multinomial logistic regression estimation, "no preference" was the reference category. The weighting variable described above was used and the model was evaluated for both multicollinearity and heteroskedasticity, which revealed that robust standard errors were needed. The model included variables measuring respondent gender, education, income, age, race/ethnicity (black and Latino), political partisanship and ideology, and non-Christian identity (Jewish and "other"). It also included measures of the gender of the respondent's current congregational leader as well as whether his or her current congregation permitted women to serve as the principal congregational leader.

Chapter 4 Additional Information

The data for Chapter 8 come from Waves 1 through 3 of the Gender and Religious Representation survey.

Dependent Variable: Support for Female Clergy. The dependent variable is a measure of support for female clergy in the congregation that the respondent attends most often. In Waves 1 and 2 of the data collection, respondents were asked: "Would you strongly prefer, somewhat prefer, somewhat NOT prefer, or strongly not prefer that the congregation you attend most often permit women to serve as the principal religious leader?" In Wave 3 the wording was varied very slightly: "Thinking of the congregation you attend most often, would you strongly prefer, somewhat prefer, somewhat NOT prefer, or strongly not prefer that women be permitted to serve as the principal religious leader?" This created a four-point ordinal variable that was then collapsed into a two-point binary "support vs. not support" variable, with 1 as "support" and 0 as "not support."

While the four-point variable would be preferable to the collapsed binary variable, the ordinal logistic estimation models failed tests of the proportional odds assumption, which necessitated the use of the two-point binary variable. The collapsed two-point variable is also desirable as our key question is what predicts *support* for female clergy. Whether the support is soft ("somewhat prefer") or solid ("strongly prefer") is less substantively interesting than whether someone does or does not prefer.

We also note that the wording for Wave 3 was altered to correct for the potential ambiguity in the question wording for Waves 1 and 2. It is possible that some respondents interpreted the question wording in Waves 1 and 2 to mean "in the congregation you attend, would you prefer that the principal religious leader most often be male or female?" An analysis of responses between Waves 1–2 and Wave 3, though, suggests that there was not a substantive difference in responses between Waves 1–2 and Wave 3. A difference of means t-test of the 4-point ordinal measure of support between Wave 1–2 and Wave 3 responses failed to produce a statistically significant difference (M=2.87, SD=0.95 for Wave 1–2, M=2.85, SD=1.168 for Wave 3, p=0.81).

Independent Variables: Congregational Context. Congregational policy regarding women as clergy is measured with the question: "Does the congregation you attend most often permit women to serve as the principal religious leader?" (Waves 1–2) and "Thinking of the congregation you attend most often, are women permitted to serve as the principal religious leader?" (Wave 3). This produced a binary variable, with 1 if women are permitted to serve as clergy in the respondent's congregation and 0 if not. We note that the wording for Wave 3 was altered to correct for the potential ambiguity in the question wording for Waves 1 and 2 as explained above. A difference of means t-test of the 4-point ordinal measure of the gender of the respondent's congregational leader between Wave 1–2 and Wave 3 responses failed to produce a statistically significant difference (M=0.56, SD=0.50 for Wave 1–2, M=0.56, SD=0.50 for Wave 3, p=0.83).

The gender of the respondent's current congregational leader is measured with the question: "Is the pastor, priest, or other principal religious leader of the congregation you attend most often male or female? [If the respondent asked for clarification, "principal religious leader" was explained to mean the chief priest, pastor, reverend, etc. of the local congregation.]" (Waves 1–2) and "Thinking of the congregation you attend most often, is the pastor, priest, or other principal religious leader male or female?" (Wave 3). The wording for Wave 3 was altered to correct for the potential ambiguity in the question wording for Waves 1 and 2, as explained above. A difference of means t-test of the binary measure of the gender of the respondent's congregational leader between Wave 1–2 and Wave 3 responses produces a small but statistically significant difference (M=0.08, SD=0.27 for Wave 1–2, M=0.12, SD=0.32 for Wave 3, p=0.05).

The gender proportion of congregational leaders in the respondent's congregation is measured with the question: "About what percent of all the ministry and small group leaders of the congregation you attend most often are female?" (Waves 1–2) and "Thinking of the congregation you attend most often, about what percent of all the ministry and small group leaders of the congregation are female?" (Wave 3). Respondents could choose "0–25%; 25–50%; 50–75%; 75–100%."

This resulted in a 4-point ordinal variable with higher values associated with a higher proportion of women serving as small group and ministry leaders. As with the other questions described in this section, the wording for Wave 3 was altered to correct for the potential ambiguity in the question wording for Waves 1 and 2 as explained above. A difference of means t-test of the binary measure of the gender of the respondent's congregational leader between Wave 1–2 and Wave 3 responses again produces a small but statistically significant difference (M=2.20, SD=0.95 for Wave 1–2, M=1.89, SD=0.82 for Wave 3, p<0.0001).

Why not specific religious traditions? It could be argued that congregational policy of gender and leadership positions would better be measured with variables for individual religious tradition, specifically dummy variables representing traditions with male-only congregational leaders. While this is a compelling option, we decided against this course for some key reasons. The first is the fact that in many cases the wider religious tradition does not set policies for individual congregations. For example, Evangelical Protestantism as a tradition includes denominations and congregations that have male-only clergy policies as well as policies that allow women to serve as clergy. There are also some Mainline Protestant denominations that still have male-only policies despite the fact that the majority of the wider tradition has opened the pulpit to women over the last several decades (CBE International 2007). Our surveys recorded the respondents' wider religious tradition but not their specific denominations.

We also know from Chaves (1997) that there is a degree of "de-coupling" in American congregations in which policy and practice on this issue are not always consistent, and thus we cannot be certain that an individual congregation actually enforces their wider denomination's policy on the matter. We ultimately believe it to be more reliable to measure individual congregational policy by the direct report of the survey respondent. Even this approach, though, is likely to have some degree of error due to social desirability concerns or simple ignorance on the part of the respondents of their congregation's policies.

On balance, however, we feel that the individual self-report approach is both more accurate and also more consistent with the methodological and analytical assumptions of self-report survey data. Out of an abundance of caution, we also ran the models presented in our chapters with controls for Catholicism, Mormonism, and Evangelicalism (the major traditions most likely to have most members in congregations *without* female leaders) but this resulted in only one substantive difference in our key findings (the p-value for religious behavior in Figure 4.6 reduces to p=0.125). Thus, it seems that the norms of the wider tradition matter less than the policies of the specific individual congregations when it comes to influencing congregant attitudes toward female clergy.

Independent Variables: Factors that Influence Support. The gender of each respondent was independently coded by the telephone interviewers in Waves 1 and 2, while gender self-identification was included in the Wave 3 internet sample. This is a binary variable with 1 as female and 0 as male. Individual level of education is a seven-point ordinal variable, with higher values associated with increased levels of education. Income is a nine-point ordinal variable, with the lowest value representing a total family income from all sources (before taxes) of less than $10,000 per year and the highest value representing more than $150,000 per year. Age is an interval-level variable created from asking the respondent's year of birth and then subtracting from 2015, the year the survey was taken. Race/ethnicity is measured with a self-report white, black, Hispanic, Asian, or some other/mixed.

Religious belief orthodoxy is a three-point ordinal scale created from the following question: "Do you think that your religion or church should preserve its traditional beliefs and practices, adjust its beliefs and practices in light of new circumstances, or adopt modern beliefs and practices?" For this question, higher values are associated with more traditional belief orthodoxy.

Religiosity (religious behavior) is a data reduction factor index variable created from responses to the following questions: "Please tell me how often you do or experience each of the following: would you say at least daily, once a week, once or twice a month, seldom, or never? Pray in private; Read the Bible or other sacred texts outside of religious services; Volunteer time to serve in a church or congregation; Share your views on God or religion with others" and "Aside from weddings and funerals, how often do you attend religious services. . . . more than once a week, once a week, once or twice a month, a few times a year, seldom, or never?" In each case, higher values are associated with increased frequency of behaviors.

Political ideology is a seven-point ordinal variable with higher values associated with more conservative ideology ("very liberal; somewhat liberal; moderate lean liberal; middle of the road; moderate lean conservative, somewhat conservative, very conservative"). Political partisanship is a seven-point ordinal variable with higher values associated with more Republican partisanship ("strong Democrat; weak Democrat; Independent lean Democrat; pure Independent; Independent lean Republican; weak Republican; strong Republican"). Due to the length of the questionnaire needed, moral foundations scores were included the internet-based Wave 3 survey only and were calculated using responses to the thirty questions included in the MFQ30 Questionnaire and coding methodology as described on the MoralFoundations website: http:// moralfoundations.org/questionnaires.

Methodology. Except for the Moral Foundations Questions, all questions were included in all three Waves of the Gender and Religious Representation Survey (the MFQ questions fielded only in Wave 3). We used a separate weighting variable specifically tailored for Wave 3 when we examined that particular dataset. In each case, the dependent variable is the same as described above—a binary variable coded 1 if the respondent supports female clergy in his or her congregation and 0 if not. Thus, we use a binary logistic multivariate regression method to estimate the various models presented in this chapter.

Chapter 6 Additional Information

Throughout this book we limit our analyses only to those who report attending religious services at least "seldom." In this particular chapter, though, we include those who report "never" attending religious services outside of weddings and funerals. This is because we are examining the effect of gender and religious leadership in childhood and adolescence on individuals, regardless of whether they currently attend religious services as adults. In a similar vein, we limit our analysis in this chapter to those who report that they attended religious services with at least some degree of regularity when growing up. In our sample, only 5.5% of respondents reported never attending religious services during childhood and adolescence. The data for Chapter 6 come from Wave 4 of the Gender and Religious Representation Survey.

Multivariate regression models. The various models estimated in this chapter used linear ordinary least squares (OLS) regression analysis to aid in the substantive interpretation. In cases where the dependent variable was binomial or ordinal, the models were estimated using binomial or ordinal logistic regression procedures to ensure that the results were substantively unchanged. We employed the survey weighting for gender, age, and race/ethnicity as described earlier. Further, each model was evaluated for multicollinearity and heteroskedasticity. Robust standard errors were used when needed to account for heteroskedasticity where present. Each model includes control variables for age, gender, race/ethnicity (binomial black and Latino variables), education, income, and non-Christian identification (Jewish and "other"). Each model also includes controls for the gender of the respondent's current congregational leader as well as whether the respondent's congregation currently permits women to serve as its primary leader. The models that estimate education and employment status also include controls for the respondent's mother's level of education and work status when the respondent was growing up as well as the respondent's political partisanship and ideology, as these have been shown to be predictive of future educational attainment and employment for women (Davis and Greenstein 2009). The models predicting view of God also include controls for political partisanship and ideology as these are associated with one's conception of God (Froese and Bader 2010).

Self-esteem measure. While global self-esteem is a concept that has many facets, research has shown that agreement with the single statement "I have high self-esteem" is just as discriminating in measuring self-esteem in public opinion surveys as using multiple measures combined into a single index variable (Baumeister et al. 2003; Robins, Hendin, and Trzesniewski 2001). Here, agreement with the self-esteem declaration is measured on a simple 1-to-4 scale, with higher values corresponding with higher levels of self-esteem.

Self-efficacy index variable. The self-efficacy index variable is a combination of responses to these three statements: "I will be able to achieve most of the goals that I have set for myself," "When facing difficult tasks, I am certain that I will accomplish them," and "Compared to other people, I can do most tasks very well." These three statements were chosen from a longer eight-item scale developed by Scherbaum, Cohen-Charash, and Kern (2006). One statement from each of the three domains (attaining goals, overcoming challenges, and task performance) was chosen due to space limitations on the survey. Respondents indicated that they either strongly agree, somewhat agree, somewhat disagree, or strongly disagree. The three variables have an average correlation with each other of 0.44, p<0.05. These were combined into a single index factor score using a standard data reduction factor analysis procedure, which was then rescaled to a 0-to-1 range to facilitate substantive interpretation. (The Eigenvalue for the single extracted component is 1.87. A Chronbach's alpha test of the combined index gives a score of 0.69, which is above the standardly accepted threshold in social science analysis to conclude the various measures are internally consistent. We can therefore be confident that these measures all capture the same basic attitude of self-efficacy.)

Educational attainment. To facilitate substantive interpretation, the education question was recoded so that responses were represented by approximate years of schooling. No schooling or only attendance in grades one through eight is assigned an 8, "high school incomplete" was assigned 11, "high school graduate" was assigned 12, "technical or trade school" was assigned 13, "some college" was assigned 14, "college degree" was assigned 16, and "post-graduate training" was assigned 19. While approximations, this permitted for the substantive interpretation of the results in terms of years of schooling. Repeating the same analysis using the original education measure changes the p-value for the substantive coefficient from 0.074 to 0.102.

View of God index variable. The view of God index variable was constructed based on that employed by Greeley (1993). Respondents were given the following prompt: "There are many different ways of thinking about God. I'm now going to read four pairs of words. For each one, please tell me which one *most closely* matches your view of God." The four options were then presented while interviewers randomly alternated the order of the words in each pair: friend/

king, judge/lover, master/spouse, and mother/father. Each statement was then recoded so that the more authoritative option corresponded with a -1, the more gracious option corresponded with a +1, and if the respondent volunteered "both," it was coded as a zero. The four variables have an average correlation with each other of 0.33, $p < 0.05$ for all combinations. These were combined into a single index factor score using a standard data reduction factor analysis procedure, which was then rescaled to a 0-to-1 range to facilitate substantive interpretation. (The Eigenvalue for the single extracted component is 1.66. A Chronbach's alpha test of the combined index gives a score of 0.50, which is slightly below the standardly accepted threshold in social science analysis to conclude the various measures are internally consistent. Given that all four variables loaded on a single factor, however, we can be fairly confident that these measures all capture the same basic attitude of self-efficacy.)

Chapter 8 additional information

The data for Chapter 8 come from Waves 1 through 3 of the Gender and Religious Representation survey.

Efficacy/identity index variable. Congregational internal efficacy, external efficacy, identity, and trust are all four-point ordinal variables indicating the degree of agreement with each of the statements listed in the text (strongly agree, somewhat agree, somewhat disagree, strongly disagree). All four variables are highly correlated and load on a single data reduction factor, indicating that for most respondents these four different variables all measure roughly the same basic orientation toward their congregations, whether positive or negative. We combined the four different measures into a single index factor score using a standard data reduction factor analysis procedure, which were then rescaled to a 0-to-1 range to facilitate substantive interpretation. (The Eigenvalue for the first extracted component is 2.57, followed by 0.67 for the second. A Chronbach's alpha test of the combined index gives a score of 0.79, which is above the standard accepted threshold in social science analysis to conclude the various measures are internally consistent. We can therefore be confident that these measures all capture the same basic attitude.)

Religiosity index variable. We use the same measures of religious behaviors as done in previous chapters: attending religious services, reading religious texts outside of religious service, praying in private, volunteering in one's congregation, and talking with other people about religion (daily, at least once a week, once or twice a month, seldom, or never). For the same reasons described above, we combine these measures into a single "religiosity" index variable using a data reduction factor analysis procedure, which we then rescale to a 0-to-1 range to facilitate substantive interpretation. (The Eigenvalue for the first extracted component is 2.82, followed by 0.75 for the second. A Chronbach's alpha test gives a score of 0.80.)

Spirituality index variable. Our measure of spirituality is a combined index variable of four measures of individual spirituality: frequency that an individual reports feeling a deep sense of spiritual peace and well-being, a deep sense of wonder and connection with the universe, God's presence and love, and guided by God in the midst of daily activities. For the same reasons we describe above, we combine these measures into a single "spirituality" index variable using a data reduction factor analysis procedure which we then rescale to a 0-to-1 range to facilitate substantive interpretation. (Eigenvalue for the first extracted component is 2.40, followed by 0.85 for the second. A Chronbach's alpha test gives a score of 0.76.)

Methodology. The various statistical analyses in this chapter utilize standard multivariate OLS regression. Diagnostics were performed in each case to check for multicollinearity and heteroskedasticity. When appropriate, robust standard errors were used to correct for heteroskedasticity, and all models were estimated using the demographic weighting procedure we discussed earlier in this appendix. Each multivariate model includes all three gender leadership variables: 1) whether the respondent's current congregational leader is male or female, 2) whether the respondent's current congregation allows women to serve as the "principal religious leader," and 3) the proportion of women in the congregation's lay leadership. We also collapse the four-point measure of gender representation in a respondent's lay leadership into a binary variable with two values: 1) 0–49% of ministry and small group leaders are female and 2) 50%–100% of ministry and small group leaders are female. This is to simplify the presentation and interpretation of the results.

Each model also includes controls for belief orthodoxy, age, race/ethnicity, education, income, and non-Christian identification (Jewish and "other" non-Christian) for the same reasons as Chapter 4: non-Christian traditions often have wider differences in theology and congregational structures that may affect how members respond to the gender of their leaders. We also control for political ideology and partisanship, given the strong relationship between religion and politics in contemporary American society (Putnam and Campbell 2012, chap. 11). All interactive relationships were tested using Stata's "margins" analytical tool.

We do not include controls for specific individual religious tradition (Evangelical, Catholic, Mainline, etc.) for the same reasons described earlier: policies at the congregational level are not uniform within the major religious traditions. For example, there are Evangelical congregations that allow women pastors and those that do not. Also, Chaves (1997) has described the "decoupling" phenomenon in which policies and practice on gender leadership are not always congruent. For these reasons we analyze the policies of the respondent's specific congregation as the more influential contextual characteristic. Re-estimating these models with controls for Catholic, Evangelical, and Mormon (the three traditions with the strongest male-only policies for the majority of their congregations), however, does not alter the substantive results of any of the findings presented in the chapter, with the exception of reducing the significance value of the interaction term to $p=0.12$ for Figures 8.2 and 8.6 and $p=0.13$ for Figure 8.5.

Numerical data for figures. The numerical data corresponding to Figures 8.7, 8.11, 8.14, and 8.15 can be found in Table A.3. These were computed by predicting the marginal values of each of the outcome variables while varying the three measures of gender representation/leadership to be either present or absent, holding all other variables constant at their mean values. These were computed using Stata's "margins" command after estimating a regression model containing the same variables found in the other models of this chapter: gender of congregational leader, whether the congregation permits female clergy, whether at least half of its lay leadership is composed of women, belief orthodoxy, political ideology, political partisanship, age, black, Latino, education, income, Jewish, and non-Christian. The models were estimated using robust standard errors when necessary to correct for heteroskedasticity.

Relative effect of female representation measures. Chapter 8 noted that of the three different measures of female representation, a congregation's policies on gender leadership and the distribution of lay leadership between men and women matter more than the frequency with which women serve as the congregation's principal religious leader. Figure A.1 illustrates this effect by examining the effect of each type of congregational gender representation for women on measures

Numerical figures corresponding to Figures 8.7, 8.11, 8.14, and 8.15

	Male-dominant leadership congregations	Female-dominant leadership congregations	Egalitarian leadership congregations
Men	Religiosity: 62.0 Spirituality: 33.6 Efficacy/identity/: 78.6	Religiosity: 61.2 Spirituality: 36.2 Efficacy/identity: 83.4	Religiosity: 62.1 Spirituality: 36.7 Efficacy/identity: 81.8
Women	Religiosity: 60.2[a] Spirituality: 35.3 Efficacy/identity: 72.7[a]	Religiosity: 73.2[b] Spirituality: 38.3 Efficacy/identity: 91.6[b]	Religiosity: 67.4 Spirituality: 37.5 Efficacy/identity: 86.1
Progressives	Religiosity: 51.9 Spirituality: 31.9 Efficacy/identity: 64.2[a]	Religiosity: 60.9 Spirituality: 36.4 Efficacy/identity: 86.8[b]	Religiosity: 56.6 Spirituality: 35.1 Efficacy/identity: 82.4
Traditionalists	Religiosity: 69.3 Spirituality: 37.3 Efficacy/identity: 83.5	Religiosity: 78.3 Spirituality: 38.6 Efficacy/identity: 91.4	Religiosity: 74.2 Spirituality: 38.9 Efficacy/identity: 86.6
Liberals	Religiosity: 55.7[a] Spirituality: 33.3 Efficacy/identity: 64.2[a]	Religiosity: 70.8[b] Spirituality: 36.7 Efficacy/identity: 87.9[b]	Religiosity: 66.3 Spirituality: 36.8 Efficacy/identity: 83.1
Conservatives	Religiosity: 65.7 Spirituality: 35.3 Efficacy/identity: 80.6	Religiosity: 75.9 Spirituality: 39.0 Efficacy/identity: 87.2	Religiosity: 70.0 Spirituality: 38.0 Efficacy/identity: 83.4
Democrats	Religiosity: 60.0 Spirituality: 34.3 Efficacy/identity: 70.5	Religiosity: 70.7[b] Spirituality: 36.2 Efficacy/identity: 87.9	Religiosity: 66.6 Spirituality: 84.8 Efficacy/identity: 83.7
Republicans	Religiosity: 62.6 Spirituality: 35.3[a] Efficacy/identity: 78.9[a]	Religiosity: 66.3 Spirituality: 39.8[b] Efficacy/identity: 87.4[b]	Religiosity: 65.2 Spirituality: 38.5 Efficacy/identity: 84.8

[a] Statistically significant at p≤0.05 between male-dominant and gender egalitarian leadership.

[b] Statistically significant at p≤0.05 between female-dominant and male-dominant leadership.

[c] Statistically significant at p≤0.05 between gender egalitarian and female-dominant leadership.

of efficacy/identity. The x-axis represents how often a congregation has a woman as the principal religious leader. On the left-hand side is "male-only clergy" and represents congregations in which women are not admitted to the priesthood. The remainder of the graph represents congregations that allow female clergy and the frequency with which it actually happens. (The graph goes only through 50% because currently only one major American denomination has women serving as clergy at least half of the time: Unitarian-Universalism. See Hersh and Malina 2017 and Quealy 2017.) The various lines represent congregations in which the lay leadership is made up of mostly men, split evenly between men and women, and mostly women.

Figure A.1 demonstrates the key point: Congregational efficacy/identity is anywhere from 73% to 80% for women in congregations that do not ordain women. This increases by about 7% for congregations that do ordain women, *even if a woman rarely, if ever, serves as the principal congregational leader.* The "added value" of having women serve as often as men, beyond it simply being

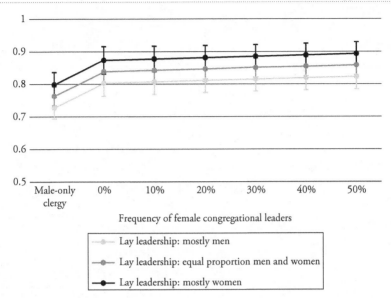

FIGURE A.1 Predicted effect of gender representation on congregational efficacy/identity among women

possible as a policy, is about 2% in terms of efficacy/identity for women in the congregation (and is not statistically significant). In contrast, a congregation in which women make up the majority of lay leaders produces levels of efficacy/identity among women an additional 7% higher than those of their counterparts in congregations where men make up the majority of the lay leadership. This effect is similar in magnitude for theological progressives and political liberals.

References

Abramowitz, Alan I. 2012. *The Polarized Public? Why American Government Is So Dysfunctional.* New York: Pearson.

Abramson, Paul R., John H. Aldrich, Brad T. Gomez, and David W. Rohde. 2015. *Change and Continuity in the 2012 and 2014 Elections.* Washington, DC: CQ Press.

Allen, Bob. 2014. "N.C. Church, First to Ordain a Woman, Calls Its First Female Pastor." *Baptist News Global.* https://baptistnews.com/2014/04/15/pioneering-n-c-church-calls-woman-pastor/ (May 9, 2016).

Allen, John L. 2015. "Why Pope Francis Won't Let Women Become Priests." *Time.* http://time.com/3729904/francis-women/ (May 5, 2016).

American Baptist Churches USA. 1989. "American Baptist Policy Statement on Ordained Ministry." http://www.abc-usa.org/wp-content/uploads/2012/06/ordain.pdf (May 9, 2016).

Amodio, David M., John T. Jost, Sarah L. Master, and Cindy M. Yee. 2007. "Neurocognitive Correlates of Liberalism and Conservatism." *Nature Neuroscience* 10(10): 1246–47.

Anastasopoulos, Lefteris. 2016. "Estimating the Gender Penalty in House of Representative Elections Using a Regression Discontinuity Design." *Electoral Studies* 43: 150–57.

Atkeson, Lonna Rae. 2003. "Not All Cues Are Created Equal: The Conditional Impact of Female Candidates on Political Engagement." *Journal of Politics* 65(4): 1040–61.

Atkeson, Lonna Rae, and Nancy Carrillo. 2007. "More Is Better: The Influence of Collective Female Descriptive Representation on External Efficacy." *Politics & Gender* 3(1): 79–101.

Bacon, John. 2016. "Pope: Women Will Be Banned from Priesthood Forever." *USA TODAY.* http://www.usatoday.com/story/news/nation/2016/11/01/pope-women-banned-priesthood-forever/93118528/ (January 27, 2017).

Bandura, Albert. 1976. *Social Learning Theory.* Englewood Cliffs, NJ: Prentice-Hall.

———. 1982. "Self-Efficacy Mechanism in Human Agency." *American Psychologist* 37(2): 122–47.

————. 1986. "The Explanatory and Predictive Scope of Self-Efficacy Theory." *Journal of Social and Clinical Psychology* 4(3): 359–73.

————. 1993. "Perceived Self-Efficacy in Cognitive Development and Functioning." *Educational Psychologist* 28(2): 117–48.

————. 1997. *Self-Efficacy: The Exercise of Control.* New York: Worth Publishers.

————. 2010. "Self-Efficacy." In *The Corsini Encyclopedia of Psychology*, edited by Irving B. Weiner and W. Edward Craighead, 1534–35. New York: John Wiley & Sons, Inc.

Banks, Adelle M. 2015a. "Adventists Stay the Course, Vote to Deny Women's Ordination." *Religion News Service.* http://religionnews.com/2015/07/08/adventists-stay-course-vote-deny-womens-ordination/ (May 5, 2016).

————. 2015b. "Male Adventist Pastors Forgo Ordination Credentials in Solidarity with Unordained Women." *Religion News Service.* http://religionnews.com/2015/10/15/male-adventist-pastors-forgo-ordination-credentials-solidarity-unordained-women/ (May 3, 2016).

————. 2017. "Unitarian Universalists Elect First Woman President." *Religion News Service.* http://religionnews.com/2017/06/27/unitarian-universalists-elect-first-woman-president/ (June 27, 2017).

Barker, David C., and Christopher Jan Carman. 2000. "The Spirit of Capitalism? Religious Doctrine, Values, and Economic Attitude Constructs." *Political Behavior* 22(1): 1–27.

BarNir, Anat, Warren E. Watson, and Holly M. Hutchins. 2011. "Mediation and Moderated Mediation in the Relationship Among Role Models, Self-Efficacy, Entrepreneurial Career Intention, and Gender." *Journal of Applied Social Psychology* 41(2): 270–97.

Barreto, Matt A., Gary M. Segura, and Nathan D. Woods. 2004. "The Mobilizing Effect of Majority–Minority Districts on Latino Turnout." *American Political Science Review* 98(1): 65–75.

Bartel, Bill. 2015. "Let Women Be Priests, Sen. Kaine Tells the Pope." *Virginian-Pilot.* http://pilotonline.com/news/government/politics/let-women-be-priests-sen-kaine-tells-the-pope/article_55c95931-5845-52e3-9b3e-2a167040c0a6.html (January 27, 2017).

Bartkowski, John. 2001. *Remaking the Godly Marriage: Gender Negotiation in Evangelical Families.* New Brunswick, NJ: Rutgers University Press.

Bartkowski, John P., and Lynn M. Hempel. 2009. "Sex and Gender Traditionalism Among Conservative Protestants: Does the Difference Make a Difference?" *Journal for the Scientific Study of Religion* 48(4): 805–16.

Baumard, Nicolas. 2016. *The Origins of Fairness: How Evolution Explains Our Moral Nature.* New York: Oxford University Press.

Baumeister, Roy F., Jennifer D. Campbell, Joachim I. Krueger, and Kathleen D. Vohs. 2003. "Does High Self-Esteem Cause Better Performance, Interpersonal Success, Happiness, or Healthier Lifestyles?" *Psychological Science in the Public Interest* 4(1): 1–44.

BBC News Services. 2013. "How Many Roman Catholics Are There in the World?" *BBC News.* http://www.bbc.com/news/world-21443313 (May 9, 2016).

Beaman, Lori, Esther Duflo, Rohini Pande, and Petia Topalova. 2012. "Female Leadership Raises Aspirations and Educational Attainment for Girls: A Policy Experiment in India." *Science* 335(6068): 582–86.

Belleville, Linda L., Craig L. Blomberg, Craig S. Keener, and Thomas R. Schreiner. 2005. *Two Views on Women in Ministry.* Revised edition. Edited by James R. Beck. Grand Rapids, Mich.: Zondervan.

Benenson, Joyce F., Henry Markovits, and Richard Wrangham. 2014. "Rank Influences Human Sex Differences in Dyadic Cooperation." *Current Biology* 24(5): R190–91.

Benson, Peter, and Bernard Spilka. 1973. "God Image as a Function of Self-Esteem and Locus of Control." *Journal for the Scientific Study of Religion* 12(3): 297–310.

Berger, Noah, and Peter Fisher. 2013. "A Well-Educated Workforce Is Key to State Prosperity." *Economic Policy Institute*. http://www.epi.org/publication/states-education-productivity-growth-foundations/ (January 30, 2017).

Berinsky, Adam J. 1999. "The Two Faces of Public Opinion." *American Journal of Political Science* 43(4): 1209–30.

Berkes, Howard. 2013. "A Woman's Prayer Makes Mormon History." *NPR.org*. http://www.npr.org/sections/thetwo-way/2013/04/08/176604202/a-womans-prayer-makes-mormon-history (June 28, 2017).

Bernstein, Robert, Anita Chadha, and Robert Montjoy. 2001. "Overreporting Voting: Why It Happens and Why It Matters." *Public Opinion Quarterly* 65(1): 22–44.

Bettinger, Eric P., and Bridget Terry Long. 2005. "Do Faculty Serve as Role Models? The Impact of Instructor Gender on Female Students." *The American Economic Review* 95(2): 152–57.

Bian, Lin, Sarah-Jane Leslie, and Andrei Cimpian. 2017. "Gender Stereotypes about Intellectual Ability Emerge Early and Influence Children's Interests." *Science* 355(6323): 389–91.

Bishop, Bill. 2009. *The Big Sort: Why the Clustering of Like-Minded America Is Tearing Us Apart*. Boston, MA: Mariner Books.

Bishop, George F., Alfred J. Tuchfarber, and Robert W. Oldendick. 1986. "Opinions on Fictitious Issues: The Pressure to Answer Survey Questions." *Public Opinion Quarterly* 50(2): 240–50.

Blair, Graeme, and Kosuke Imai. 2012. "Statistical Analysis of List Experiments." *Political Analysis* 20(1): 47–77.

Blumberg, Antonia. 2017. "Muslim Women Are Opening a New, Inclusive Mosque in California." *Huffington Post*. http://www.huffingtonpost.com/entry/muslim-women-are-opening-a-new-inclusive-mosque-in-california_us_58e40a50e4b0f4a923b30ec7.

Bolzendahl, Catherine I., and Daniel J. Myers. 2004. "Feminist Attitudes and Support for Gender Equality: Opinion Change in Women and Men, 1974–1998." *Social Forces* 83(2): 759–89.

Boorstein, Michelle. 2015a. "Archbishop Urges Pope Francis's Synod on the Family: Consider Allowing Female Deacons." *Washington Post*. https://www.washingtonpost.com/news/acts-of-faith/wp/2015/10/06/archbishop-urges-pope-franciss-synod-on-the-family-consider-allowing-women-deacons/ (May 5, 2016).

———. 2015b. "Seventh-Day Adventists Vote against Female Ordination." *Washington Post*. https://www.washingtonpost.com/local/social-issues/seventh-day-adventists-vote-against-female-ordination/2015/07/08/42920f7e-25c8-11e5-b77f-eb13a215f593_story.html (May 9, 2016).

Boorstein, Michelle, and Wesley Robinson. 2014. "Founder of Mormon Women's Movement Excommunicated by All-Male Church Panel." *Washington Post*. https://www.washingtonpost.com/local/founder-of-mormon-womens-movement-excommunicated-by-all-male-church-panel/2014/06/23/b3f29b76-fb11-11e3-932c-0a55b81f48ce_story.html (May 5, 2016).

Bosma, Niels, Jolanda Hessels, Veronique Schutjens, Mirjam Van Praag, and Ingrid Verhuel. 2012. "Entrepreneurship and Role Models." *Journal of Economic Psychology* 33(2): 410–24.

Brader, Ted, Joshua A. Tucker, and Dominik Duell. 2013. "Which Parties Can Lead Opinion? Experimental Evidence on Partisan Cue Taking in Multiparty Democracies." *Comparative Political Studies* 46(11): 1485–1517.

Brady, Jeff. 2015. "In Defiance of the Church, Some Catholic Women Seek Priesthood." *NPR. org*. http://www.npr.org/2015/09/16/440254032/in-defiance-of-the-church-some-catholic-women-seeking-priesthood (May 5, 2016).

Briggs, Sheila, and Mary McClintock Fulkerson. 2014. *The Oxford Handbook of Feminist Theology*. Reprint edition. New York: Oxford University Press.

Brinkerhoff, Merlin B., and Marlene MacKie. 1985. "Religion and Gender: A Comparison of Canadian and American Student Attitudes." *Journal of Marriage and Family* 47(2): 415–29.

Brooks, Clem, and Catherine Bolzendahl. 2004. "The Transformation of US Gender Role Attitudes: Cohort Replacement, Social-Structural Change, and Ideological Learning." *Social Science Research* 33(1): 106–33.

Bryant, Alyssa N. 2003. "Changes in Attitudes toward Women's Roles: Predicting Gender-Role Traditionalism Among College Students." *Sex Roles* 48(3–4): 131–42.

Buchanan, Robert F., Renee L. Warning, and Robert P. Tett. 2012. "Trouble at the Top: Women Who Don't Want to Work for a Female Boss." *Journal of Business Diversity* 12(1): 33–46.

Bureau of Labor Statistics. 2014. "Women in the Labor Force: A Databook." https://www.bls.gov/opub/reports/womens-databook/archive/womenlaborforce_2013.pdf.

Buri, John R., and Rebecca A. Mueller. 1993. "Psychoanalytic Theory and Loving God Concepts: Parent Referencing Versus Self-Referencing." *The Journal of Psychology* 127(1): 17–27.

Burke, Edmund. 2009. *Reflections on the Revolution in France*. Reissue edition. Ed. L. G. Mitchell. New York: Oxford University Press.

Burns, Nancy, Kay Lehman Schlozman, and Sidney Verba. 2001. *The Private Roots of Public Action: Gender, Equality, and Political Participation*. Cambridge, Mass.: Harvard University Press.

Bussey, Kay, and Albert Bandura. 1984. "Influence of Gender Constancy and Social Power on Sex-Linked Modeling." *Journal of Personality and Social Psychology* 47(6): 1292–1302.

———. 1999. "Social Cognitive Theory of Gender Development and Differentiation." *Psychological Review* 106(4): 676–713.

Bussey, Kay, and David G. Perry. 1982. "Same-Sex Imitation: The Avoidance of Cross-Sex Models or the Acceptance of Same-Sex Models?" *Sex Roles* 8(7): 773–84.

Campbell, Catherine Galko. 2013. *Persons, Identity, and Political Theory: A Defense of Rawlsian Political Identity*. New York: Springer.

Campbell, David E., and Christina Wolbrecht. 2006. "See Jane Run: Women Politicians as Role Models for Adolescents." *Journal of Politics* 68(2): 233–47.

Campbell, Toni A., and David E. Campbell. 1997. "Faculty/Student Mentor Program: Effects on Academic Performance and Retention." *Research in Higher Education* 38(6): 727–42.

Carney, Eliza Newlin. 2016. "Is 2016 Another 'Year of the Woman?'" *The American Prospect*. http://prospect.org/article/2016-another-%E2%80%9Cyear-woman%E2%80%9D.

Carrell, Scott E., Marianne E. Page, and James E. West. 2009. *Sex and Science: How Professor Gender Perpetuates the Gender Gap*. National Bureau of Economic Research. Working Paper. http://www.nber.org/papers/w14959 (January 30, 2017).

Carroll, Jackson W., Barbara Hargrove, and Adair T. Lummis. 1983. *Women of the Cloth: A New Opportunity for the Churches*. San Francisco: Harper & Row.

Carroll, Susan J., and Richard L. Fox, eds. 2013. *Gender and Elections: Shaping the Future of American Politics*. 3rd edition. New York: Cambridge University Press.

Catania, Joseph A., David R. Gibson, Barbara Marin, Thomas J. Coates, and Ruth M. Greenblatt. 1990. "Response Bias in Assessing Sexual Behaviors Relevant to HIV Transmission." *Evaluation and Program Planning* 13(1): 19–29.

Cauterucci, Christina. 2016. "The Number of Women of Color in the Senate Is About to Quadruple." *Slate*. http://www.slate.com/blogs/xx_factor/2016/11/09/the_number_of_women_of_color_in_the_senate_is_about_to_quadruple.html (January 27, 2017).

CBE International. 2007. "US Denominations and Their Stances on Women in Leadership." http://www2.cbeinternational.org/new/E-Journal/2007/07spring/denominations%20first%20installment--FINAL.pdf (May 4, 2016).

Chang, Patricia M. Y. 1997. "In Search of a Pulpit: Sex Differences in the Transition from Seminary Training to the First Parish Job." *Journal for the Scientific Study of Religion* 36(4): 614–27.

Chanley, Virginia A., Thomas J. Rudolph, and Wendy M. Rahn. 2000. "The Origins and Consequences of Public Trust in Government: A Time Series Analysis." *Public Opinion Quarterly* 64(3): 239–56.

Chapman, Morris H. 2016. "The Truth about the SBC & Texas." http://www.baptist2baptist.net/PDF/TruthAboutSBCandTexas.pdf (February 6, 2016).

Charlton, Joy. 1997. "Clergywomen of the Pioneer Generation: A Longitudinal Study." *Journal for the Scientific Study of Religion* 36(4): 599–613.

Chase, Lisa. 2014. "An Oral History of the Day Women Changed Congress." *ELLE*. http://www.elle.com/life-love/society-career/history-of-nytimes-photo-house-of-representatives-1991 (January 27, 2017).

Chaves, Mark. 1997. *Ordaining Women: Culture and Conflict in Religious Organizations*. Cambridge, Mass.: Harvard University Press.

Chaves, Mark, and James Cavendish. 1997. "Recent Changes in Women's Ordination Conflicts: The Effect of a Social Movement on Intraorganizational Controversy." *Journal for the Scientific Study of Religion* 36(4): 574–84.

Chaves, Mark, and Alison Eagle. 2015. "National Congregations Study." http://www.soc.duke.edu/natcong/Docs/NCSIII_report_final.pdf (May 3, 2016).

Ciabattari, Teresa. 2001. "Changes in Men's Conservative Gender Ideologies: Cohort and Period Influences." *Gender & Society* 15(4): 574–91.

Citrin, Jack, Donald Philip Green, and David O. Sears. 1990. "White Reactions to Black Candidates: When Does Race Matter?" *The Public Opinion Quarterly* 54(1): 74–96.

Clark, Catherine. 2017. "Orthodox Church Debate over Women Deacons Moves One Step Closer to Reality." http://religionnews.com/2017/03/09/orthodox-church-debate-over-women-deacons-moves-one-step-closer-to-reality/ (July 21, 2017).

Clark, Christopher J. 2014. "Collective Descriptive Representation and Black Voter Mobilization in 2008." *Political Behavior* 36(2): 315–33.

Clark, Paul W., Craig A. Martin, and Alan J. Bush. 2001. "The Effect of Role Model Influence on Adolescents' Materialism and Marketplace Knowledge." *Journal of Marketing Theory and Practice* 9(4): 27–36.

Clausen, Aage R. 1968. "Response Validity: Vote Report." *Public Opinion Quarterly* 32(4): 588–606.

Cohen, Claire. 2017. "Donald Trump Sexism Tracker: Every Offensive Comment in One Place." *The Telegraph*. http://www.telegraph.co.uk/women/politics/donald-trump-sexism-tracker-every-offensive-comment-in-one-place/ (January 27, 2017).

Comşa, Mircea, and Camil Postelnicu. 2013. "Measuring Social Desirability Effects on Self-Reported Turnout Using the Item Count Technique." *International Journal of Public Opinion Research* 25(2): 153–72.

Cooperman, Alan, Greg Smith, Elizabeth Sciupac, and Erin O'Connell. 2014. "U.S. Catholics View Pope Francis as a Change for the Better." http://www.pewforum.org/files/2014/03/Pope-Francis-change-for-the-better-full-report.pdf (May 17, 2016).

Cooperman, Alan, and Gregory Smith. 2015. "America's Changing Religious Landscape." *Pew Research Center for the People and the Press*. http://www.pewforum.org/2015/05/12/americas-changing-religious-landscape/.

Corbett, Christianne, and Catherine Hill. 2012. *Graduating to a Pay Gap: The Earnings of Women and Men One Year after College Graduation*. American Association of University Women. http://www.aauw.org/research/graduating-to-a-pay-gap/ (February 12, 2017).

Cott, Nancy F., ed. 2004. *No Small Courage: A History of Women in the United States*. New York: Oxford University Press.

Cragun, Ryan T., Stephen M. Merino, Michael Nielson, Brent D. Beal, Matthew Stearmer, and Bradley Jones. 2016. "Predictors of Opposition to and Support for the Ordination of Women: Insights from the LDS Church." *Mental Health, Religion & Culture* 19(2): 124–37.

Craig, Stephen C., and Michael A. Maggiotto. 1982. "Measuring Political Efficacy." *Political Methodology* 8(3): 85–109.

Crandall, Barbara. 2012. *Gender and Religion: The Dark Side of Scripture*. 2nd edition. New York: Bloomsbury Academic.

Cunningham, Loren, David Joel Hamilton, and Janice Rogers. 2000. *Why Not Women: A Biblical Study of Women in Missions, Ministry, and Leadership*. Seattle: YWAM Publishing.

Cutler, David M., and Adriana Lleras-Muney. 2006. *Education and Health: Evaluating Theories and Evidence*. National Bureau of Economic Research. Working Paper. http://www.nber.org/papers/w12352 (January 30, 2017).

Davis, Shannon N., and Theodore N. Greenstein. 2009. "Gender Ideology: Components, Predictors, and Consequences." *Annual Review of Sociology* 35: 87–105.

De Roos, Simone A., Jurjen Iedema, and Siebren Miedema. 2004. "Influence of Maternal Denomination, God Concepts, and Child-Rearing Practices on Young Children's God Concepts." *Journal for the Scientific Study of Religion* 43(4): 519–35.

Deckman, Melissa M., Sue E. S. Crawford, Laura R. Olson, and John C. Green. 2003. "Clergy and the Politics of Gender." *Journal for the Scientific Study of Religion* 42(4): 621–31.

Dickie, Jane R., Amy K. Eshleman, Dawn M. Merasco, Amy Shepard, Michael Vander Wilt, and Melissa Johnson. 1997. "Parent-Child Relationships and Children's Images of God." *Journal for the Scientific Study of Religion* 36(1): 25–43.

Djupe, Paul A. 2014. "The Effects of Descriptive Associational Leadership on Civic Engagement: The Case of Clergy and Gender in Protestant Denominations." *Journal for the Scientific Study of Religion* 53(3): 497–514.

Djupe, Paul A., and Christopher P. Gilbert. 2003. *The Prophetic Pulpit: Clergy, Churches, and Communities in American Politics*. Lanham, Md.: Rowman & Littlefield Publishers.

———. 2008. *The Political Influence of Churches*. Cambridge; New York: Cambridge University Press.

Djupe, Paul A., and Laura R. Olson. 2013. "Stained-Glass Politics and Descriptive Representation: Does Associational Leadership by Women Engender Political Engagement among Women?" *Politics, Groups, and Identities* 1(3): 329–48.

Djupe, Paul A., Jacob R. Neiheisel, and Anand E. Sokey. 2017. "Did Disagreement over Trump Drive People Out of Churches?" *Religion in Public Blog*, April 11. https://religioninpublic. blog/2017/04/11/did-disagreement-over-trump-drive-people-out-of-churches/ (January 16, 2018).

Dolan, Kathleen. 1998. "Voting for Women in the 'Year of the Woman.'" *American Journal of Political Science* 42(1): 272–93.

———. 2006. "Symbolic Mobilization? The Impact of Candidate Sex in American Elections." *American Politics Research* 34(6): 687–704.

Donnellan, M. Brent, Kali H. Trzesniewski, and Richard W. Robins. 2014. "Measures of Self-Esteem." In *Measures of Personality and Social Psychological Attitudes: Measures of Social Psychological Attitudes*, edited by Gregory J. Boyle, Donald H. Saklofske, and Gerald Matthews, 131–57. Cambridge, MA: Academic Press.

Dovi, Suzanne. 2007. *The Good Representative*. Hoboken, NJ: Wiley-Blackwell.

Druckman, James N. 2015. "Research and Undergraduate Teaching: A False Divide? Symposium Introduction." *PS: Political Science & Politics* 48(1): 35–38.

DuBois, David L., and Naida Silverthorn. 2005. "Natural Mentoring Relationships and Adolescent Health: Evidence From a National Study." *American Journal of Public Health* 95(3): 518–24.

Eby, Lillian T., Tammy D. Allen, Sarah C. Evans, Thomas Ng, and David L. DuBois. 2008. "Does Mentoring Matter? A Multidisciplinary Meta-Analysis Comparing Mentored and Non-Mentored Individuals." *Journal of Vocational Behavior* 72(2): 254–67.

Elliot, Andrew J., and Patricia G. Devine. 1994. "On the Motivational Nature of Cognitive Dissonance: Dissonance as Psychological Discomfort." *Journal of Personality and Social Psychology* 67(3): 382–94.

Elliott, Andrea. 2005. "Woman Leads Muslim Prayer Service in New York." *The New York Times*. http://www.nytimes.com/2005/03/19/nyregion/woman-leads-muslim-prayer-service-in-new-york.html (May 9, 2016).

Ellison, Christopher G. 1995. "Rational Choice Explanations of Individual Religious Behavior: Notes on the Problem of Social Embeddedness." *Journal for the Scientific Study of Religion* 34(1): 89–97.

England, Paula. 2010. "The Gender Revolution: Uneven and Stalled." *Gender & Society* 24(2): 149–66.

Erola, Jani, Sanni Jalonen, and Hannu Lehti. 2016. "Parental Education, Class and Income over Early Life Course and Children's Achievement." *Research in Social Stratification and Mobility* 44: 33–43.

Fahrenthold, David A. 2016. "Trump Recorded Having Extremely Lewd Conversation about Women in 2005." *Washington Post*. https://www.washingtonpost.com/politics/trump-recorded-having-extremely-lewd-conversation-about-women-in-2005/2016/10/07/3b9ce776-8cb4-11e6-bf8a-3d26847eeed4_story.html (January 27, 2017).

Fan, Pi-Ling, and Margaret Mooney Marini. 2000. "Influences on Gender-Role Attitudes during the Transition to Adulthood." *Social Science Research* 29(2): 258–83.

Fetzer, Joel S. 1998. "Religious Minorities and Support for Immigrant Rights in the United States, France, and Germany." *Journal for the Scientific Study of Religion* 37(1): 41–49.

Finke, Roger, and Amy Adamczyk. 2008. "Cross-National Moral Beliefs: The Influence of National Religious Context." *Sociological Quarterly* 49(4): 617–52.

Finke, Roger, and Rodney Stark. 2005. *The Churching of America, 1776–2005: Winners and Losers in Our Religious Economy*. Revised edition. New Brunswick, NJ: Rutgers University Press.

Fisher, Mary Pat. 2006. *Women in Religion*. New York: Pearson.

Forbes, H. D. 1997. *Ethnic Conflict: Commerce, Culture, and the Contact Hypothesis*. New Haven, Conn.: Yale University Press.

Fowler, Robert Booth, Allen D. Hertzke, Laura R. Olson, and Kevin R. Den Dulk. 2013. *Religion and Politics in America: Faith, Culture, and Strategic Choices*. 5th edition. Boulder, Colo.: Westview Press.

Francis, Leslie J. 2002. "God Images, Personal Wellbeing and Moral Values." In *Imagining God: Empirical Explorations from an International Perspective*. Münster, Germany: LIT Verlag Münster.

Francis, Leslie J., Harry M. Gibson, and Mandy Robbins. 2001. "God Images and Self-Worth among Adolescents in Scotland." *Mental Health, Religion & Culture* 4(2): 103–8.

Friesen, Amanda, and Paul A. Djupe. 2017. "Conscientious Women: The Dispositional Conditions of Institutional Treatment on Civic Involvement." *Politics & Gender* 13(1): 57–80.

Froese, Paul, and Christopher Bader. 2010. *America's Four Gods: What We Say about God—and What That Says about Us*. New York: Oxford University Press.

Froese, Paul, and Christopher D. Bader. 2007. "God in America: Why Theology Is Not Simply the Concern of Philosophers." *Journal for the Scientific Study of Religion* 46(4): 465–81.

Fry, Richard, and Renee Stepler. 2017. "Women May Never Make up Half of the U.S. Workforce." *Pew Research Center*. http://www.pewresearch.org/fact-tank/2017/01/31/women-may-never-make-up-half-of-the-u-s-workforce/ (February 3, 2017).

Furnée, Carina A., Wim Groot, Van Den Brink, and Henriëtte Maassen. 2008. "The Health Effects of Education: A Meta-Analysis." *European Journal of Public Health* 18(4): 417–21.

Gay, Claudine. 2001. "The Effect of Black Congressional Representation on Political Participation." *American Political Science Review* 95(03): 589–602.

Ghosh, Rajashi, and Thomas G. Reio Jr. 2013. "Career Benefits Associated with Mentoring for Mentors: A Meta-Analysis." *Journal of Vocational Behavior* 83(1): 106–16.

Gibson, Donald E. 2004. "Role Models in Career Development: New Directions for Theory and Research." *Journal of Vocational Behavior* 65(1): 134–56.

Gibson, Donald E, and Diana I. Cordova. 1999. "Women's and Men's Role Models: The Importance of Exemplars." In *Mentoring Dilemmas: Developmental Relationships Within Multicultural Organizations*. New York: Psychology Press, 115–34.

Gilbert, Lucia A., June M. Gallessich, and Sherri L. Evans. 1983. "Sex of Faculty Role Model and Students' Self-Perceptions of Competency." *Sex Roles* 9(5): 597–607.

Gilens, Martin. 1998. "Racial Attitudes and Race-Neutral Social Policies: White Opposition to Welfare and the Politics of Racial Inequality." In *Perception and Prejudice: Race and Politics in the United States*. New Haven, CT: Yale University Press, 171–201.

Gilligan, Carol. 1982. *In a Different Voice: Psychological Theory and Women's Development*. 2nd edition. Cambridge, Mass.: Harvard University Press.

Gilmore, Stephanie, ed. 2008. *Feminist Coalitions: Historical Perspectives on Second-Wave Feminism in the United States.* Urbana: University of Illinois Press.

Glick, Peter, and Susan T. Fiske. 2001. "An Ambivalent Alliance: Hostile and Benevolent Sexism as Complementary Justifications for Gender Inequality." *American Psychologist* 56(2): 109–18.

Glynn, Adam N. 2013. "What Can We Learn with Statistical Truth Serum? Design and Analysis of the List Experiment." *Public Opinion Quarterly* 77(1): 159–72.

Goren, Paul, Christopher M. Federico, and Miki Caul Kittilson. 2009. "Source Cues, Partisan Identities, and Political Value Expression." *American Journal of Political Science* 53(4): 805–20.

Graham, Jesse, Jonathan Haidt, and Brian A. Nosek. 2009. "Liberals and Conservatives Rely on Different Sets of Moral Foundations." *Journal of Personality and Social Psychology* 96(5): 1029–46.

Grant, Tobin. 2015. "Most Women Belong to a Religious Community That Prohibits Them from Being Leaders." *Religion News Service.* http://religionnews.com/2015/07/09/most-women-belong-to-a-religious-community-that-prohibits-them-from-being-leaders/ (May 3, 2016).

———. 2016. "Gender Pay Gap among Clergy Worse than National Average—A First Look at the New National Data." *Religion News Service.* http://religionnews.com/2016/01/12/gender-pay-gap-among-clergy-worse-than-national-average-a-first-look-at-the-new-national-data/ (May 3, 2016).

Graves-Fitzsimmons, Guthrie. 2016. "Methodists Consider Revoking Female Ordination (SATIRE)." *Religion News Service.* https://twitter.com/RNS/status/728638104463024128 (May 27, 2016).

Greeley, Andrew. 1989. *Religious Change in America.* Cambridge, Mass.: Harvard University Press.

———. 1993. "Religion and Attitudes toward the Environment." *Journal for the Scientific Study of Religion* 32(1): 19–28.

Green, John C., Mark J. Rozell, and Clyde Wilcox, eds. 2006. *The Values Campaign?: The Christian Right and the 2004 Elections.* Washington, DC: Georgetown University Press.

Hackett, Gail, Donna Esposito, and M. Sean O'Halloran. 1989. "The Relationship of Role Model Influences to the Career Salience and Educational and Career Plans of College Women." *Journal of Vocational Behavior* 35(2): 164–80.

Hadaway, C. Kirk, Penny Long Marler, and Mark Chaves. 1993. "What the Polls Don't Show: A Closer Look at U.S. Church Attendance." *American Sociological Review* 58(6): 741–52.

Haidt, Jonathan. 2012. *The Righteous Mind: Why Good People Are Divided by Politics and Religion.* New York: Pantheon.

Haidt, Jonathan, and Jesse Graham. 2007. "When Morality Opposes Justice: Conservatives Have Moral Intuitions That Liberals May Not Recognize." *Social Justice Research* 20(1): 98–116.

Hankins, Barry. 2009. *American Evangelicals: A Contemporary History of a Mainstream Religious Movement.* Lantham, MD: Rowman & Littlefield Publishers.

Harrison, Mark. 2014. "Letter to Kate Kelly." https://www.washingtonpost.com/apps/g/page/local/letter-to-kate-kelly/1118/ (May 5, 2016).

Heilman, Uriel. 2015. "New Cohort of Clergy Tests Orthodox Readiness for Women Rabbis." *Jewish Telegraphic Agency.* http://www.jta.org/2015/05/12/news-opinion/united-states/new-cohort-of-clergy-tests-orthodox-readiness-for-women-rabbis (May 5, 2016).

Hersh, Eitan D., and Gabrielle Malina. 2017. "Partisan Pastor: The Politics of 130,000 American Religious Leaders." http://www.eitanhersh.com/uploads/7/9/7/5/7975685/hersh_malina_draft_061117.pdf.

Hertel, Bradley R., and Michael J. Donahue. 1995. "Parental Influences on God Images among Children: Testing Durkheim's Metaphoric Parallelism." *Journal for the Scientific Study of Religion* 34(2): 186–99.

Hess, Cynthia, Jessica Milli, Jeff Hayes, and Ariene Hegewisch. 2015. "The Status of Women in the States: 2015." *Women in the States*. http://www.iwpr.org/publications/pubs/the-status-of-women-in-the-states-2015-full-report (January 27, 2017).

Hetherington, Marc J. 1998. "The Political Relevance of Political Trust." *American Political Science Review* 92(4): 791–808.

———. 2006. *Why Trust Matters: Declining Political Trust and the Demise of American Liberalism*. Princeton, NJ: Princeton University Press.

Hetherington, Marc J., and Thomas J. Rudolph. 2015. *Why Washington Won't Work: Polarization, Political Trust, and the Governing Crisis*. Chicago: University Of Chicago Press.

Heywood, Andrew. 2012. *Political Ideologies: An Introduction*. 5th edition. New York: Palgrave Macmillan.

Hill, John P., and Mary Ellen Lynch. 1983. "The Intensification of Gender-Related Role Expectations during Early Adolescence." In *Girls at Puberty*, eds. Jeanne Brooks-Gunn and Anne C. Petersen. Boston: Springer, 201–28. http://link.springer.com/chapter/10.1007/978-1-4899-0354-9_10 (January 30, 2017).

Hill, M. Anne, and Elizabeth King. 1995. "Women's Education and Economic Well-Being." *Feminist Economics* 1(2): 21–46.

Hoffmann, Florian, and Philip Oreopoulos. 2009. "A Professor Like Me: The Influence of Instructor Gender on College Achievement." *Journal of Human Resources* 44(2): 479–94.

Holbrook, Allyson L., and Jon A. Krosnick. 2010. "Social Desirability Bias in Voter Turnout Reports Tests Using the Item Count Technique." *Public Opinion Quarterly* 74(1): 37–67.

Holden, Gary. 1992. "The Relationship of Self-Efficacy Appraisals to Subsequent Health Related Outcomes." *Social Work in Health Care* 16(1): 53–93.

Hopkins, Daniel J. 2009. "The Diversity Discount: When Increasing Ethnic and Racial Diversity Prevents Tax Increases." *The Journal of Politics* 71(01): 160–77.

Huddy, Leonie, Joshua Billig, John Bracciodieta, Lois Hoeffler, Patrick J. Moynihan, and Patricia Pugliani. 1997. "The Effect of Interviewer Gender on the Survey Response." *Political Behavior* 19(3): 197–220.

Hummer, Robert A., and Elaine M. Hernandez. 2013. "The Effect of Educational Attainment on Adult Mortality in the U.S." *Population Reference Bureau*. http://www.prb.org/Publications/Reports/2013/us-educational-attainment-mortality.aspx (January 30, 2017).

Iannaccone, Laurence R. 1994. "Why Strict Churches Are Strong." *American Journal of Sociology* 99(5): 1180–1211.

Imai, Kosuke. 2011. "Multivariate Regression Analysis for the Item Count Technique." *Journal of the American Statistical Association* 106(494): 407–16.

Institute for Women's Policy Research. 2016. "Pay Equity & Discrimination." http://www.iwpr.org/initiatives/pay-equity-and-discrimination (May 9, 2016).

Ironson, Gail, Rick Stuetzle, Dale Ironson, Elizabeth Balbin, Heidemarie Kremer, Annie George, Neil Schneiderman, and Mary Ann Fletcher. 2011. "View of God as Benevolent and Forgiving or Punishing and Judgmental Predicts HIV Disease Progression." *Journal of Behavioral Medicine* 34(6): 414–25.

Janus, Alexander L. 2010. "The Influence of Social Desirability Pressures on Expressed Immigration Attitudes." *Social Science Quarterly* 91(4): 928–46.

Jick, Todd D. 1979. "Mixing Qualitative and Quantitative Methods: Triangulation in Action." *Administrative Science Quarterly* 24(4): 602–11.

Johnson, Kathryn A., Yexin Jessica Li, Adam B. Cohen, and Morris A. Okun. 2013. "Friends in High Places: The Influence of Authoritarian and Benevolent God-Concepts on Social Attitudes and Behaviors." *Psychology of Religion and Spirituality* 5(1): 15–22.

Johnston, Lucas F. 2014. *Religion and Sustainability: Social Movements and the Politics of the Environment*. Bristol, CT: Routledge.

Jones, Susan S. 2009. "The Development of Imitation in Infancy." *Philosophical Transactions of the Royal Society B: Biological Sciences* 364(1528): 2325–35.

Jonge, Chad P. Kiewiet de, and David W. Nickerson. 2013. "Artificial Inflation or Deflation? Assessing the Item Count Technique in Comparative Surveys." *Political Behavior* 36(3): 659–82.

Jost, John T., Jamie L. Napier, Hulda Thorisdottir, Samuel D. Gosling, Tibor P. Palfai, and Brian Ostafin. 2007. "Are Needs to Manage Uncertainty and Threat Associated With Political Conservatism or Ideological Extremity?" *Personality and Social Psychology Bulletin* 33(7): 989–1007.

Jost, John T., Mahzarin R. Banaji, and Brian A. Nosek. 2004. "A Decade of System Justification Theory: Accumulated Evidence of Conscious and Unconscious Bolstering of the Status Quo." *Political Psychology* 25(6): 881–919.

Jost, John T., Jack Glaser, Arie W. Kruglanski, and Frank J. Sulloway. 2003. "Political Conservatism as Motivated Social Cognition." *Psychological Bulletin* 129(3): 339–75.

Jost, John T., Brian A. Nosek, and Samuel D. Gosling. 2008. "Ideology: Its Resurgence in Social, Personality, and Political Psychology." *Perspectives on Psychological Science* 3(2): 126–36.

Jost, John T., and Jim Sidanius, eds. 2004. *Political Psychology: Key Readings*. New York: Psychology Press.

Judge, Timothy A., and Joyce E. Bono. 2001. "Relationship of Core Self-Evaluations Traits—Self-Esteem, Generalized Self-Efficacy, Locus of Control, and Emotional Stability—with Job Satisfaction and Job Performance: A Meta-Analysis." *Journal of Applied Psychology* 86(1): 80–92.

Julian, Tiffany, and Robert Kominski. 2011. "Education and Synthetic Work-Life Earnings Estimates." https://www.census.gov/prod/2011pubs/acs-14.pdf.

Kahn, Mattie. 2017. "Thanks to Maggie Hassan, Little Girls in New Hampshire Think Only Women Can Be Governors." *ELLE*. http://www.elle.com/culture/career-politics/news/a47128/maggie-hassan-interview-americans-with-disabilities/ (August 16, 2017).

Kam, Cindy D. 2005. "Who Toes the Party Line? Cues, Values, and Individual Differences." *Political Behavior* 27(2): 163–82.

Kamo, Yoshinori. 2000. "'He Said, She Said': Assessing Discrepancies in Husbands' and Wives' Reports on the Division of Household Labor." *Social Science Research* 29(4): 459–76.

Kane, Emily W. 2000. "Racial and Ethnic Variations in Gender-Related Attitudes." *Annual Review of Sociology* 26: 419–39.

Kane, Emily W., and Laura J. Macaulay. 1993. "Interviewer Gender and Gender Attitudes." *Public Opinion Quarterly* 57(1): 1–28.

Kane, James G., Stephen C. Craig, and Kenneth D. Wald. 2004. "Religion and Presidential Politics in Florida: A List Experiment." *Social Science Quarterly* 85(2): 281–93.

Karimi, Saeid, Harm J.A. Biemans, Thomas Lans, Mohammad Chizari, Martin Mulder, and Karim Naderi Mahdei. 2013. "Understanding Role Models and Gender Influences on Entrepreneurial Intentions Among College Students." *Procedia—Social and Behavioral Sciences* 93: 204–14.

Karp, Jeffrey A., and Susan A. Banducci. 2008. "Political Efficacy and Participation in Twenty-Seven Democracies: How Electoral Systems Shape Political Behaviour." *British Journal of Political Science* 38(2): 311–34.

Karp, Jeffrey A., and David Brockington. 2005. "Social Desirability and Response Validity: A Comparative Analysis of Overreporting Voter Turnout in Five Countries." *Journal of Politics* 67(3): 825–40.

Katosh, John P., and Michael W. Traugott. 1981. "The Consequences of Validated and Self-Reported Voting Measures." *Public Opinion Quarterly* 45(4): 519–35.

Kennel-Shank, Celeste. 2017. "Disciples of Christ Elect First Woman of Color to Lead a Mainline Denomination." *The Christian Century.* https://www.christiancentury.org/article/disciples-christ-elect-first-woman-color-lead-mainline-denomination (July 18, 2017).

King, James E., and Martha R. Crowther. 2004. "The Measurement of Religiosity and Spirituality: Examples and Issues from Psychology." *Journal of Organizational Change Management* 17(1): 83–101.

Kling, Kristen C., Janet Shibley Hyde, Carolin J. Showers, and Brenda N. Buswell. 1999. "Gender Differences in Self-Esteem: A Meta-Analysis." *Psychological Bulletin* 125(4): 470–500.

Knoll, Benjamin R. 2009. "'And Who Is My Neighbor?' Religion and Immigration Policy Attitudes." *Journal for the Scientific Study of Religion* 48(2): 313–31.

———. 2013. "Implicit Nativist Attitudes, Social Desirability, and Immigration Policy Preferences." *International Migration Review* 47(1): 132–65.

Kohut, Andrew, Scott Keeter, Carroll Doherty, Michael Dimock, and Leah Christian. 2012. "Assessing the Representativeness of Public Opinion Surveys." http://www.people-press.org/files/legacy-pdf/Assessing%20the%20Representativeness%20of%20Public%20Opinion%20Surveys.pdf (May 6, 2016).

Koleva, Spassena P., Jesse Graham, Ravi Iyer, and Peter H. Ditto. 2012. "Tracing the Threads: How Five Moral Concerns (Especially Purity) Help Explain Culture War Attitudes." *Journal of Research in Personality* 46(2): 184–94.

Kreuter, Frauke, Stanley Presser, and Roger Tourangeau. 2008. "Social Desirability Bias in CATI, IVR, and Web Surveys The Effects of Mode and Question Sensitivity." *Public Opinion Quarterly* 72(5): 847–65.

Krogstad, Jens Manuel, and Mark Hugo Lopez. 2017. "Black Voter Turnout Fell in 2016, Even as a Record Number of Americans Cast Ballots." *Pew Research Center.* http://www.pewresearch.org/fact-tank/2017/05/12/black-voter-turnout-fell-in-2016-even-as-a-record-number-of-americans-cast-ballots/ (September 4, 2017).

Krumpal, Ivar. 2011. "Determinants of Social Desirability Bias in Sensitive Surveys: A Literature Review." *Quality & Quantity* 47(4): 2025–47.

Krysan, Maria. 1998. "Privacy and the Expression of White Racial Attitudes: A Comparison across Three Contexts." *Public Opinion Quarterly* 62(4): 506–44.

Kuklinski, James H., Michael D. Cobb, and Martin Gilens. 1997. "Racial Attitudes and the 'New South.'" *The Journal of Politics* 59(2): 323–49.

Kunda, Ziva. 1990. "The Case for Motivated Reasoning." *Psychological Bulletin* 108(3): 480–98.

Kuruvilla, Carol. 2014. "These Are The Religious Denominations That Ordain Women." *The Huffington Post*. http://www.huffingtonpost.com/2014/09/26/religion-ordain-women_n_5826422.html (May 3, 2016).

———. 2015. "6 Questions With a Black Mormon Feminist." *Huffington Post*. http://www.huffingtonpost.com/entry/6-questions-with-a-black-mormon-feminist_us_55e75b1ee4b0b7a9633b833c (May 3, 2016).

Kymlicka, Will. 1995. *Multicultural Citizenship: A Liberal Theory of Minority Rights*. Oxford; New York: Oxford University Press.

LaBrie, Joseph W., and Mitchell Earleywine. 2000. "Sexual Risk Behaviors and Alcohol: Higher Base Rates Revealed Using the Unmatched-count Technique." *The Journal of Sex Research* 37(4): 321–26.

LaFrance, Marianne, and Jennifer L. Harris. 2004. "Gender and Verbal and Nonverbal Communication." In *Praeger Guide to the Psychology of Gender*, Praeger, 133–50.

Lambert, Christina D., and Sharon E. Robinson Kurpius. 2004. "Relationship of Gender Role Identity and Attitudes with Images of God." *American Journal of Pastoral Counseling* 7(2): 55–75.

Lasheras, Cristina, Angeles M. Patterson, Carmen Casado, and Serafina Fernandez. 2001. "Effects of Education on the Quality of Life, Diet, and Cardiovascular Risk Factors in an Elderly Spanish Community Population." *Experimental Aging Research* 27(3): 257–70.

Latu, Ioana M., Marianne Schmid Mast, Joris Lammers, and Dario Bombari. 2013. "Successful Female Leaders Empower Women's Behavior in Leadership Tasks." *Journal of Experimental Social Psychology* 49(3): 444–48.

Lavanga, Claudio. 2016. "Pope Creates Vatican Commission to Consider Female Deacons." *NBC News*. http://www.nbcnews.com/news/world/pope-francis-creates-vatican-commission-consider-female-deacons-n621561 (January 27, 2017).

Lawless, Jennifer L. 2004. "Politics of Presence? Congresswomen and Symbolic Representation." *Political Research Quarterly* 57(1): 81–99.

———. 2015. "Female Candidates and Legislators." *Annual Review of Political Science* 18(1): 349–66.

Lawless, Jennifer L., and Richard L. Fox. 2005. *It Takes a Candidate: Why Women Don't Run for Office*. New York: Cambridge University Press.

Lehman, Edward C. 1980. "Patterns of Lay Resistance to Women in Ministry." *Sociological Analysis* 41(4): 317–38.

———. 1981. "Organizational Resistance to Women in Ministry." *Sociological Analysis* 42(2): 101–18.

———. 1985. *Women Clergy: Breaking through Gender Barriers*. New Brunswick, NS: Transaction Publishers.

———. 1986. "The Local/Cosmopolitan Dichotomy and Acceptance of Women Clergy: A Replication and Extension of Roof." *Journal for the Scientific Study of Religion* 25(4): 461–82.

———. 1987. "Research on Lay Church Members Attitudes toward Women Clergy: An Assessment." *Review of Religious Research* 28(4): 319–29.

———. 1993. *Gender and Work: The Case of the Clergy*. Albany: State University of New York Press.

———. 2002. "Women's Path into Ministry: Six Major Studies." http://faithcommunitiestoday.org/sites/all/themes/pulpitandpew/files/Lehman.pdf (May 3, 2016).

Lelkes, Yphtach, Jon A. Krosnick, David M. Marx, Charles M. Judd, and Bernadette Park. 2012. "Complete Anonymity Compromises the Accuracy of Self-Reports." *Journal of Experimental Social Psychology* 48(6): 1291–99.

Locke, Edwin A., and Gary P. Latham, eds. 2012. *New Developments in Goal Setting and Task Performance*. New York: Routledge.

Lockwood, Penelope. 2006. "'Someone Like Me Can Be Successful': Do College Students Need Same-Gender Role Models?" *Psychology of Women Quarterly* 30: 36–46.

Lodge, Milton, Marco R. Steenbergen, and Shawn Brau. 1995. "The Responsive Voter: Campaign Information and the Dynamics of Candidate Evaluation." *American Political Science Review* 89(02): 309–26.

Lodge, Milton, and Charles S. Taber. 2013. *The Rationalizing Voter*. New York: Cambridge University Press.

Lugo, Luis et al. 2013. "A Portrait of Jewish Americans." *Pew Research Center's Religion & Public Life Project*. http://www.pewforum.org/files/2013/10/jewish-american-full-report-for-web.pdf (May 9, 2016).

Lummis, Adair T., and Paula D. Nesbitt. 2000. "Women Clergy Research and the Sociology of Religion." *Sociology of Religion* 61(4): 443–53.

MacLean, Nancy. 2008. *The American Women's Movement, 1945–2000: A Brief History with Documents*. Boston: Bedford/St. Martin's.

Macy, Gary. 2007. *The Hidden History of Women's Ordination: Female Clergy in the Medieval West*. New York: Oxford University Press.

Malhotra, Neil, and Jon A. Krosnick. 2007. "The Effect of Survey Mode and Sampling on Inferences about Political Attitudes and Behavior: Comparing the 2000 and 2004 ANES to Internet Surveys with Nonprobability Samples." *Political Analysis* 15(3): 286–323.

Malone, Clare. 2016. "From 1937 to Hillary Clinton, How Americans Have Felt About a Woman President." *FiveThirtyEight*. https://fivethirtyeight.com/features/from-1937-to-hillary-clinton-how-americans-have-felt-about-a-female-president/ (January 27, 2017).

Mansbridge, Jane. 1999. "Should Blacks Represent Blacks and Women Represent Women? A Contingent 'Yes.'" *The Journal of Politics* 61(03): 628–57.

Margolis, Michele F. 2018. *From Politics to Pews: How Partisanship and the Political Environment Shape Religious Identity*. Chicago, IL: Chicago University Press.

Marlowe, David, and Douglas P. Crowne. 1961. "Social Desirability and Response to Perceived Situational Demands." *Journal of Consulting Psychology* 25(2): 109–15.

Marsh, Charles. 2006. *The Beloved Community: How Faith Shapes Social Justice from the Civil Rights Movement to Today*. New York: Basic Books.

Martínez, Juan Agustín Franco, Macario Rodríguez-Entrena, and María Jesús Rodríguez-Entrena. 2012. "The Ordination of Women in the Catholic Church: A Survey of Attitudes in Spain." *Journal of Gender Studies* 21(1): 17–34.

Martinez, Michael D., and Stephen C. Craig. 2010. "Race and 2008 Presidential Politics in Florida: A List Experiment." *The Forum* 8(2): Article 4.

Masci, David. 2014. "The Divide over Ordaining Women." *Pew Research Center*. http://www.pewresearch.org/fact-tank/2014/09/09/the-divide-over-ordaining-women/ (May 3, 2016).

Matthewes-Green, Frederica. 2007. "Women's Ordination." *Antiochian Orthodox Christian Archdiocese*. http://antiochian.org/node/17953 (July 21, 2017).

Matusiak, John. 2017. "Ordination of Women—Questions & Answers." *Orthodox Church in America.* https://oca.org/questions/priesthoodmonasticism/ordination-of-women   (July 21, 2017).

McKenna, Josephine. 2016. "Pope Francis Names Panel to Study Ordaining Women Deacons." *Religion News Service.* http://religionnews.com/2016/08/02/pope-francis-names-panel-to-study-ordaining-women-deacons/ (January 27, 2017).

———. 2017. "Catholic Groups Launch Conversation about Female Deacons | Religion News Service." *Religion News Service.* http://religionnews.com/2017/06/15/catholic-groups-launch-conversation-about-female-deacons/ (June 16, 2017).

McLemore, Philip G. 2016. "Becoming the Beloved of the Lord: Maturing through the Stages of Spiritual Growth." *Sunstone: Mormon Experience, Scholarship, Issues, and Art* (Winter 183).

McLeod, Saul. 2012. "Low Self Esteem." *Simply Psychology.* http://www.simplypsychology.org/self-esteem.html (January 30, 2017).

McMillan, Becky. 2002. "What Do Clergy Do All Week?" *Pulpit and Pew.* http://pulpitandpew.org/what-do-clergy-do-all-week (May 10, 2016).

Melander, Clint. 2015. "Area Business Weekends." http://www.mormonstories.org/wp-content/uploads/2017/02/151204_Area_Business_Weekends_REVISION2.pdf.

Mellowes, Marilyn. 2010. "God in America—The Black Church." *God in America.* http://www.pbs.org/godinamerica/black-church/ (May 9, 2016).

Meltzoff, Andrew N., and Wolfgang Prinz, eds. 2011. *The Imitative Mind: Development, Evolution and Brain Bases.* Reissue edition. Cambridge: Cambridge University Press.

Miller, Emily McFarlan. 2016a. "Methodists Postpone Debate of Gay Issues That Could Split Denomination." *Religion News Service.* http://religionnews.com/2016/05/19/united-methodists-create-lgbt-commission/ (May 27, 2016).

———. 2016b. "Supporters of Women as Priests See Hope in Pope's Openness to Deacons." *Religion News Service.* http://religionnews.com/2016/09/02/supporters-of-women-as-priests-see-hope-in-popes-openness-to-deacons/ (January 27, 2017).

Miller, Sharon Hodde. 2013. "The Seminary Gender Gap." *Christianity Today.* http://www.christianitytoday.com/women/2013/may/seminary-gender-gap.html (July 18, 2017).

Miller, Warren E., and J. Merrill Shanks. 1996. *The New American Voter.* Cambridge, MA: Harvard University Press.

Moghe, Sonia, and Yon Pomrenze. 2016. "Orthodox Woman Is First to Take Title of Rabbi." *CNN.* http://www.cnn.com/2016/04/05/living/first-orthodox-woman-rabbi-feat/index.html (May 5, 2016).

Mowday, Richard T., and Robert I. Sutton. 1993. "Organizational Behavior: Linking Individuals and Groups to Organizational Contexts." *Annual Review of Psychology* 44(1): 195–229.

Multon, Karen D., Steven D. Brown, and Robert W. Lent. 1991. "Relation of Self-Efficacy Beliefs to Academic Outcomes: A Meta-Analytic Investigation." *Journal of Counseling Psychology* 38(1): 30–38.

Nesbitt, Paula D. 1997. *Feminization of the Clergy in America: Occupational and Organizational Perspectives.* 1New York: Oxford University Press.

Netchaeva, Ekaterina, Maryam Kouchaki, and Leah D. Sheppard. 2015. "A Man's (Precarious) Place Men's Experienced Threat and Self-Assertive Reactions to Female Superiors." *Personality and Social Psychology Bulletin* 41(9): 1247–59.

Neumark, David, and Rosella Gardecki. 1996. *Women Helping Women? Role-Model and Mentoring Effects on Female Ph.D. Student in Economics.* National Bureau of Economic Research. Working Paper. http://www.nber.org/papers/w5733 (January 31, 2017).

Newton-Small, Jay. 2016. "How Anita Hill Paved the Way for Women in Government." *Time.* http://time.com/4280829/anita-hill-hbo-drama-clarence-thomas-congress-women/ (January 27, 2017).

Nixon, Lucia A., and Michael D. Robinson. 1999. "The Educational Attainment of Young Women: Role Model Effects of Female High School Faculty." *Demography* 36(2): 185–94.

Nynäs, Peter and Andrew Kam-Tuck Yip, eds. 2016. *Religion, Gender and Sexuality in Everyday Life.* Philadelphia, PA: Routledge.

O'Brien, Laurie T., Aline Hitti, Emily Shaffer, Amanda R. Van Camp, Donata Henry, and Patricia N. Gilbert. 2017. "Improving Girls' Sense of Fit in Science: Increasing the Impact of Role Models." *Social Psychological and Personality Science* 8(3): 301–9.

Ochman, Jan M. 1996. "The Effects of Nongender-Role Stereotyped, Same-Sex Role Models in Storybooks on the Self-Esteem of Children in Grade Three." *Sex Roles* 35(11–12): 711–35.

Oliver, J. Eric, and Janelle Wong. 2003. "Intergroup Prejudice in Multiethnic Settings." *American Journal of Political Science* 47(4): 567–82.

Olson, Laura R., Wendy Cadge, and James T. Harrison. 2006. "Religion and Public Opinion about Same-Sex Marriage." *Social Science Quarterly* 87(2): 340–60.

Olson, Laura R., Sue E. S. Crawford, and Melissa M. Deckman. 2005. *Women with a Mission: Religion, Gender, and the Politics of Women Clergy.* 2nd edition. Tuscaloosa: University of Alabama Press.

Oostenbroek, Janine, Thomas Suddendorf, Mark Nielson, Jonathan Redshaw, Siobhan Kennedy-Costantini, Jacqueline Davis, Sally Clark, and Virginia Slaughter. 2016. "Comprehensive Longitudinal Study Challenges the Existence of Neonatal Imitation in Humans." *Current Biology* 26(10): 1334–38.

Orth, Ulrich, Richard W. Robins, and Keith F. Widaman. 2012. "Life-Span Development of Self-Esteem and Its Effects on Important Life Outcomes." *Journal of Personality and Social Psychology* 102(6): 1271–88.

Paquette, Danielle. 2015. "Why More Young Women Than Ever Before Are Skipping Church." *Washington Post,* May 27. https://www.washingtonpost.com/news/wonk/wp/2015/05/27/why-more-young-women-than-ever-are-skipping-church/ (May 19, 2016).

Patten, Ellen. 2015. "On Equal Pay Day, Key Facts about the Gender Pay Gap." *Pew Research Center.* http://www.pewresearch.org/fact-tank/2015/04/14/on-equal-pay-day-everything-you-need-to-know-about-the-gender-pay-gap/ (January 27, 2017).

———. 2016. "Racial, Gender Wage Gaps Persist in U.S. Despite Some Progress." *Pew Research Center.* http://www.pewresearch.org/fact-tank/2016/07/01/racial-gender-wage-gaps-persist-in-u-s-despite-some-progress/ (January 27, 2017).

Payne, Philip Barton. 2009. *Man and Woman, One in Christ: An Exegetical and Theological Study of Paul's Letters.* Grand Rapids, Mich.: Zondervan.

Payton, Mark E., Matthew H. Greenstone, and Nathaniel Schenker. 2003. "Overlapping Confidence Intervals or Standard Error Intervals: What Do They Mean in Terms of Statistical Significance?" *Journal of Insect Science* 3(1): 34.

Peek, Charles W., George D. Lowe, and L. Susan Williams. 1991. "Gender and God's Word: Another Look at Religious Fundamentalism and Sexism." *Social Forces* 69(4): 1205–21.

Perry, David G., and Kay Bussey. 1979. "The Social Learning Theory of Sex Differences: Imitation Is Alive and Well." *Journal of Personality and Social Psychology* 37(10): 1699–1712.

Pew Research Center. 2015. "Women and Leadership." *Pew Research Center's Social & Demographic Trends Project.* http://www.pewsocialtrends.org/2015/01/14/women-and-leadership/ (January 27, 2017).

Phillips, Derek L., and Kevin J. Clancy. 1972. "Some Effects of 'Social Desirability' in Survey Studies." *American Journal of Sociology* 77(5): 921–40.

Piatt, Christian. 2014. "5 Reasons You Need a Female Pastor." *OnFaith.* http://www.faithstreet. com/onfaith/2014/03/27/5-reasons-you-need-a-female-pastor/31461 (May 3, 2016).

Pierce, Jon L., Donald G. Gardner, Larry L. Cummings, and Randall B. Dunham. 1989. "Organization-Based Self-Esteem: Construct Definition, Measurement, and Validation." *The Academy of Management Journal* 32(3): 622–48.

Pivec, Holly. 2006. "The Feminization of the Church." *Biola Magazine.* http://magazine.biola. edu/article/06-spring/the-feminization-of-the-church/ (June 3, 2016).

Poggioli, Sylvia. 2016. "Seizing on Pope's Remarks, Women Meet in Rome to Discuss Female Priesthood." *NPR.org.* http://www.npr.org/sections/parallels/2016/06/04/480624491/ seizing-on-popes-remarks-women-meet-in-rome-to-discuss-female-priesthood (June 6, 2016).

Povoledo, Elisabetta, and Laurie Goodstein. 2016. "Pope Francis Says Panel Will Study Whether Women May Serve as Deacons." *The New York Times.* http://www.nytimes.com/2016/05/13/ world/europe/pope-says-hes-open-to-studying-whether-women-can-serve-as-deacons.html (May 27, 2016).

Powell, Richard J. 2013. "Social Desirability Bias in Polling on Same-Sex Marriage Ballot Measures." *American Politics Research* 41(6): 1052–70.

Powers, Daniel A., and Christopher G. Ellison. 1995. "Interracial Contact and Black Racial Attitudes: The Contact Hypothesis and Selectivity Bias." *Social Forces* 74(1): 205–26.

Press, Julie E., and Eleanor Townsley. 1998. "Wives' and Husbands' Housework Reporting: Gender, Class, and Social Desirability." *Gender & Society* 12(2): 188–218.

Preuhs, Robert R. 2007. "Descriptive Representation as a Mechanism to Mitigate Policy Backlash Latino Incorporation and Welfare Policy in the American States." *Political Research Quarterly* 60(2): 277–92.

Price-Mitchell, Marilyn. 2015. *Tomorrow's Change Makers: Reclaiming the Power of Citizenship for a New Generation.* Bainbridge Island, WA: Eagle Harbor Publishing.

Pritt, Ann F. 1998. "Spiritual Correlates of Reported Sexual Abuse among Mormon Women." *Journal for the Scientific Study of Religion* 37(2): 273–85.

Purvis, Sally B. 1995. *The Stained-Glass Ceiling: Churches and Their Women Pastors.* Louisville, Ky.: Westminster John Knox Press.

Putnam, Robert D. 2016. *Our Kids: The American Dream in Crisis.* New York: Simon & Schuster.

Putnam, Robert D, and David E. Campbell. 2012. *American Grace: How Religion Divides and Unites Us.* New York: Simon & Schuster.

Pyszczynski, Tom, Jeff Greenberg, Sheldon Solomon, Jamie Arndt, and Jeff Schimel. 2004. "Why Do People Need Self-Esteem? A Theoretical and Empirical Review." *Psychological Bulletin* 130(3): 435–68.

Quealy, Kevin. 2017. "Your Rabbi? Probably a Democrat. Your Baptist Pastor? Probably a Republican. Your Priest? Who Knows." *The New York Times.* https://www.nytimes.com/interactive/2017/06/12/upshot/the-politics-of-americas-religious-leaders.html (June 16, 2017).

Quimby, Julie L., and Angela M. De Santis. 2006. "The Influence of Role Models on Women's Career Choices." *The Career Development Quarterly* 54(4): 297–306.

Redlawsk, David P. 2002. "Hot Cognition or Cool Consideration? Testing the Effects of Motivated Reasoning on Political Decision Making." *The Journal of Politics* 64(04): 1021–44.

Redlawsk, David P., Caroline J. Tolbert, and William Franko. 2010. "Voters, Emotions, and Race in 2008: Obama as the First Black President." *Political Research Quarterly* 63(4): 875–89.

Reingold, Beth, and Heather Foust. 1998. "Exploring the Determinants of Feminist Consciousness in the United States." *Women & Politics* 19(3): 19–48.

Reingold, Beth, and Jessica Harrell. 2010. "The Impact of Descriptive Representation on Women's Political Engagement: Does Party Matter?" *Political Research Quarterly* 63(2): 280–94.

Robins, Richard W., Holly M. Hendin, and Kali H. Trzesniewski. 2001. "Measuring Global Self-Esteem: Construct Validation of a Single-Item Measure and the Rosenberg Self-Esteem Scale." *Personality and Social Psychology Bulletin* 27(2): 151–61.

Roof, Wade Clark. 2009. "American Presidential Rhetoric from Ronald Reagan to George W. Bush: Another Look at Civil Religion." *Social Compass* 56(2): 286–301.

Rosenfeld, Paul, Stephanie Booth-Kewley, Jack E. Edwards, and Marie D. Thomas. 1996. "Responses on Computer Surveys: Impression Management, Social Desirability, and the Big Brother Syndrome." *Computers in Human Behavior* 12(2): 263–74.

Ross, Catherine E., and Marieke Van Willigen. 1997. "Education and the Subjective Quality of Life." *Journal of Health and Social Behavior* 38(3): 275–97.

Rubin, Herbert J., and Irene S. Rubin. 2011. *Qualitative Interviewing: The Art of Hearing Data.* 3rd edition. Thousand Oaks, Calif.: SAGE Publications, Inc.

Ryan, Camille L., and Kurt Bauman. 2016. "Educational Attainment in the United States: 2015." http://www.census.gov/content/dam/Census/library/publications/2016/demo/p20-578.pdf.

Saldaña, Johnny. 2012. *The Coding Manual for Qualitative Researchers.* 2nd edition. Los Angeles: SAGE Publications Ltd.

Sanbonmatsu, Kira. 2003. "Gender-Related Political Knowledge and the Descriptive Representation of Women." *Political Behavior* 25(4): 367–88.

Sánchez, Bernadette, Patricia Esparza, and Yarí Colón. 2008. "Natural Mentoring under the Microscope: An Investigation of Mentoring Relationships and Latino Adolescents' Academic Performance." *Journal of Community Psychology* 36(4): 468–82.

Sapiro, Virginia, and Pamela Johnston Conover. 1997. "The Variable Gender Basis of Electoral Politics: Gender and Context in the 1992 US Election." *British Journal of Political Science* 27(4): 497–523.

Scherbaum, Charles A., Yochi Cohen-Charash, and Michael J. Kern. 2006. "Measuring General Self-Efficacy: A Comparison of Three Measures Using Item Response Theory." *Educational and Psychological Measurement* 66(6): 1047–63.

Schneider, Carl, and Dorothy Schneider. 1997. *In Their Own Right: The History of American Clergywomen.* New York: Crossroad.

Schunk, Dale H. 1991. "Self-Efficacy and Academic Motivation." *Educational Psychologist* 26(3–4): 207–31.

Seager, Richard Hughes. 2012. *Buddhism in America.* New York: Columbia University Press.

Seidman, Irving. 2012. *Interviewing as Qualitative Research: A Guide for Researchers in Education and the Social Sciences, Fourth Edition.* New York: Teachers College Press.

Sentilles, Sarah. 2009. *A Church of Her Own: What Happens When a Woman Takes the Pulpit.* Boston, MA: Mariner Books.

Severns, Maggie. 2016. "Trump Reiterates: Video Was 'Locker Room Talk.'" *Politico.com.* http://politi.co/2dHCANF (January 27, 2017).

Seymour, Jeffrey M., Michael R. Welch, Karen Monique Gregg, and Jessica Collett. 2014. "Generating Trust in Congregations: Engagement, Exchange, and Social Networks." *Journal for the Scientific Study of Religion* 53(1): 130–44.

Shariff, Azim F., and Ara Norenzayan. 2011. "Mean Gods Make Good People: Different Views of God Predict Cheating Behavior." *The International Journal for the Psychology of Religion* 21(2): 85–96.

Shaw, Susan. 2015. "Still the Second Sex." *The Huffington Post.* http://www.huffingtonpost.com/susan-m-shaw/still-the-second-sex_b_7798106.html (May 3, 2016).

Shepherd, Gordon, Lavina Fielding Anderson, and Gary Shepherd, eds. 2015. *Voices for Equality: Ordain Women and Resurgent Mormon Feminism.* Draper, UT: Greg Kofford Books, Inc.

Shields, Chelsea. 2015. "How I'm Working for Change inside My Church." Presented at the Ted Fellows Retreat 2015. https://www.ted.com/talks/chelsea_shields_how_i_m_working_for_change_inside_my_church.

Shoemaker, Christopher M. 2003. "A Small Work: The Story of Helenor Alter Davisson, Methodism's First Ordained Woman." *Methodist History* 41(2): 3–11.

Shogan, Colleen J. 2007. *The Moral Rhetoric of American Presidents.* Revised edition. College Station, TX: Texas A&M University Press.

Silton, Nava R., Kevin J. Flannelly, Kathleen Galek, and Christopher G. Ellison. 2014. "Beliefs About God and Mental Health Among American Adults." *Journal of Religion and Health* 53(5): 1285–96.

Silver, Brian D., Barbara A. Anderson, and Paul R. Abramson. 1986. "Who Overreports Voting?" *The American Political Science Review* 80(2): 613–24.

Silverstone, Peter H., and Mahnaz Salsali. 2003. "Low Self-Esteem and Psychiatric Patients: Part I—The Relationship between Low Self-Esteem and Psychiatric Diagnosis." *Annals of General Hospital Psychiatry* 2: 2.

Simon, Rita J., and Pamela S. Nadell. 1995. "In the Same Voice or Is It Different?: Gender and the Clergy." *Sociology of Religion* 56(1): 63–70.

Smidt, Corwin E. 2016. *Pastors and Public Life: The Changing Face of American Protestant Clergy.* New York: Oxford University Press.

Smidt, Corwin, Lyman Kellstedt, and James L. Guth, eds. 2009. *The Oxford Handbook of Religion and American Politics.* New York: Oxford University Press.

Smith, Christian. 1991. *The Emergence of Liberation Theology: Radical Religion and Social Movement Theory.* Chicago: University Of Chicago Press.

———, ed. 1996. *Disruptive Religion: The Force of Faith in Social Movement Activism.* New York: Routledge.

Smith, Gregory Allen. 2008. *Politics in the Parish: The Political Influence of Catholic Priests.* Washington, DC: Georgetown University Press.

Smith, Krista Lynn, and Daphne Pedersen Stevens. 2003. "Attitudes of Laypersons toward Female Clergy and Priests: Testing Two Theological Arguments against Ordination." *The Social Science Journal* 40(3): 419–29.

Smith, Tom W. 1998. "A Review of Church Attendance Measures." *American Sociological Review* 63(1): 131–36.

Sniderman, Paul M., and Edward G. Carmines. 1999. *Reaching beyond Race*. Cambridge, MA: Harvard University Press.

Southern Baptist Convention. 1984. "Resolution on Ordination and the Role of Women in Ministry." http://www.sbc.net/resolutions/1088/resolution-on-ordination-and-the-role-of-women-in-ministry (May 9, 2016).

Sowislo, Julia Friederike, and Ulrich Orth. 2013. "Does Low Self-Esteem Predict Depression and Anxiety? A Meta-Analysis of Longitudinal Studies." *Psychological Bulletin* 139(1): 213–40.

Spencer, Renée, and Belle Liang. 2009. "'She Gives Me a Break from the World': Formal Youth Mentoring Relationships between Adolescent Girls and Adult Women." *The Journal of Primary Prevention* 30(2): 109–30.

Stack, Peggy Fletcher. 2015. "Mormon Women to Have More Say in Plans for Weekly Services." *Salt Lake Tribune*. http://www.sltrib.com/home/2627089-155/mormon-women-to-have-more-say (June 28, 2017).

Stajkovic, Alexander D., and Fred Luthans. 1998. "Self-Efficacy and Work-Related Performance: A Meta-Analysis." *Psychological Bulletin* 124(2): 240–61.

Stecker, Frederick. 2011. *The Podium, the Pulpit, and the Republicans: How Presidential Candidates Use Religious Language in American Political Debate*. Santa Barbara, Calif.: Praeger.

Stout, Christopher T., and Reuben Kline. 2011. "I'm Not Voting for Her: Polling Discrepancies and Female Candidates." *Political Behavior* 33(3): 479–503.

Strauss, Anselm L. 1987. *Qualitative Analysis for Social Scientists*. New York: Cambridge University Press.

Streb, Matthew J., Barbara Burrell, Brian Frederick, and Michael A. Genovese. 2008. "Social Desirability Effects and Support for a Female American President." *Public Opinion Quarterly* 72(1): 76–89.

Stroope, Samuel. 2011. "Caste, Class, and Urbanization: The Shaping of Religious Community in Contemporary India." *Social Indicators Research* 105(3): 499–518.

Sullins, Paul. 2000. "The Stained Glass Ceiling: Career Attainment for Women Clergy." *Sociology of Religion* 61(3): 243–66.

Tajfel, Henri, and John Turner. 1986. "The Social Identity Theory of Intergroup Behavior." In *Psychology of Intergroup Relations*, edited by Stephen Worchel and William G. Austin, 7–24. Chicago: Nelson-Hall.

Tamborini, Christopher R., Chang Hwan Kim, and Arthur Sakamoto. 2015. "Education and Lifetime Earnings in the United States." *Demography* 52(4): 1383–1407.

Teachman, Jay D. 1987. "Family Background, Educational Resources, and Educational Attainment." *American Sociological Review* 52(4): 548–57.

Thomas, Kathrin, David Johann, Silvia Kritzinger, Caroline Plescia, and Eva Zeglovits. 2017. "Estimating Sensitive Behavior: The ICT and High-Incidence Electoral Behavior." *International Journal of Public Opinion Research* 29(1): 157–71.

Time Magazine. 1992. "From Anita Hill to Capitol Hill." *Time Magazine*. http://content.time.com/time/subscriber/article/0,33009,977008,00.html (January 27, 2017).

Tolbert, Caroline J., and John A. Grummel. 2003. "Revisiting the Racial Threat Hypothesis: White Voter Support for California's Proposition 209." *State Politics and Policy Quarterly* 3(2): 183–202.

Torjesen, Karen Jo. 1993. *When Women Were Priests: Women's Leadership in the Early Church and the Scandal of Their Subordination in the Rise of Christianity*. San Francisco: HarperCollins.

Traugott, Michael W., and John P. Katosh. 1979. "Response Validity in Surveys of Voting Behavior." *The Public Opinion Quarterly* 43(3): 359–77.

Trzesniewski, Kali H., Brent M. Donnellan, Terrie E. Moffitt, Richard W. Robins, Richie Poulton, Avshalom Caspi. 2006. "Low Self-Esteem during Adolescence Predicts Poor Health, Criminal Behavior, and Limited Economic Prospects during Adulthood." *Developmental Psychology* 42(2): 381–90.

Twenge, Jean M., Julie J. Exline, Joshua B. Grubbs, Ramya Sastry, and W. Keith Campbell. 2015. "Generational and Time Period Differences in American Adolescents' Religious Orientation, 1966–2014." *PLoS ONE* 10(5): e0121454.

Ulbig, Stacy G. 2007. "Gendering Municipal Government: Female Descriptive Representation and Feelings of Political Trust." *Social Science Quarterly* 88(5): 1106–23.

UNESCO. 2011. "Education Counts: Toward the Millennium Development." http://unesdoc.unesco.org/images/0019/001902/190214e.pdf.

Unger, Rhoda K. 1979. "Toward a Redefinition of Sex and Gender." *American Psychologist* 34(11): 1085–94.

Verba, Sidney, Kay Lehman Schlozman, and Henry Brady. 1995. *Voice and Equality: Civic Voluntarism in American Politics*. Cambridge, Mass.: Harvard University Press.

Walch, Tad. 2014. "LDS Church Confirms Women's Meeting Now Part of General Conference | Deseret News." *Deseret News*. http://www.deseretnews.com/article/865614355/LDS-Church-confirms-womens-meeting-now-part-of-general-conference.html (June 28, 2017).

———. 2015. "In a Significant Move, Women to Join Key, Leading LDS Church Councils." *Deseret News*. http://www.deseretnews.com/article/865634860/In-a-significant-move-women-to-join-key-leading-LDS-Church-councils.html (June 28, 2017).

Wallace, Ruth A. 1992. *They Call Her Pastor: A New Role for Catholic Women*. Albany: State University of New York Press.

Warner, Judith. 2014. "Fact Sheet: The Women's Leadership Gap—Center for American Progress." https://www.americanprogress.org/issues/women/reports/2014/03/07/85457/fact-sheet-the-womens-leadership-gap/ (January 27, 2017).

Wayne, Carly, Nicholas Valentino, and Marzia Oceno. 2016. "How Sexism Drives Support for Donald Trump." *Washington Post*. https://www.washingtonpost.com/news/monkey-cage/wp/2016/10/23/how-sexism-drives-support-for-donald-trump/ (January 27, 2017).

Weissberg, Robert. 1978. "Collective vs. Dyadic Representation in Congress." *American Political Science Review* 72(02): 535–47.

Welch, Eric W., Charles C. Hinnant, and M. Jae Moon. 2005. "Linking Citizen Satisfaction with E-Government and Trust in Government." *Journal of Public Administration Resesarch and Theory* 15(3): 371–91.

Welch, James S. 2013. "The Importance of Self-Efficacy in Ethical Education for Business Undergraduates." *Southern Journal of Business and Ethics* 5: 214–23.

Whiten, Andrew, Gillian Allan, Siobahn Devlin, Natalie Kseib, Nicola Raw, and Nicola McGuigan. 2016. "Social Learning in the Real-World: 'Over-Imitation' Occurs in Both Children and Adults Unaware of Participation in an Experiment and Independently of Social Interaction." *PLOS ONE* 11(7): e0159920.

Wiesner-Hanks, Merry E. 2010. *Gender in History: Global Perspectives.* 2nd edition. Malden, Mass; Oxford: Wiley-Blackwell.

Wiktorowicz, Quintan, ed. 2003. *Islamic Activism: A Social Movement Theory Approach.* Bloomington: Indiana University Press.

Wilcox, Clyde. 1990. "Religion and Politics among White Evangelicals: The Impact of Religious Variables on Political Attitudes." *Review of Religious Research* 32(1): 27–42.

Willard, Dallas. 2010. *How I Changed My Mind about Women in Leadership: Compelling Stories from Prominent Evangelicals.* Ed. Alan F. Johnson. Grand Rapids, Mich.: Zondervan.

Williams, Christine L., and E. Joel Heikes. 1993. "The Importance of Researcher's Gender in the In-Depth Interview: Evidence from Two Case Studies of Male Nurses." *Gender and Society* 7(2): 280–91.

Wilson, Fiona, Jill Kickul, and Deborah Marlino. 2007. "Gender, Entrepreneurial Self-Efficacy, and Entrepreneurial Career Intentions: Implications for Entrepreneurship Education." *Entrepreneurship Theory and Practice* 31(3): 387–406.

Wimbush, James C., and Dan R. Dalton. 1997. "Base Rate for Employee Theft: Convergence of Multiple Methods." *Journal of Applied Psychology* 82(5): 756–63.

Winston, Kimberly. 2015. "Modern Orthodox Judaism Says 'No' to Women Rabbis." *Religion News Service.* http://religionnews.com/2015/11/02/modern-orthodox-judaism-says-no-women-rabbis/ (May 3, 2016).

Wiseman, Travis, and Nabamita Dutta. 2016. *Religion and the Gender Wage Gap: A U.S. State-Level Study.* Rochester, NY: Social Science Research Network. SSRN Scholarly Paper. http://papers.ssrn.com/abstract=2738523 (May 27, 2016).

Witham, Larry A. 2005. *Who Shall Lead Them?: The Future of Ministry in America.* New York: Oxford University Press.

Witter, Robert A., Morris A. Okun, William A. Stock, and Marilyn J. Haring. 1984. "Education and Subjective Well-Being: A Meta-Analysis." *Educational Evaluation and Policy Analysis* 6(2): 165–73.

Wolak, Jennifer. 2015. "Candidate Gender and the Political Engagement of Women and Men." *American Politics Research* 43(5): 872–96.

Wolbrecht, Christina, and David E. Campbell. 2007. "Leading by Example: Female Members of Parliament as Political Role Models." *American Journal of Political Science* 51(4): 921–39.

Women's Ordination Conference. 2017. "About Our Work | Women's Ordination Conference." http://www.womensordination.org/about-us/about-our-work/ (January 27, 2017).

Wong-McDonald, Ana, and Richard L. Gorsuch. 2004. "A Multivariate Theory of God Concept, Religious Motivation, Locus of Control, Coping, and Spiritual Well-Being." *Journal of Psychology and Theology* 32(4): 318.

Zaller, John R. 1992. *The Nature and Origins of Mass Opinion.* New York: Cambridge University Press.

Zigerell, L. J. 2011. "You Wouldn't Like Me When I'm Angry: List Experiment Misreporting." *Social Science Quarterly* 92(2): 552–62.

Zikmund, Barbara Brown, Adair T. Lummis, and Patricia Mei Yin Chang. 1998. *Clergy Women: An Uphill Calling.* Louisville, Ky.: Westminster John Knox Press.

Zimmerman, Barry J. 2000. "Self-Efficacy: An Essential Motive to Learn." *Contemporary Educational Psychology* 25(1): 82–91.

Zimmerman, Emily B., Steven H. Woolf, and Amber Haley. 2015. *Understanding the Relationship Between Education and Health: A Review of the Evidence and an Examination of Community Perspectives.* U.S. Department of Health and Human Services. https://www.ahrq.gov/professionals/education/curriculum-tools/population-health/zimmerman.html (January 30, 2017).

Index

Note: Figures and tables are indicated by *f* and *t* respectively following page numbers.